"Finally, a book on the immigration challer̄ Soerens and Hwang have experienced both ᴵ come with caring about people in difficult circumstances. This book is deeply personal in a way that helps us all be compassionate, yet it does not dumb down the challenge we all face with our natural propensity for shallow platitudes and partisan politicking. This book helps us find our way as Americans and as Christians to understanding the real issues, and it will help us shape a comprehensive public policy direction that honors both law and love."

Dr. Joel C. Hunter, senior pastor, Northland Church, Orlando, Florida

"A daring and desperate call to remember the story of God that begins with baby Moses being floated down a river in the middle of Pharaoh's genocide and climaxes with God's Son entering the world as a homeless refugee in the middle of Herod's bloodshed. It is a story of immigrants and strangers. This book invites us to participate in the radical inclusion and grace of God. *Welcoming the Stranger* is written with the urgent sense that we cannot wait for politicians to tell us how to treat immigrants but we simply need to pick up the Bible and reimagine what it means to be the people of God. Here is a reminder that as a people of rebirth our love does not stop at the borders of nations."

Shane Claiborne, author, activist and recovering sinner

"*Welcoming the Stranger* is a must-read for one who desires to take a fresh biblical look at the issue of immigration in the U.S. I believe this is the compassion and justice issue of our day, and we need to do careful work so we are accurate and biblical in our solutions. I wholeheartedly endorse Jenny and Matt's wonderful work and commend it to you for your study."

William J. Hamel, president, Evangelical Free Church of America

"Justice, compassion and truth are too often missing from the immigration debate in this country. *Welcoming the Stranger* provides all three with comprehensive information on every aspect of the current problem, its roots and common-sense solutions. Every Christian seeking an informed response to this critical issue should read this book."

Jim Wallis, president, Sojourners, and author of *The Great Awakening*

"Here is a book for every Christian and every church leadership team interested in one of the greatest mercy/justice issues of our time: how will the church care for immigrants in our midst? The authors write with sensitivity concerning the volatile emotions on all sides of the debates as they offer essential information designed to help us formulate responses to this very complex issue. *Welcoming the Stranger* inspired me to expand my heart of compassion and take action."

Paul Borthwick, adjunct professor of missions, Gordon College, Wenham, Massachusetts

"Thinking of immigration policy requires that we think first about the kingdom of God—God's rule and reign; his plan, will, agenda and story. Only then will we be able to think well through the secondary lenses of nation-states, tribes and ethnicities. The parable of the good Samaritan, while easy to understand, has fallen victim to global, political and economic complexities. *Welcoming the Stranger,* without being simplistic, clears our thoughts and lights a way forward to love and serve twelve million undocumented neighbors."

Todd Hunter, church planter, The Anglican Mission in the Americas, past president of Alpha USA and Vineyard Churches USA, and author of *Christianity Beyond Belief*

"Immigration is one of the most pressing issues facing our country today. Some twelve million undocumented immigrants live among us, but their lives are largely in the shadows. They are our neighbors and we are theirs. The ethical challenges that face us all are numerous in the legal, economic, educational and health areas. What would God have us do regarding these new neighbors? Matthew Soerens and Jenny Hwang have made an invaluable contribution to Christians through their book *Welcoming the Stranger.* With great precision and fairness, they lead us through the difficult and thorny ethical issues of immigration. They provide personal stories and abundant statistics. Most of all, they bring God's Word to challenge us to obey God and to welcome the strangers among us. This book is must-reading for every Christian and every congregation that desires to love the strangers in our midst."

Lindy Scott, professor of Spanish and Latin American studies, Whitworth University, and coauthor of *Los Evangélicos: Portraits of Latin American Protestantism in the United States*

MATTHEW SOERENS & JENNY HWANG

Foreword by Leith Anderson

WELCOMING

THE

STRANGER

Justice, Compassion & Truth in the Immigration Debate

IVP Books

An imprint of InterVarsity Press
Downers Grove, Illinois

InterVarsity Press
P.O. Box 1400, Downers Grove, IL 60515-1426
World Wide Web: www.ivpress.com
E-mail: email@ivpress.com

InterVarsity Press® is the book-publishing division of InterVarsity Christian Fellowship/USA®, a student movement active on campus at hundreds of universities, colleges and schools of nursing in the United States of America, and a member movement of the International Fellowship of Evangelical Students. For information about local and regional activities, write Public Relations Dept., InterVarsity Christian Fellowship/USA, 6400 Schroeder Rd., P.O. Box 7895, Madison, WI 53707-7895, or visit the IVCF website at <www.intervarsity.org>.

Design: Janelle Rebel
Images: Shannon Stapleton/Reuters/Corbis

ISBN 978-0-8308-3359-7

Printed in the United States of America ∞

Library of Congress Cataloging-in-Publication Data

Soerens, Matthew, 1983-
  Welcoming the stranger: justice, compassion, and truth in the
  immigration debate / Matthew Soerens and Jenny Hwang.
      p. cm.
  Includes bibliographical references and index.
  ISBN 978-0-8308-3359-7 (pbk.: alk. paper)
  1. Church work with immigrants—United States. 2. Emigration and
  immigration—Religious aspects—Christianity. 3. United
  States—Emigration and immigration. 4. Immigrants—Religious
  life—United States. I. Hwang, Jenny, 1980- II. Title.
  BV639.I4.S554 2009
  261.8'36—dc22

                                                          2008046023

P 23 22 21 20 19 18 17 16 15 14 13 12 11 10 9 8 7 6

Y 28 27 26 25 24 23 22 21 20 19 18 17 16 15 14 13 12

To our parents,

Dave and Jane Soerens and Byong-tak and Jong-hye Hwang,

with love and gratitude

CONTENTS

Foreword by Leith Anderson 9

1 The Immigration Dilemma 11

2 Aliens Among You: Who Are Undocumented Immigrants? 26

3 Nation of Immigrants: A Historical Perspective
on Immigration to the United States 45

4 Immigrating the Legal Way: Our Immigration System Today 64

5 Thinking Biblically About Immigration 82

6 Concerns About Immigration 93

7 The Value of Immigration to the United States 115

8 The Politics and Policies of Immigration Reform 138

9 The Church and Immigration Today 159

10 A Christian Response to the Immigration Dilemma 176

Appendix 1: Discussion Questions 187

Appendix 2: World Relief Statement
in Support of Comprehensive Immigration Reform 194

Appendix 3: Ministries and Organizations Serving
Immigrants and Refugees in the United States 200

Appendix 4: Ministries and Organizations Addressing
the Root Causes of Immigration 205

Appendix 5: Selected Resources for Learning More
About the Immigration Issue 207

Appendix 6: Tools for Political Advocacy 211

Acknowledgments 213

Notes 216

Index 231

FOREWORD

My mother is dying. This week she will conclude her long life in America, thousands of miles across the Atlantic Ocean from where she was born and grew to adulthood.

Her father died early in the last century of pernicious anemia, a disease that most of us have never heard of and that would be easily treated today. Her widowed mother couldn't support herself and three daughters under six years old so she moved back with her parents. Nearly twenty years later my grandmother met and married an American and moved to the United States. But my mother had to stay behind because of U.S. immigration laws and quotas. Unlike her younger sisters my mother was an adult, and immigration for her was harder. She waited a year or two and then received a visa, sailing the North Atlantic to Philadelphia and to her new country.

When I was a little boy I went with my mother to the post office every January where she was required by law to register as an alien. On our family vacations to Canada she always waited for us on the U.S. side of the border out of fear there might be problems returning if she left the country. Eventually she became an American citizen.

For the past seven years she has lived in a nursing home in Boca Raton, Florida, where much of the staff is foreign born. The hallway buzz ranges from Haitian Creole to Jamaican English. Her physician is from Southeast Asia. They love my mother. They give her care I cannot provide. They are kind and gracious. These immigrant caregivers pray for her, quote the Bible and sing hymns. They are the best of believers.

As my mother's final hours are counting down they come to her room in a steady stream. Some come to see her on their days off. Because my mother has outlived most of her friends, these who are not native born have become my mother's final friends.

I love these immigrants. I need these immigrants.

You see, every immigrant story is a personal story. Behind the statistics and politics are stories of mothers and fathers, sons and daughters, husbands and wives. There are millions of stories that vary as much as race, nationality, gender and faith.

When you read about all the complexity of immigration and think about what needs to be done, love the immigrants.

Leith Anderson
President
National Association of Evangelicals

THE IMMIGRATION DILEMMA

Most evangelicals are caught in between wanting to have responsible border policy with compassion for the alien. It makes coming up with a fair balance here very difficult.
Reverend Richard Cizik, in *The Washington Times*, January 14, 2007

Nearly everyone seems to agree that we have an immigration problem in the United States. The exact nature of the problem, though, is heatedly disputed. From one perspective, our nation is facing an unprecedented invasion of illegal aliens, who violate our laws upon entry and then become a drain on social services and public education systems, depress wages and displace native-born American workers, and then contribute to increases in poverty and crime rates. A flier for candidates for the Carpentersville, Illinois, city council prior to the elections of fall 2006 expresses the frustrations of many Americans:

> Are you tired of waiting to pay for your groceries while Illegal Aliens pay with food stamps and then go outside and get in a $40,000 car?
> Are you tired of paying taxes when Illegal Aliens pay NONE!
> Are you tired of reading that another Illegal Alien was arrested for drug dealing?
> Are you tired of having to punch 1 for English?
> Are you tired of seeing multiple families in our homes?
> Are you tired of not being able to use Carpenter Park on the weekend, because it is over run by Illegal Aliens?
> Are you tired of seeing the Mexican Flag flown above our Flag?[1]

Others see the current state of immigration as a problem for very different reasons. They see millions of people who have, usually for economic reasons, accepted displacement from their home countries to pursue a better life for themselves and their families in the United States, just as generations of immigrants have done before them. Tragically, from this perspective, these people are not welcomed into our society, but are scapegoated and forced into a shadowy existence by broken immigration laws, even though they contribute to our nation's economy by performing a host of jobs, most of which few native-born Americans would be willing to do. Undocumented immigrant Elvira Arellano spent a year living inside a Methodist church in Chicago, Illinois, in an ultimately unsuccessful attempt to avoid deportation that would separate her from her eight-year-old, U.S.-citizen son. She has become something of a spokesperson for this perspective:

> Out of fear and hatred of an enemy you cannot find you have set out to destroy our lives and our families. As you knocked on my door, you are knocking on thousands of doors, ripping mothers and fathers away from their terrified children. You have a list of 17 million Social Security no-match numbers, and you are following that list as if we were terrorists and criminals instead of workers with families. You are denying us work and the seniority and benefits we have earned, and you are taking the property we have saved for and bought.[2]

From either of these perspectives, the immigration dilemma seems frustratingly simple. As both sides rail against the other, and against the government, where Congress has proposed competing bills but has yet to pass into law any substantial changes in immigration policy, we are left with the status quo: an estimated 11 to 12 million people with no valid immigration status living and, usually, working in the United States.

Less vocal in the debate are the many who suspect that this is actually a complicated, nuanced issue. Partisans of a particular policy position are apt to view the issue as very simple—right versus wrong, us versus them.

Yet, as political scientist Amy Black notes, it is these "easy" issues that often prove the most complex and the hardest to resolve, since our presumptions keep us from hearing the other side.[3] Within this debate, a growing middle recognizes this is not a simple issue. They want a more thoughtful, informed understanding of the issues than offered by the two-minute screaming matches by advocates of differing perspectives on cable news channels and talk radio.

Those of us who seek to follow Christ, in particular, face a challenge in sorting through the rhetoric to understand how we can reflect God's justice as well as his love and compassion in designing a national immigration policy, and in the ways we relate individually to the immigrants and refugees in our communities. On first glance at the issue, we recognize that immigrants are people made in God's image who should be treated with respect; at the same time, we believe God has instituted the government and the laws that it puts into place for a reason, and that as Christians we are generally bound to submit to the rule of law. Many are left conflicted, unsure of what our faith requires of us on this pressing issue.

Through the work of World Relief, the Christian ministry where we both work that serves refugees and immigrants throughout the United States, we might find ourselves on a regular basis in a church, speaking with people about issues of immigration and citizenship, or in a congressperson's office, talking with staffers about the need to fix the immigration system. Sometimes we speak in Spanish or with translation in Lithuanian, Arabic or Cantonese to an audience of immigrants eager to naturalize. Other times we are speaking in front of a predominantly nonimmigrant church group, usually in an adult education class, answering questions about immigration policy. When we are in front of an audience of nonimmigrant evangelicals or before congressional staffers who are helping our political leaders form immigration policy, we find that many are asking the same questions we have often asked ourselves. This book seeks to address some of the most common questions and misconceptions that we and other Christians have wrestled with as we consider the immigration "problem."

This book is written out of our own personal experiences with this dilemma, tracing through much of the investigation to which our own questions have led us in seeking to understand immigration policy—and, more important, immigrants and refugees themselves—through the lens of our faith. While it would be disingenuous to pretend that we do not have strong opinions about how we (as individuals, as the church and as a society) should approach this issue, our foremost interest is not to convince the reader of the virtue of any particular piece of legislation. Rather, we hope this book will encourage our sisters and brothers to take a step back from the rhetoric and combine a basic understanding of how immigration works and has worked in the United States with a biblical worldview. We do not believe there is one Christian prescription to solve the immigration issue (though there may be decidedly un-Christian ways to view the issue), and there is plenty of space within the church for charitable disagreement on issues such as this.

Learning Through Relationships

More than just a policy question, immigration is also very personal to each of us, because of the many immigrants and refugees whom we have come to know. These relationships have transformed our own perspectives. Each immigrant, and each nonimmigrant affected by immigration, has a distinct story that cannot be summarized by abstract statistics or polling data.

I (Matthew) have been particularly marked by getting to know some of my neighbors. My first friend in the neighborhood where I live, whom I met even before I moved in, is Jean.* He is now a high school sophomore in a suburb of Chicago, but he was born in Rwanda shortly before genocide broke out in that small East African country in 1994. He fled with his family to Tanzania, then to the Congo and then finally to Zambia, where he lived for nearly a decade. In 2005, Jean and his family were

---

*Here and throughout this book we have, in some cases, changed names and identifying details of those whose stories we include to maintain their privacy. Anyone whose story is told in this book has given us permission to use it.

accepted by the U.S. government as refugees to be resettled in the United States. With the help of churches, volunteers, the Rwandese community already in the United States, and World Relief, they are making a new life for themselves step by step. His mother and father work very hard in difficult, low-paying jobs at all hours of the day and night to pay the bills and even to pay the U.S. government back for their seven trans-atlantic airline tickets. Jean is less concerned with his family's finances than about fitting in at his school, mastering American English (his fifth language, which he is concerned he speaks with an accent) and finding a lawn-mowing job for the summer. He is tired of sharing a bed-room with his four sisters, and he talks often about what he misses of Africa, but he thanks God that he is safe.

Another neighbor, Elena, has a very different story. She came to the United States from Mexico in 1990 at age twenty-six, crossing the border illegally with the very expensive assistance of a *coyote* (a people smuggler), hoping to find a job that would let her make ends meet—something she could not find in Mexico. She has now lived and worked here for more than fifteen years, is involved in her church (a Catholic parish that has nearly as many people in its Spanish-language masses each weekend as in its English masses), has married and divorced in the United States, and is now raising two children on a very limited income. She speaks enough English to work the drive-thru at the fast food restaurant across the street, but she is far from fluent and often comes by to ask for help reading a let-ter in English from her children's school; she often also brings delicious enchiladas or *chilaquiles*.

Elena is very proud that her children speak English but sometimes la-ments their reluctance to speak Spanish. She prays for a legalization of some sort, or that her U.S.-born children will eventually be able to help her get a green card. She notes the small amount of assistance that the African refugees like Jean's family receive from the government, for which she is ineligible, even though she too struggles to support her family. Still, she is happy to be here. "I live better here than in Mexico," she says. "Here, nothing lacks"—an astonishing statement, given that she sometimes falls behind on the rent payments for the very modest one-bedroom apartment that she shares with three others in her family, cannot afford a car, and has no health insurance—"I have work. In Mexico, there is no work."

Two doors down from Elena lives an African American family that moved from a rough neighborhood on the west side of Chicago, seeking to avoid the gang violence there. The mother, Serena, works at a fast food restaurant and is preparing to take the GED high school equivalency exam. She gets along fine with her neighbors—she even gives Elena's daughter a ride to school on rainy days—but she does not think it is right that the Mexican immigrants come illegally and take jobs when her husband is out of work. She too notices the help that the African refugees receive from churches and wonders why something like that is not available for someone who was born in this country.

Living in relationships with immigrants, refugees and other low-income people has forced us to grapple with the question of what it means for us, as followers of Christ, to love our neighbors as we love ourselves. It has also awakened us to the ethically complex questions of immigration and refugee policy—whom do we let in, what do we do with those who came in even though our government did not allow them in, and what effect will our policies have on those already here and struggling to get by? Of course, our attempts to address these questions have been shaped by our own personal journeys.

My Personal Journey: Matthew's Story

I grew up in an evangelical home, with parents who were (and are) very committed to their faith in Jesus Christ. We attended a nondenominational church where politics were seldom if ever mentioned. I suspect, though, that a survey would have shown that a large majority of my congregation, including my family and me, identified with a generally conservative political stance—particularly on issues such as abortion or homosexual marriage, but also probably on issues of immigration policy.

I had little exposure to immigrants growing up in the small city of

Neenah, Wisconsin. While Hmong people from Laos had been resettled in neighboring towns, I never interacted with them. There were a few Mexican and Asian immigrants in my town, but almost everyone in my elementary school was descended from white immigrants from Europe at least two or three generations back, if not more. My own ancestors came from Holland in the mid-1800s, long enough ago that the immigrant experience felt very removed from my reality; what I knew about immigrants and immigration I knew primarily from television. As I relocated to the Chicago area for college, I realized that immigrants and refugees were all around me, yet I still did not know them.

Ironically, I began to think a lot more about U.S. immigration while outside the United States. I spent a summer living and volunteering in San José, Costa Rica. There I played sports, tutored and led Bible studies in a community of immigrants from Nicaragua. Much like Mexicans and Central Americans who go north to find a better economic situation in the United States, hundreds of thousands of Nicaraguans have gone south, both legally and illegally, to take advantage of a more vibrant economy in Costa Rica—and like immigrants in the United States, Nicaraguans in Costa Rica are not always warmly welcomed.

I returned to Central America a few years later where I worked with World Relief and their local affiliate, *Pueblos en Acción Comunitaria*, as they sought to help farmers in rural Nicaragua raise their incomes by providing small loans. In my time there, I saw firsthand the extreme poverty and chronic unemployment that motivate many people to emigrate. Particularly when lured by promises and rumors (true or untrue) of generous salaries and unparalleled opportunity in the United States, many of the people I met hoped one day to find a better life in the north for their families, even if that meant going *mojado* (literally, wet—as in having crossed the Río Grande River illegally). Seeing the conditions in which many Nicaraguans live—for many, on less than $1 per day—I could hardly blame them for entertaining this option.

When I returned to the United States, I accepted a job with World Relief's office in the suburbs of Chicago, where I was able to use my Spanish language skills to partner with churches to assist immigrants and refugees in integrating into our society. In the process, I have gotten to know many immigrants and refugees, heard their stories and begun to understand why they left their home countries for the United States. My specific job description as an immigration legal counselor has also let me learn a great deal about our country's immigration laws, exposing my own previous ignorance: I have been surprised to discover that much of what I believed about immigration was inaccurate.

On graduation from college, I also decided to move into the diverse apartment complex where Jean, Elena and Serena live. My move was based, at least in part, out of a desire to really understand who my new neighbors are, to try to love them as myself (though I have not always done this well), and to share with them the grace and love that I have experienced in Christ. Within my apartment complex, located in a well-to-do suburb of Chicago, I have neighbors born in Mexico, Sudan, Somalia, Rwanda, Burundi, Sierra Leone, Burma, Vietnam and India, as well as many Caucasians (like myself) and African Americans whose ancestors came to this country decades or centuries ago. Being a part of this community has allowed me to put human faces on the immigration dilemma and has led me deeper into questions of how I ought to think about and act on the immigration "problem."

My Personal Journey: Jenny's Story

I grew up in a Christian home where both of my parents were immigrants from South Korea. My older brother and I were born in Philadelphia, Pennsylvania, a few years after my parents immigrated to the United States.

My dad has one of the most amazing stories of resilience and strength of any immigrant I have ever met. His grandfather and father owned a large, well-regarded newspaper in Korea in the early 1900s. Through this company a love for journalism grew in my family. During the Korean War of 1950, the Communist forces invaded Korea and proceeded to kill all the media personnel first. My grandfather was killed during the war, and my father, still an infant, was left with his mother, who eventually became sick and died when he was ten years old. My father was an orphan and extremely poor in a country where rice and spare portions of vegetables were the meals of the day, and where a single pair of shoes with holes was supposed to last you years through the winter snow and summer heat. My grandmother, however, was a Christian. (A large number of Koreans were being brought to faith by American missionaries who were entering Korea in large numbers at the time.) Her faith in God led my father to also accept Jesus Christ as his savior at a very young age. His faith in God sustained him through his parents' death and as he lived with his uncle, who was also poor and struggled to support my father through school.

In order to support himself my father tutored his fellow classmates and helped the teacher after school to earn money for food and school supplies. He eventually became president of his class in high school. Having loved cars all throughout his childhood, he applied for a grant to go to Japan to visit the car manufacturing factories there. He received the grant and went to tour the Japanese car manufacturing facilities, which deepened his love for cars. Upon his return, he wrote a report for the company that employed him. My dad learned how to fix cars in his local neighborhood and eventually entered a national car-repair competition where he won first place. One of the judges during the competition noticed my father and asked him if he would like to go with him to the United States. My father's dream since he was a young child was to go to the United States, a land where the "streets were paved with gold" and there was an abundance of food and opportunity to pursue his dreams. In Korea, he didn't really have a place he could call home, and it would have been extremely difficult for him to climb up in society.

He readily accepted and landed in the United States with the dream of one day opening up his own business. He started working for Volkswagen and then for the Ford Motor Company as a mechanic, then went back to Korea for a few years, where he met my mother. They were married and both immigrated to the United States. Through hard work and the grace of God, my father fulfilled his lifelong dream by eventually owning his own auto mechanic shop.

Life in the United States was not as easy as he thought, however. When he first immigrated to the United States, he went to the supermarket and bought a can of breadcrumbs with a picture of fried chicken on the front. He was so ecstatic because he did not know fried chicken was so cheap and easy to eat! He hurriedly went home and eagerly opened the can, only to peer in and see bread crumbs staring back at him. He saved money, ate fast food and lived in a small apartment. He also regularly attended church and found a sense of community there. While life was not easy, he was always very grateful to God for the opportunity to immigrate to the United States, and he did everything he could to express his thanks by raising his children to love God, serving in the church and giving back to his community.

My father has a deep, abiding love of this country grounded in the opportunities he was given when he first arrived. During his citizenship interview, the interviewing officer commended my father for his hard work ethic and his easy grasp of English, saying he was a model immigrant and that the United States was proud to have people like him here. My father has never missed a day of work and uses his auto mechanic services to help those in need in the community. He still loves journalism and writes frequently for the local Korean newspaper, and he is a well-respected leader in his church and among his friends.

While the immigrant experience of my father is a story I share often with friends and colleagues, I also grew up in the United States having to form my identity as a full American, born and bred in this country, yet with a cultural background and appearance distinct from the dominant culture. I was not an immigrant myself but grew up in an immigrant home where the hardships my parents endured to "make it" in this country formed my personal identity and my faith in Christ. Growing up as a minority, I wondered whether people would ever just think of me as an American without having my appearance predispose them to think I was a "foreigner." In fact, in order to fit in, I didn't want to learn the Korean language growing up and struggled with whether to be proud of my Korean heritage. Even though I speak English fluently, love American football and have been educated here, people are surprised sometimes that I can speak English as well as I can, and they have often asked me "where are you *really* from?"

The political debate over immigration in the United States was not something to which I paid particular attention until later in life. While in college, I had studied migration issues at a macrolevel and always had a general interest in immigration due to my background. When I studied and worked in Madrid, Spain, I realized that immigration affects not just the United States but other industrialized countries, too, as their populations age and as migrants take jobs traditionally occupied by their native workforce.

I started working at World Relief on advocacy for refugee and immigration issues. I had my own reservations and initial misgivings about why the system was so broken in the first place and how it had even come to this point. My advocacy work in Washington, D.C., dispelled much of the misinformation I had previously believed.

More important, my work exposed me to the human side of the story. Stories of undocumented immigrants who had no way to regularize their status yet had been here for over ten years working in the same job, or of family members who were initially here legally yet were separated for long periods due to processing delays, softened my heart and mind to investigate the issue further. Living in Baltimore, I knew that a growing immigrant population there was challenging the traditional ideas and expectations of what the city should "look like," and I knew this issue was affecting not just Baltimore but communities all across America and throughout the world. I realized more and more as I studied immigration how truly broken the system was and what role the church could play by bringing to light the human aspects of an issue mired in numbers and politics.

I also realized that immigration issues and immigrants themselves were never going to go away. If the church does not respond now, it will eventually have to respond in one way or another. Will our response be one that we can look back on a century later and say we were proud to have taken? We must, as God's stewards, respond in a way that is based on facts and reflects God's justice and compassion. World Relief's position in the immigration debate grew out of its work with immigrants in the United States, and it was through this position that I grew to have a deeper understanding of the issue beyond the rhetoric.

Charting the Course

Through this book, we will attempt to put a human face on the immigration issue by introducing you to a number of immigrants and refugees, many of whom have become our friends. It is easy to forget, when talking about a complex issue like immigration, rife with competing statistics used liberally by both sides of the debate, that we are essentially talking about human beings, each one made in God's image. C. S. Lewis reminds us that each human being—the foreign born certainly not excluded—is an immortal being with a destiny much greater than this life alone, and in this sense is "the holiest object presented to your senses."[4] Our faith prohibits us from seeing any person as anything less than human and therefore sacred.

The terminology we use in English to refer to foreigners is quite unhelpful for keeping the uniqueness and sacredness of humanity in our minds. According to the dictionary, the language of our immigration laws, and even some translations of the Bible, it is entirely proper to refer to a person from another country as an *alien*, and no disrespect is inherently intended. Yet the fact that the term is now more commonly used to describe an extraterrestrial means that our minds go to Hollywood-induced images of three-headed green Martians when we hear about aliens, not to human beings with families and faith, made in God's image just like ourselves.

We prefer to refer to people as "undocumented" rather than "illegal." We do not deny that it is illegal to enter the United States without a valid visa and inspection, nor do we condone any illegal activity. However, while entry without inspection (or overstaying a temporary visa) is illegal, this does not define the person's identity. Many of us have broken a law at one time or another (we can both confess to having sped down the highway on more than one occasion), but if a single (or even, in the case of our speeding, repeated) act were to define our identity, we would probably all be "illegals." Such terminology, in common usage, lumps immigrants—whose entering or overstaying unlawfully usually does not require any malicious intent—with criminals like murderers, rapists and kidnappers. It is too easy to dehumanize such immigrants when we lump them with such unsavory characters.* So, rather than referring to people as illegal aliens, we have generally opted to refer to people as undocumented immigrants throughout this text.

The next chapter will, we hope, help us recapture the human element of the immigration dilemma, focusing on who immigrants and refugees are, why they come to our country and how they are received when they get here. We particularly focus on the 11 to 12 million people who have no legal right to be present, as they, even more than immigrants who are here legally, bear most of the ill will stirred up by the immigration debate, and are probably the most likely to be dismissed as different from ourselves.

In chapter three, we present a concise history of our nation's immigration history—from the earliest settlers to Ellis Island to the new waves of immigrants that began to reach our shores after the last major immigration reform was passed in 1965. We cannot adequately understand the current situation without understanding what has occurred in the past. In particular, we want to look at where our churches have been on this complex issue—which, as it does today, has always stirred passions.

In chapter four, drawing on Matthew's experience as an immigration counselor, we explain our current immigration legal system—one that is quite complex and that can be difficult to understand even for those who work with it day-to-day. A basic understanding of how our immigration laws work (and do not work) today is crucial if we are to understand why

---

*That said, even murderers, rapists and kidnappers are made in the image of God, so we should not dehumanize them either.

so many people have come to the United States illegally.

Chapter five takes a step back and examines immigration from a biblical and theological perspective, reviewing the many immigrants in Scripture and what the Bible has to say about interacting with immigrants. While we will, of course, not find a specific prescription for U.S. immigration policy spelled out in the Bible, we can certainly identify principles that help us ascertain how God would have us, as followers of Christ, address this complex topic. Above all, we suggest that the ethic of loving our neighbor—including the immigrant and refugee—is central to God's desire for us as we wrestle with this issue.

In chapter six, we address many of the most common concerns about immigration—both legal and illegal—including those from a Christian perspective. In particular, we focus on the apparent dilemma between wanting to welcome immigrants as Scripture commands us and following and upholding the laws, which is also a biblical mandate.

Chapter seven considers the impact of immigration on our country. We examine the U.S. economy and show how many industries depend on immigrant labor. We also present immigration from a global perspective, so the reader can gain a broader understanding of how it is affecting not just the United States but also many countries throughout the world.

Chapter eight provides a summary of the proposals that have been considered in recent years to deal with immigration. Drastically different ideas have been debated in the U.S. Congress, from mass deportation and criminalization to amnesty for all. What have come closer to becoming law—though there have been no major changes as of this writing—are compromise bills that include both stricter border enforcement as well as an earned legalization for at least some of the undocumented, requiring them to pay a fine and meet other criteria in order to receive their legal status. We draw on Jenny's experience in representing World Relief's position in Washington as we walk through the most recent policy proposals.

In chapter nine, we examine how many of the churches and denominations in our country—particularly those of the evangelical persuasion with which we both identify—are approaching the immigration dilemma. Many of the major streams of Christianity—both Protestant and Catholic, evangelical and liberal mainline—have put forth some sort of statement on immigration, and we can learn much from the thoughtful theological reasoning contained in these. We will also examine how immigration is changing the church itself in America today and what this means for how the church should respond to immigrants.

Finally, chapter ten provides some suggestions for moving forward. There are many responses: by serving and getting to know our immigrant neighbors through volunteering; by advocating for more just governmental policies; by educating our churches and communities; and by addressing the larger structural issues that lead to poverty, war and environmental disasters in other countries and thus to the waves of immigration that we face today.

We hope that you will be convinced—not necessarily of which policy to support, but at least, as a follower of Christ, that we each are called to love and serve our foreign-born neighbors. Appendixes at the end of the book provide resources for getting started in this process.

We expect that we have readers looking at this immigration dilemma from a wide range of perspectives. We may have already offended some of you just in the first chapter, as immigration is a highly charged topic. Our sincere prayer is that you will continue to journey with us to explore these difficult questions, and that each of us, personally and corporately as the church, would seek God's heart on this issue. To begin, we need to understand who the immigrants at the center of this controversy *are*, which is the topic of the next chapter.

ALIENS AMONG YOU

WHO ARE UNDOCUMENTED IMMIGRANTS?

We have no idea who these people are, where they're going, or what they want.
U.S. Representative Gabrielle Giffords, Democrat of Arizona, discussing undocumented immigrants while campaigning during the 2006 congressional elections, in *The Chicago Tribune*, September 26, 2006

The millions of undocumented immigrants living in the United States—11 to 12 million of them, according to researchers—are at the center of the immigration dilemma.[1] For many Americans, the issue is compounded by a great confusion about who these undocumented immigrants are: Why do they come here? Where do they come from? What do they do once they are here, and what effect do they have on our communities?

The reality for many of us is that we have very limited meaningful interaction with immigrants and even less interaction with undocumented immigrants. Today, immigrants live in just about every corner of the United States. While, historically, most immigrants once lived in large cities like New York, Chicago, Los Angeles and Miami, increasingly immigrants are also showing up in small towns in places like Iowa, North Carolina, Wisconsin and Idaho. Still, many Christians could count on one hand the number of immigrants they would consider friends.

Sifting Through the Rhetoric

For those who do not know many immigrants personally, much of what is known comes from secondary sources—particularly anecdotal stories passed around the water cooler at work, the coffee pot at church, or the Internet and television. Much of what we hear is just inaccurate. For example, an e-mail that has been circulating for several years, citing the *Los Angeles Times* as its source, claims that "95 percent of warrants for murder in Los Angeles are for illegal aliens," "75 percent of people on the Most Wanted List in Los Angeles are illegal aliens," and "over [two-thirds] of all births in Los Angeles County are to illegal alien Mexicans on [Medicaid] whose births were paid for by taxpayers."[2] In reality, as Chuck Colson points out in a column calling on Christians to think more critically and compassionately about immigration, none of these "facts" are true, nor did they come from the *Los Angeles Times*.[3]

Most of us are savvy enough not to believe everything we read in a forwarded e-mail or on the Internet, but we are more likely to trust what we hear on television or radio. Yet even here, we find that not everything reported about immigrants is accurate. For example, Lou Dobbs, host of a popular television program on CNN (the self-proclaimed "most trusted name in news"), has made his strong opposition to illegal immigration a central theme of his television program; in the process, his program has on multiple occasions reported disparaging and untrue information. In April 2005, Dobbs introduced a report by proclaiming, "The invasion of illegal aliens is threatening the health of many Americans."[4] The report proceeded to state that there had been 7,000 cases of leprosy (also known as Hansen's disease) in the United States over the past three years, compared to just 900 cases total in the previous forty years.[5] The reality, according to federal government statistics, is that there were only 137 reported cases of Hansen's disease in the previous year, and there has been no significant change in the prevalence of the disease over the past several years whatsoever; the figure of 7,000 reported cases is really for the last *thirty* years, and the prevalence actually peaked in 1983.[6]

Similarly, Dobbs reported in May 2006 that illegal immigrants comprised "about a third of our prison population," and complained about the cost of their incarceration. In reality, about 6 percent of prisoners in federal and state prisons are noncitizens, which includes both documented and undocumented immigrants.[7] The crime rate among immigrants is actually lower than among native-born U.S. citizens, contrary to the popular perception.[8] Since millions of people watched these reports on CNN and accepted them as fact, it is understandable that popular perception is often incorrect.

In addition to relaying false information, those opposed to immigration tend to rely on isolated, anecdotal situations to build stereotypes. Author James Russell, for example, begins his book (a critique of the role of American churches in guiding immigration policy) with the story of an undocumented immigrant in Oregon who raped a Catholic nun and then strangled her to death with her own rosary beads.[9] Russell suggests from this appalling but isolated case that all undocumented immigrants are to be feared, establishing an unfair and illogical prejudice. Such stereotypes get generalized and repeated by those most vigorously opposed to immigration, such as Chris Simcox, cofounder of the anti-illegal-immigration Minuteman Project, who stated in 2003 that Central American and Mexican immigrants are "evil people" who "have no problem slitting your throat and taking your money or selling drugs to your kids or raping your daughter."[10]

Most American Christians reject such obviously prejudiced and hateful statements, but it is easy, if we hear false statistics and stereotypes repeated frequently enough, to subconsciously suspect they are at least partially true. As followers of Christ, we need to carefully consider what we read, see and hear and, as Chuck Colson suggests, be careful not to go "beyond worrying about illegal immigration to demonizing the immigrants themselves."[11] "Regardless of where one stands on the policy debate, the dehumanization of immigrants is at clear odds with Christian values of compassion, mercy and dignity."[12]

Who Are Immigrants?

If immigrants are not necessarily who we hear they are on television or radio, we are still left wondering: who are these people? Statistics about the undocumented population are always going to be estimates, as those without immigration status are sometimes wary to participate in surveys or census questionnaires. Still, we consider the demographic information from the Pew Research Center, a nonpartisan research institute that we have cited for several statistics below, to be among the most reliable, unbiased data.

I (Matthew) have also included a number of stories from immigrants, most of whom are my friends and acquaintances and, for that reason, are geographically concentrated near my home in Illinois. Indeed, anecdotal evidence can be easily twisted, but the stories I have selected generally represent the diversity of immigrant experiences I have encountered in my neighborhood and through my work as an immigration counselor. All of the stories in this chapter and throughout the book are factual, personal stories, shared with the individuals' consent, but to guard their privacy we have changed names and identifying details in some cases.

Immigrants: Documented and Undocumented

In any discussion about undocumented immigrants, it is important to remember that most foreign-born people in the United States have legal status. Of an estimated 37 million people born outside but living inside the United States, about 35 percent are already naturalized U.S. citizens and 33 percent are Lawful Permanent Residents. An additional 2 percent of immigrants have temporary resident status; many of them will adjust their status to permanent resident status eventually. Thus, most foreign-born individuals—about seven out of every ten—are entirely legal. The rest of the immigrants currently in the United States—about 31 percent— have no legal status, meaning either that they entered the country without inspection or overstayed a temporary visa.[13]

Immigrants with legal status come from all over the world and are found across social strata. My own family includes a number of such immigrants. My uncle Dan was born in southern India but immigrated to the United States in 1981 to join his mother, who had been granted an employment-based visa to do research in the United States. He later at-

29

tended seminary in Michigan and served as a pastor for many years. He became naturalized in 1996, several years after marrying my aunt. Their two children, my cousins, were born in the United States and thus are American citizens by birth.

My cousin Josh was serving in the U.S. Air Force and was stationed in Japan when he met Jun, the woman who would eventually become his wife. When Josh was assigned to an Air Force base in Arizona, he applied for a green card on Jun's behalf, so that she could join him in the United States.

My sister-in-law Maria-Jose is from Chile. After studying to be a psychologist in her home country, she accepted a scholarship to study counseling at a Christian graduate school near Seattle, Washington, and came to the United States on a temporary student visa. During her time in Seattle, Maria-Jose met my brother, Tim, and they decided to marry. Though it was not her original intention when she arrived, Maria-Jose decided to remain in the United States to marry my brother. She recently received her green card, allowing her to work and reside permanently in the United States.

Why They Come

Immigrants—whether with or without legal status—come to the United States for many reasons. Many are drawn to the United States to find a better-paying job to support themselves and their families; others come to reunite with family members; still others come seeking the freedoms guaranteed in the United States but not, certainly, in every other country of the world. For many, the incentive to come includes multiple factors. Some immigrants secure a visa to come legally, but many others are unable to obtain a visa to live and work in the United States. Some with no legal option for entry enter illegally, crossing a border without the required governmental inspection, while others can secure a temporary visitor visa and enter legally, but then violate the terms of their visa by overstaying.

Pedro, Martha and Family—Economic Realities

My friends Pedro and Martha are somewhat typical undocumented immigrants. They are both originally from Morelos, a small Mexican state just south of the capital city. They married young and have long struggled economically, as many do in Mexico, where more than 10 percent of the population lives on less than two dollars per day.[14] Early in their marriage, Martha recalls, they had nothing to eat besides simple corn tortillas and salt. They considered migrating then, a few decades ago, to find better work and a better future in the United States, but under U.S. immigration law their financial situation made it extremely unlikely that they would be granted visas.

Pedro found work in a factory, making fabrics for export to the United States and other countries; it was hard work at a relatively low wage, but the family was able to support themselves. The couple had four children over the years. It was a challenging life, but they were surviving. Then the factory where Pedro worked went bankrupt and closed, and Pedro lost his job. Pedro found other jobs, but could not make enough income to support the family. Afraid to ask her husband for money that she knew they did not have, but unwilling to see her children drop out of school, Martha began to take out loans for their children's school expenses. Eventually, she had to tell her husband that they were severely indebted, with interest payments for the school loans using up the better part of the income that Pedro was bringing in.

Desperate, the couple decided there was no option other than to have Pedro head north; their seventeen-year-old son, Harold, decided to accompany him. Martha would stay behind along with the three other children. Pedro had relatives—two sisters and some cousins—living in the Chicago suburbs, who offered a temporary place to stay and to help them find work. They would send money back to pay off the debt and support the rest of the family.

The family took out one more loan, enough to cover the $3,800 Pedro would have to pay a *coyote*, or smuggler, to bring him and his son illegally into the United States. Pedro and Harold set out. Their group consisted of two smugglers, one male and one female, and eighteen migrants. As they crossed the Mexico-Arizona border in the desert, the group was spotted by U.S. Border Patrol agents and ran in different directions. Harold remembered his father's advice: "Whatever happens, we stay together." They ended up together, but they were separated from part of their group, including the more experienced smuggler. They now had no way to arrive in Phoenix, as had been the plan, so they jumped on a slow-moving freight train, holding on for twelve hours and trying desperately to stay awake.

When they finally arrived in Phoenix, several days later than planned, Pedro was able to call Martha by telephone and assure her that, though tired and traumatized by the journey, they were okay. Only then did Martha complete the payment to the smuggler.

Pedro and Harold were taken by van from Phoenix to Chicago, where they were reunited with Pedro's sisters and cousins. They provided them a place to stay and helped them to secure false Social Security cards, since, having entered illegally, they were not eligible to obtain authentic work documents. Very soon after arrival, both Pedro and Harold became busboys in a family restaurant, each working about fifty hours a week. It was hard work, but they were grateful for employment. They lived very frugally, sharing a small space with family members, and were able to send money home to Martha and the children.

With each paycheck, a sizable portion of Pedro and Harold's income is deducted for payroll taxes, but Pedro knows he will likely never receive any benefit for all the money he is paying into Social Security or Medicare, since he has been using a false Social Security card.

When another of Pedro's sons, Homero, decided to come north and join his father and brother in the United States, the family rented their first apartment, a small one-bedroom unit not far from where I live. Since Pedro and Harold had developed a reputation as very hard workers, the manager of the restaurant where they work was eager to hire Homero as well. In 2006, a few months after Homero arrived, with half of the family now living and working in the United States, Martha decided to make the journey as well. She agonized over the decision, but she felt it was ultimately best for her family that she go, work and earn additional money, and eventually try to bring the two younger children as well. Leaving her ten- and eleven-year-old son and daughter with her sister in Morelos, Martha set out for the United States.

Like her family members before her, Martha went with a smuggler and many other immigrants. As they crossed the border into New Mexico, though, they were apprehended by Border Patrol agents, temporarily detained, and then brought back to Mexico. Three days later, Martha tried again, and ultimately arrived at her new home, reunited with her husband and elder sons. The journey was so traumatic and difficult, though—trekking for days through the desert, having been mistreated and drugged with some sort of pill by the smugglers, and having been caught by immigration officials—that she had second thoughts about bringing her two younger children. "I don't want that for my children," she told me, and yet she is desperate to be with them, and for them to have the education available to them in the United States, vastly superior to what they receive in Mexico.

Martha wasted no time in finding work, either, working twelve hours per day between a fast-food restaurant and a hotel where she cleans guest rooms. She, too, pays her taxes. Their family lives humbly, with four people in a one-bedroom apartment, each working far more hours per week than I do for just slightly more than the minimum wage. They desperately miss their youngest children: Martha sometimes talks about selling their home in Morelos to cover the expense of a smuggler, since there is no legal way for them to enter.

Their lack of legal status also makes a normal existence very difficult. They live in fear of being deported ("I'm always afraid that they'll send me back," Pedro confesses). Homero was recently pulled over by the police while driving from work because the rosary beads hanging from his rearview mirror apparently limited visibility and violated a local ordinance. Having caught him for that small charge, the officer also fined him for what amounted to several days' of his income for driving without a valid driver's license. As an undocumented immigrant in Illinois, of course, Homero is not eligible for a driver's license.*

---

*In a certain sense, Homero might consider himself fortunate: in our community in Illinois a routine traffic stop does not generally trigger questions about immigration status or referrals for deportations, as it could in certain other municipalities in the United States.

Undocumented Immigrants and Taxes

Many undocumented workers use a false Social Security card to acquire work. Payroll taxes are then deducted from each paycheck and sent to the Social Security Administration. The federal government certainly realizes the money it is receiving out of such paychecks does not match any valid Social Security number—it receives about $6 to $7 billion each year in no-match Social Security contributions, which it acknowledges come primarily from unauthorized immigrants.[15] At a time when our Social Security system is facing a crisis, however, few people seem particularly concerned about extra money flowing into the system, subsidizing our grandparents and other retired folks.

It is probably not coincidental that the Social Security card, unlike most government documents such as a driver's license or passport, employs very little modern technology that would make it difficult to falsify; in fact, it looks like it was made on blue construction paper with a typewriter. While there has not yet been the political will to grant employment authorization to undocumented workers, at least in recent years, many politicians have also been wary about imposing a nationwide verification system. Such a system could result in millions of undocumented immigrants losing their jobs and have, as a result, potentially disastrous effects on the American economy, many of whose companies rely on low-wage undocumented labor. Recently, however, there has been discussion about implementing a fraud-proof employment eligibility verification system.

While the perception persists that undocumented immigrants are paid "under the table," in cash, with their income unreported and untaxed—and indeed some are—the majority of undocumented immigrants (the Social Security Administration estimates three out of four) do have Social Security, Medicare and income taxes deducted from their payroll—though, under current law, they are ineligible for any Social Security or Medicare benefits and for almost all federal- or state-government benefits funded through their income taxes.[16] Of course, just as do all consumers, all undocumented immigrants also pay sales tax and, whether directly as homeowners or indirectly through their monthly rent payments, property taxes.

In fact, many undocumented immigrants actually file tax returns each year. Their false Social Security numbers are not valid for filing taxes, but the Internal Revenue Service offers special Individual Taxpayer Identification Numbers (ITINs) to those who do not have valid Social Security numbers, with a commitment that the IRS will not communicate with immigration enforcement authorities. "We want your money whether you are here legally or not and whether you earned it legally or not," IRS commissioner Mark Everson told *The New York Times* in 2007.[17] Since 1996, when the ITIN first became available, more than 11 million numbers have been issued, and in 2005, tax returns with at least one household member reporting an ITIN number accounted for more than $5 billion in federal taxes paid.[18] While many criticize undocumented immigrants because of certain societal costs related to illegal immigration, they are often slow to recognize that immigrants often pay more in taxes than they take in services, and that they contribute overall to the U.S. economy.

Still, for all the unique difficulties, Pedro, Martha and their family are relatively content in their new life. "Back there, we didn't even have enough to eat." Now, their apartment is often full of relatives and friends, myself included, who enjoy Martha's delicious cooking. As I sat in their small kitchen, taking notes and enjoying my dinner, a fiber-optic Christmas tree emitted a repetitive, slightly annoying Christmas carol. Pedro explained that they had never been able to afford a Christmas tree in Mexico, but now they could. "I feel like I'm in glory here," Martha says. She just wishes her younger children could also be here.

Delfina—A Perilous Journey

Although their journey was difficult, Pedro and Martha are actually fortunate to have arrived safely in the United States. Many who endeavor the dangers of crossing the southern border illegally face injury or even death. In recent years, as the Mexican border has been controlled more vigorously, especially near major cities such as San Diego, California, and El

Paso, Texas, migrants have moved into the desert to cross. On a typical day at least one person dies while attempting it.[19]

Others survive the journey, but not intact. Delfina is a young migrant from Chihuahua, Mexico, whom I met near the border in El Paso. A single mother, she was struggling to support her children by working in a factory along the border that made car parts for export to the United States. Earning $50 per week and working long hours, Delfina heard she could make $500 per week cleaning houses if she went to Albuquerque, New Mexico. Leaving her children with her sister and promising to return, Delfina decided to make the journey.

She crossed the Rio Grande undetected and spent the first night sleeping in a park, but she was not yet in Albuquerque. Like Pedro, she tried to board a freight train—but she slipped, and the train cut her toes off of her right foot. When I met her, Delfina was waiting for her foot to heal enough that she could return to Mexico to be with her children.

Yaneth—When Visas Are Not Possible

The journey can be far more difficult, risky and expensive for those not from Mexico. About 2.5 million people—an estimated 22 percent of all undocumented workers—come from Latin American countries other than Mexico, particularly from Central America.[20] In most Central American countries, incomes are a fraction even of what they are in Mexico, providing all the more incentive to migrate.

Yaneth, who now lives near Washington, D.C., is typical of many Central American migrants. She graduated from high school in El Salvador and her husband, Walter, had gone to college. Though they both had jobs with the government, their combined salaries were not enough to feed their children more than one meal a day. Desperate, Yaneth's husband tried twice to apply for a visa to the United States. Since he did not have a close family member in the U.S. and did not otherwise qualify to apply for a green card, he applied for a tourist visa. Because he had very few assets, the U.S. consulate denied his application both times he applied. He went illegally instead and quickly found work.

After four years of separation, and after Yaneth also tried unsuccessfully to obtain a visa, her husband sent $9,000 to pay a smuggler to bring her all the way from El Salvador to the United States, crossing illegally through Guatemala and Mexico. The trip took fifty days, most of it in the back of a covered pick-up truck cramped with dozens of other migrants. Yaneth says that she cried the entire journey, thinking of her three children left behind, whom she hoped to support better from abroad.

Now Yaneth supervises a cleaning team for an apartment complex. She is sending money back so her children can get an education and, she hopes, have a good life in El Salvador. She would like to bring them to the United States, but if that is not possible she says she will return eventually. Nearly one-third of Latino immigrants say that they plan to return to their home country eventually, while most would like to stay in the U.S. for good.[21] Ironically, recent efforts aimed at minimizing illegal immigration—particularly increased funding for Border Patrol activities, along with more serious consequences for illegal reentry (a permanent bar to legal status)—have actually had the effect of keeping undocumented immigrants in, since there is now more risk attached to coming and going across the border as many migrants once did.[22]

Bal—When Spouses' Statuses Differ

While many undocumented immigrants cross the border illegally, nearly half—between 40 percent and 50 percent—enter the United States legally, on a valid visa, and then overstay or otherwise violate the terms of that visa.[23] Their journeys are typically far less perilous, but these undocumented immigrants face many of the same challenges once they arrive.

It is also important to realize that, though many people equate undocumented immigrants with citizens of Mexico, only a slight majority of undocumented immigrants, about 56 percent, come from Mexico.[24] There are also millions from Asia, Europe, Canada and Africa.

Bal is one of an estimated 1.5 million undocumented Asian immigrants in the United States, accounting for about 13 percent of the undocumented population.[25] He legally entered the United States through

Austin, Texas, in 1988 with a visa because he was working as a crewman for a shipping company. After entering, Bal completed his contract with the shipping company. In the United States, he was offered a construction job, with a monthly salary equal to what he would earn in one year in the Philippines, his home country. He accepted it, though it violated the terms of his visa, and he has been in the United States ever since.

Bal has tried on multiple occasions to obtain legal status, even paying thousands of dollars to "immigration consultants" who promised him a green card. Under current law, though, Bal has no right to apply for permanent legal status; the supposed experts swindled him. Sadly, there are many such "consultants" or *notarios*, usually not legally authorized to practice immigration law, willing to lie to and take advantage of undocumented immigrants like Bal, who is desperate (but legally ineligible) for legal status.*

In 1995, Bal met another Filipino immigrant, Shirly, whom he eventually married. Shirly came into the United States legally as well, on a temporary work visa, but Shirly never fell out of legal status. She worked as a nurse and eventually was able to adjust her status and obtain a green card through her employer, allowing her to live and work permanently in the United States. In 2007, Shirly took the next step in her American dream by becoming a naturalized U.S. citizen.

Shirly hoped that, as a U.S. citizen, she would be able to help her undocumented husband obtain legal status, especially since he has been in the United States for nearly twenty years and has been paying his taxes. While in certain cases undocumented individuals can obtain legal status

---

*In order to avoid receiving inaccurate and possibly unethical legal advice, immigrants should not accept immigration advice from anyone other than an immigration attorney or a nonprofit organization that is recognized by the Board of Immigration Appeals (BIA). A list of BIA-recognized organizations and accredited individuals at those organizations is maintained by the Executive Office for Immigration Review of the U.S. Department of Justice and can be found at <www.justice .gov/eoir/statspub/raroster.htm>. Churches and other nonprofit organizations that want to assist immigrants with immigration legal services should undergo the training necessary to become recognized by the BIA, because without adequate knowledge, well-meaning people can actually do irrevocable harm to an immigrant seeking advice.

through a U.S.-citizen spouse, Bal does not have this option under current law. He could apply for legal status if he returned to the Philippines, but the moment he leaves the United States he would trigger a ten-year bar to reentering the United States legally. His only option (except for waiting in the Philippines, separated from his wife, for ten years) is to apply for a waiver based on the extreme hardship to his U.S.-citizen wife.[26] Those waiver requests are often denied, particularly by the U.S. consulate in Manila, in which case the undocumented immigrant has triggered a bar to reentry and has no option for appeal. Bal and Shirly are thus faced with the difficult decision to risk ten years of separation or for Bal to continue without legal status.

Bal and Shirly's situation—with at least one U.S. citizen in a family with undocumented immediate family members—is actually very common. At least one in three undocumented families has one or more household members who are U.S. citizens.[27] Were the undocumented member of the family to be deported—which is entirely possible under current law—their U.S.-citizen family members (children, in many cases) would either need to live apart from them or relocate themselves to another country, presuming the relative's country of citizenship would allow them in.

Lyudmyla—Legal Status Limbo

While many immigrants come to the United States primarily for economic reasons, other immigrants come for other reasons and yet sometimes find themselves unable to obtain permanent resident status. Lyudmyla immigrated to the United States to be reunited with her husband, who had come eight years earlier and been granted asylum because, as an ethnic minority in Ukraine, he had faced persecution. Lyudmyla left a good job as the owner of a small restaurant to be with her husband.

When she arrived in the Chicago area in 2005, though, she found that her husband had changed a great deal in the eight years they had been separated. When he became abusive, Lyudmyla decided she needed to get out; she found a women's shelter where she lived for a while. Knowing very few people in a new country and with limited English, she found a caring community in a nearby nondenominational church, where she also heard for the first time about a relationship with Jesus and eventually accepted Christ as her savior.

Having entered legally as the spouse of an asylee, Lyudmyla later found out that, by divorcing her abusive husband, she had lost her right to apply for a green card.* She found herself in legal limbo.

Lyudmyla considered returning to the Ukraine, but she feared she would not know how to grow in her newfound faith there, where there are few evangelical Christians. "Sometimes I think that the only way is for me to go back," Lyudmyla told me, "but then when I think of how I would survive there as a Christian, without a church, without any support from the government for Christianity . . . that's why I stay here." With the support of her church community, Lyudmyla has gone to cosmetology school and learned English, but her life in the United States has been very difficult. She struggles to make the monthly rent payment, as her ambiguous legal status makes it difficult to find work. She says that it is only because of her faith that she can press on: "I believe God brought me in here for some reason, so I [would be] saved, and I know that he's not going to forsake me or leave me."

Sandra—Undocumented Children

Some undocumented immigrants, like my friend Sandra, do not choose to come to the United States at all—they simply accompany their parents. Sandra entered the United States illegally in 1992 at the age of six. Her first few years of life, in Mexico, had been very difficult. Her father refused to allow her to go to school, instead sending her to the street corner to sell oranges. He drank too much and mistreated Sandra's mother. Eventually, Sandra's mother decided to escape: she took Sandra and her older sister and made the journey to California, settling near San Francisco, where they had family. In 1993, shortly after their arrival, Sandra's

---

*Lyudmyla may have avenues to request legal status using some novel legal arguments, but she risks that her request could be denied, which could mean her deportation. As of this writing, she is weighing her options in consultation with her attorney.

U.S.-citizen uncle petitioned for his sister (Sandra's mother) and her minor children (Sandra and her sister), but it would be many years before that petition could possibly lead to legal status.

Sandra attended school and readily learned English. While many immigrants have difficulty learning English—only about 35 percent of Hispanic immigrants report speaking "pretty well" or "very well"—their children, like Sandra, almost always speak English very well.[28] Despite access to an education, though, Sandra's life in the U.S. was far from easy: she lived in a dangerous neighborhood, wrought with gangs, drugs and violence, and her family had few economic resources. As undocumented immigrants, they were ineligible for public benefits, such as welfare or food stamps, so their primary income was from Sandra's mother's work as a nanny.

Sandra's mother's limited income was not enough to support the family, though, so Sandra began working as well when she was about fourteen. She worked shifts of up to twelve hours some weekends at a restaurant, getting paid in cash and never being allowed a break. She and her coworkers—all undocumented—were taken advantage of, but as undocumented workers, they had few better options. Very involved in the youth group at her charismatic Apostolic church, Sandra turned to God. "When I would have hard days at work," Sandra says, "church was the only thing that kept me going."

Sandra resolved then that she would not do this sort of work all of her life. Despite working nearly a full-time schedule at the restaurant, Sandra dedicated herself to her schoolwork, and she excelled academically. Her high school teachers encouraged her to consider college, something that she had never before considered. Many people in her neighborhood did not even graduate from high school, and few went on to college, but Sandra became excited about the possibility. "I really wanted to get a degree, so that I could go back and help my family and my neighborhood," Sandra explains.

It was when she went to talk to her high school's guidance counselor about the possibility of college that Sandra understood for the first time

Immigrants and Public Benefits

A misconception we hear regularly about undocumented immigrants is that they come to the U.S. to take advantage of our country's generous public aid programs, such as welfare (Temporary Aid for Needy Families), food stamps, public housing, Supplementary Security Income for the disabled, the Earned Income Tax Credit and low-income, state health insurance programs like Medicaid. In reality, undocumented immigrants are not eligible for any of these programs. Although public benefit eligibility varies somewhat from one state to another, the only benefits for which an undocumented immigrant *might* be eligible in most states are emergency and prenatal healthcare, immunizations and treatment for communicable diseases, certain nutritional programs aimed primarily at children, and noncash emergency disaster relief (such as in the wake of Hurricane Katrina).[29] Also, because of the Supreme Court's 1982 decision in *Plyler v. Doe,* children, regardless of immigration status, are allowed to attend public schools. No undocumented immigrant, though, can legally receive any cash benefit from the government.

In fact, even many immigrants *with* legal status who entered the country after 1996 are ineligible for most public benefits. Although they may have a Lawful Permanent Resident (green) card, they are not eligible for food stamps or for any cash benefit until they have been Lawful Permanent Residents for at least five years.[30] While there are exceptions for refugees, asylees and a few other distinct groups, most immigrants must wait until they are eligible to apply for citizenship to qualify for public benefits. Even after five years of Lawful Permanent Residency, immigrants who received their legal status through a sponsoring U.S.-citizen family member and then receive public benefits risk that their sponsoring family member could be sued by the government for the value of those benefits.[31]

While the perception persists that people migrate to milk America's social safety net, the reality is that almost all immigrants come to the United States to work. The employment rate for adult male undocumented immigrants is an estimated 96 percent, significantly higher than for either work-authorized immigrants or for U.S.-citizen males.[32]

what it meant that she was undocumented: the college counselor told her that it would be nearly impossible for her to go to college. Despite an impressive high school résumé, her lack of a valid Social Security number meant she was ineligible for financial aid, and there was no way her family could pay for college.

Heartbroken, Sandra asked God why he would bring her to this country. In the midst of her prayer, she said she felt that God was showing her that he would provide a way for her to go to college.

God provided in a unique way. Based on her high grades, Sandra was accepted into a college preparation summer program at Stanford University for low-income students, which did not inquire about immigration status. The program then helped her to attain a scholarship to attend Wheaton College, an evangelical liberal arts college in Illinois.

Sandra excelled at Wheaton, maintaining a nearly perfect grade point average, serving in the student government and tutoring low-income children at a public housing project in Chicago, a neighborhood similar to where she had grown up in the San Francisco Bay area. She also has worked to begin a summer college preparation program for low-income high school students at Wheaton, modeled on what she experienced at Stanford, but from a distinctly Christian perspective.

Sandra's story has a happier ending than most: she obtained a green card in 2006 and is no longer undocumented. The petition that her U.S.-citizen uncle filed for her mother in 1993 finally became current—within days of Sandra's twenty-first birthday, such that Sandra was still eligible under the petition. By paying a $1,000 fine for having entered unlawfully, Sandra was able to adjust status and now has a green card.* She is eager to apply for citizenship when she is eligible in a few years. Sandra's older sis-

---

*The law that allowed Sandra to adjust status even though she had entered without inspection by paying a $1,000 fine, Section 245(i) of the Immigration & Nationality Act, expired in 2001, but Sandra was "grandfathered in" since her uncle's petition was submitted prior to the expiration of the law. For an immigrant in a similar situation today, but whose petition was not yet submitted when the law expired, adjustment of status to become a Lawful Permanent Resident would no longer be an option.

ter, who entered with her as a small child, is not so fortunate: she turned twenty-one before the visa became available, and thus no longer qualified under the petition; she remains undocumented.

Conclusion

The immigrants whose stories I have included in this chapter—Pedro and Martha, Delfina, Yaneth, Bal, Lyudmyla, and Sandra—are representative of the many undocumented immigrants with whom I (Matthew) have interacted over the past several years in my work with World Relief and living in a neighborhood with many immigrants. As I have gotten to know them, I have found them to be good friends, neighbors and, often, brothers and sisters in Christ. They are not perfect, but they are also certainly not the criminals that the media often portrays them to be. Like me, they are concerned about their family, their faith and the day-to-day realities of paying rent and affording groceries.

As a legal counselor, my job is to inform the immigrants who come to me for advice about what the law says. In rare cases, the law provides them an option to obtain legal status, but more often I have to break to them the bad news that, under current law, they have no real options. This realization made me wonder: how is it that my ancestors, who I am told came much for the same reasons as those described here, were able to immigrate to the United States? In the next chapter, we will look at how American immigration (and immigration policy) has changed over time.

NATION OF IMMIGRANTS

A HISTORICAL PERSPECTIVE ON
IMMIGRATION TO THE UNITED STATES

Do not oppress an alien; you yourselves know how it feels to be aliens, because you were aliens in Egypt.
Exodus 23:9

The biblical mandate to take special concern for foreigners, which we will look at in more depth in chapter five, is frequently paired with God's injunction to the people of Israel to remember their own history. They knew how it felt to be strangers living in a foreign land—Egypt—and God said that their own immigrant experience should inform how they were to treat sojourners in their land.

The problem, God knew, was that we human beings are apt to forget our own history. Our tendency, as pastor and author Rob Bell notes, is to think, once we have moved out of a difficult place and into a more comfortable situation, that we have done it ourselves, forgetting where we have come from and God's grace in bringing us through it.[1] To help keep their immigrant history in front of them, God imposed on the Israelites something of a liturgy, to be repeated to the priest when bringing forward an offering:

> When you have entered the land the LORD your God is giving you as
> an inheritance and have taken possession of it and settled in it . . . you

shall declare before the LORD your God: "My father was a wandering Aramean, and he went down into Egypt with a few people and lived there and became a great nation, powerful and numerous. But the Egyptians mistreated us and made us suffer, putting us to hard labor. Then we cried out to the LORD, the God of our fathers, and the LORD heard our voice and saw our misery, toil and oppression. So the LORD brought us out of Egypt with a mighty hand and an outstretched arm, with great terror and with miraculous signs and wonders. He brought us to this place and gave us this land, a land flowing with milk and honey; and now I bring the firstfruits of the soil that you, O LORD, have given me." Place the basket before the LORD your God and bow down before him. And you and the Levites and the aliens among you shall rejoice in all the good things the LORD your God has given to you and your household. (Deut 26:1, 5-11)

The Israelites were commanded to rehearse their history, lest they forget it. In doing so, Bell says, the Israelites were saying, "If I ever forget that my ancestors were homeless refugees, I will have lost my connection with the God who was good to my ancestors and who has been good to me."[2]

American Christians are in a unique position in that, as spiritual descendants of the Israelites, we too are commanded to remember and learn from their history as immigrants in Egypt. At the same time, we have the unique distinction of being a nation of immigrants, where more than 99 percent of the population—everyone except for those few whose ancestry is entirely Native American—has an immigrant history. As did the Israelites, we need to remember our history—where God has brought us and our ancestors from—to remember God's grace, especially as we think about how God would have us interact with immigrants reaching our country today.

America as a Land of Immigrants

Immigration holds an important place in our national mythology and lore. Our ancestors, generations of grandparents have told their grandchildren, came to this county with nothing, worked extraordinarily hard, and realized the American Dream. Historian Nancy Foner describes the common sentiment about immigrants of a century or two ago, which has been perpetuated and sometimes glorified by films, television and literature: "They worked hard; they strove to become assimilated; they pulled themselves up by their own Herculean efforts; . . . they had strong family values and colorful roots. They were, in short, what made America great."[3]

Curiously, though our collective image of the immigration of a century or two ago has become more romanticized with time, many Americans do not have the same warm feelings toward contemporary immigrants. Historian Roger Daniels suggests that most Americans hold a dualistic opinion about immigration, "on the one hand reveling in the nation's immigrant past and on the other rejecting much of its immigrant present."[4] They make a firm distinction between the immigrants of Ellis Island and earlier eras—who, they are quick to note, immigrated the legal way—and those who are coming today, some of them illegally, and most of them not from Europe but from Latin America and Asia.

Immigrants today, whatever their manner of entry, come primarily for the same reasons that immigrants have always come to our country. Though immigration policies have changed quite drastically over the last two centuries, immigrants themselves are still pushed out of their countries of origin by poverty, war and persecution and are still drawn to the United States by promises of jobs and economic advancement, freedom and family reunification. These "push" and "pull" factors explain most, if not all, of immigration to the United States from the time of the first settlers to today.

Likewise, the rhetoric around immigration and immigrants themselves has not changed much. Immigrants have always been simultaneously praised and resented, welcomed and scapegoated, from the earliest days of our country's existence to the present. Consider the following quote:

Why should [immigrants] establish their Language and Manners to the Exclusion of ours? Why should Pennsylvania, founded by the English, become a Colony of Aliens who will shortly be so numerous as to [change] us instead of our Anglifying them, and will never adopt our Language or Customs, any more than they can acquire our complexion?[5]

These words could feasibly come today from some media personalities who have made their dissatisfaction with contemporary immigration a central theme of their broadcasts, but the words were actually Benjamin Franklin's, writing in 1751 about the mass arrival of German immigrants into Pennsylvania. Anti-immigrant attitudes, and concerns that immigrants will not assimilate, are nothing new (though few Americans of German origin speak their ancestral tongue today and few could distinguish their skin tone from that of Americans with British blood).

Much of the lore of immigration is built around the Statue of Liberty, standing majestically on Liberty Island in New York Harbor, where millions of immigrants entered the United States for the first time. The words of a sonnet by Emma Lazarus, penned in 1883 and later inscribed on the base of the Statue of Liberty, have immortalized the idea of America as a refuge of freedom and opportunity:

Give me your tired, your poor,
Your huddled masses yearning to breathe free,
The wretched refuse of your teeming shore.
Send these, the homeless, tempest-tost to me,
I lift my lamp beside the golden door![6]

The poem suggests an era when immigrants, even the poor and outcast of their home countries, were welcomed into the United States—but just a year prior to the poem's publication, in 1882, the U.S. Congress had passed the first significant federal law restricting immigration, the Chinese Exclusion Act, which legally forbade Chinese immigrants from entering the United States for more than sixty years. The very same year, the federal government also passed, for the first time, laws banning the immigration of any "lunatic, idiot, or any person unable to take care of himself or herself without becoming a public charge"—excluding precisely many of the tired, poor, huddled masses that Lazarus would write about the following year.[7]

Throughout American history, pro- and anti-immigrant voices have coexisted, and public policy has generally responded to whichever voice commanded the majority of public opinion at the time. The various perspectives on the immigration debate cannot adequately be described as "conservative" or "liberal," nor as Republican or Democrat: the debate has, throughout history just as it does now, divided otherwise homogeneous ideological blocs.[8]

To understand the contemporary debate over immigration, we must first understand at least a little bit of the historical context. What follows is a brief, and certainly not conclusive, review of the various waves of immigration to the United States.*

Immigration in the Early Days of the United States

As Benjamin Franklin's concerns about German assimilation suggest, immigration to the United States has had its opponents since even before the United States became an independent country. Most of the founding fathers, though, looked favorably on continued immigration, recognizing there was plenty of space to fill in the nascent nation. George Washington's words, addressed to Irish immigrants in 1783, are representative:

> The bosom of America is open to receive not only the opulent and respectable stranger, but the oppressed and persecuted of all nations and religions, whom we shall welcome to participate in all of our rights and privileges, if by decency and propriety of conduct they appear to merit the employment.[9]

Following these ideals, Congress imposed no significant restrictions on immigration until after the Civil War, though there were some changes in

---

*Appendix 5 suggests a variety of books and other resources about the history of immigration to the United States for those interested in delving deeper.

law during this time that affected the foreign born. For example, a 1790 law limited naturalization—the process of becoming a U.S. citizen—to free, white people. A few years later, the Alien and Sedition Acts of 1798, pushed through by John Adams and his Federalist Party out of wariness of French immigrants, gave the government the right to deport immigrants whom it believed to be a danger to the United States or who came from countries at war with the United States.[10] Even with these changes, though, new immigration remained open to all.

Among the earliest immigrants, of course, were also men and women from Africa, who were enslaved and taken against their will to the New World. An estimated 645,000 Africans were involuntarily displaced and forced to work as slaves in what is now the United States, with millions more being sent to other parts of the Western Hemisphere.[11] It is important to remember this tragic element of our country's immigrant history, particularly since involuntary migration—now termed human trafficking—continues to be a problem today.

The First Great European Wave: 1820-1860

Throughout American history, immigration levels have ebbed and flowed, depending both on what was happening in the United States and what was happening in other parts of the world. As is still often the case, events in the particular country of origin often precipitated large waves of immigration: in the 1840s, for example, a massive famine caused by the failure of the potato crop in Ireland provided the push that many Irish needed to leave their homeland and come to the United States, where farmland was abundant.[12] German immigration spiked around the same time, as people fled a government that had stomped out an attempted revolution in 1848, seeking the liberty and democracy offered by the United States.[13]

These Irish and German immigrants, in particular, created a wave of immigration unlike anything the United States had seen up to this point. Over 5 million immigrants arrived between 1820 and 1860, about twenty times more than the number of immigrants who had arrived in the previous forty-four years since the nation's independence.[14] By 1860, 13.2 percent of the population of the United States was foreign born, a percentage that would roughly stay the same through the 1920s.[15] Beyond the sheer numbers, most of the German and Irish immigrants of this era were also distinct from the previous generations of immigrants in that they were primarily Roman Catholic, not Protestant.

This surge in non-Protestant immigration fueled a sharp rise in anti-immigrant sentiment among earlier generations of immigrants, mostly Protestant Christians of various denominations. Many Protestant laypeople genuinely believed, following the rhetoric of some church leaders, that Roman Catholicism represented "an invading enemy, audaciously conspiring, under the mask of *holy religion*, against the liberties of our country."[16] This anti-Catholic rhetoric led to a rash of arson against Catholic churches and convents, beginning in the 1830s, that lasted several decades, while continued and increasing Irish and German immigration meant that the number of Catholics—and thus the alleged threat—kept on growing.[17]

This anti-Catholic and anti-immigrant hysteria had political manifestations as well. A political movement known officially as the American Party—though more popularly known as the "Know Nothing" party*— relied on anti-Catholic and anti-immigrant rhetoric and policy proposals to grow to 1.25 million members and to have elected seven governors, eight U.S. senators, and 104 representatives by 1856, though federal immigration policy was not substantially altered by their presence.[18] The movement fell apart only when its membership sharply divided over the issue of slavery in the years leading up to the Civil War.

The Treaty of Guadalupe Hidalgo: 1848

Even while immigration was booming from western Europe, the demographic characteristics of the United States were also changing because of U.S. military activity along the southern border. On February 2, 1848, ap-

---

*The "Know Nothing" party acquired that name because, as a secret society, members were instructed to respond to outside questions about their organization with, "I know nothing."

proximately 100,000 foreign-born individuals became U.S. citizens in a single day—not because they crossed the border, but because the border itself migrated south and crossed them.[19] On that day, the United States and Mexico signed the Treaty of Guadalupe Hidalgo, putting an end to the Mexican-American War that had raged since 1846. The terms of the treaty ceded more than half of what had been Mexican territory—including modern day California, Nevada, Utah and parts of Colorado, Arizona, Wyoming and New Mexico—to the United States. Those Mexican citizens living in the territory were granted the right to automatically become U.S. citizens by simply taking an oath of allegiance, without undergoing any naturalization process.[20]

The Mexican-American War began when the Mexican government, unhappy with the annexation of Texas, broke off diplomatic relations with its northern neighbor. U.S. President James K. Polk responded by offering to buy California and New Mexico from Mexico for $25 million; when Mexico refused the offer, the United States declared war—and in the end, forced Mexico into a treaty that gave the U.S. not just California and New Mexico but several other future states for just $15 million.[21] The war, and the treaty that ended it, were the result of an idea known as "Manifest Destiny," which claimed that the United States had the God-given responsibility to expand its territory—spreading democracy in the process.

The treaty, though, and the war that preceded it, were not uncontroversial. Ulysses S. Grant considered the war to be "one of the most unjust ever waged by a stronger against a weaker nation."[22] Abraham Lincoln, in one of his earliest speeches on the floor of the U.S. Congress, asserted his belief that the war constituted an unprovoked attack against Mexico and warned that President James K. Polk, who insisted that the U.S.'s military incursions had been just and warranted, would feel "the blood of this war, like the blood of Abel . . . crying to Heaven against him."[23]

Whether just or unjust, the treaty that ended the Mexican-American War shifted the border south and made many Mexicans into Americans practically with the stroke of a pen. With the prominence of Mexicans in today's immigration debates, it is important to remember that not all people of Mexican descent are recent immigrants: some are living in the same locations that their ancestors have lived for centuries. In fact, contrary to general perception, about seventy percent of Hispanics* living in the United States in 2000 were U.S. citizens, most of them by birth.[24]

Chinese Immigration and Exclusion: 1848-1890

Mexico signed away the rights to California with the Treaty of Guadalupe Hidalgo unaware that, just nine days before the document was signed, gold had been found there. It did not take long, though, before news of the potentially lucrative discovery spread throughout the world.[25]

Hundreds of thousands eagerly set out to strike it rich in California—including many of the European immigrants arriving around this time in New York and the Mexicans and Native Americans who were already on the land. As news spread beyond the United States, other immigrants came as well, in some cases having been actively recruited. Among these new immigrants were many Chinese men, lured by promising advertisements such as this:

> Americans are rich people. They want the Chinaman to come and will make him welcome. There will be big pay, large houses, and food and clothing of the finest description. . . . Money is in great plenty and to spare in America. Such as wishes to have wages and labor guaranteed can obtain the security by application at this office.[26]

The Chinese, mostly men and mostly from the region of Canton, poured into California for several decades, lured first by the promises of gold and later by the employment created by construction of the Union Central Pacific Railroad.[27] Many had no intention to stay permanently in the United States, seeking to make money in the United States and then

---

*The term *Hispanic*, which we use here interchangeably with the term *Latino*, includes individuals of Mexican descent but also those from Spanish-speaking countries in Central America, South America and the Caribbean.

to return to their families in China. By 1870, the census counted 60,000 Chinese living in the United States, most of them in California.[28]

As has proven to be a theme throughout American history with immigrants from throughout the world, though, the Chinese were welcomed when their labor was needed, but once work became scarce, the welcome wore thin. Particularly on completion of the railroad in 1869, public sentiment on the West Coast turned against the Chinese, who were viewed as racially inferior and as taking jobs from U.S. citizens.[29] In many cases, as historian Jean Pfaelzer has documented, Chinese immigrants were forcibly driven from their homes and were in other cases victims of lynching and other violence.[30] Californian legislators began to pass a series of ordinances and laws designed to drive out the Chinese: for example, the state legislature passed bills making it illegal for the Chinese to obtain a business license, fish, or marry a white person.[31] Local ordinances aimed specifically at the Chinese immigrant population and their particular customs were also passed in various places, such as an ordinance in Santa Cruz that declared, "no person shall carry baskets or bags attached to poles carried upon back or shoulders on public sidewalks."[32]

As West Coast legislators carried the anti-Chinese hysteria with them to Washington, the U.S. Congress authorized a joint congressional committee to investigate Chinese immigration in 1876. The final congressional report stated, among other inflammatory statements, that there "was not sufficient brain capacity in the Chinese race to furnish motive power for self-government" and that "there is no Aryan or European race which is not far superior to the Chinese," and on these bases recommended a full halt to immigration from China.[33]

While there was no immediate action on these recommendations, by 1882 a bill passed the Congress and was eventually signed by President Chester A. Arthur that prohibited the entry of any new Chinese laborers—a bill that would become known as the Chinese Exclusion Act.[34] The Chinese Exclusion Act marked the first significant federal legislation limiting immigration, such that historian Roger Daniels considers the signing of the bill to be "the moment when the golden doorway of admission to the

United States began to narrow."[35] New immigration by people from China would be closed until the bill was repealed in 1943, at which time the Chinese—though not most other Asians—were finally allowed to naturalize.[36]

That the law prohibited entry of the Chinese, though, is not to say that no new Chinese immigrants entered the United States after 1882. Many came as "paper sons"—presenting birth certificates to suggest that they were the children of American-born citizens of Chinese descent, and thus citizens themselves according to the laws that governed the derivation of citizenship from a father to a child.[37] This phenomenon, as immigration attorney and policy advocate Fred Tsao points out, demonstrates a reality that is important to the current immigration debate: that "if you set up restrictions . . . particularly restrictions on established patterns of immigration, you'll find [that] people will find ways to get around them."[38]

The Second Great European Wave: 1880-1920

As the earlier wave of European immigrants—primarily the Irish and the Germans—began to ebb, a new wave began, with immigrants now arriving from southern and eastern Europe, particularly Italians, Poles and people of Jewish descent fleeing Russia. These immigrants, whose arrival book-ended the turn of the twentieth century, are often remembered as the Ellis Island immigrants, because, beginning in 1892, they were processed into the United States through Ellis Island in New York Harbor. Between 1881 and 1920, an estimated 23.4 million immigrants entered the United States—many times more than had entered in all of the country's history prior to that time—and the percentage of the population that was foreign born was steadily between 13 and 15 percent, far more than it has ever been since that time.*[39]

The Italians were primarily peasant farmers from southern Italy. The population of Italy had been growing substantially during this time pe-

---

*In 2000, based on census data, an estimated 11.1 percent of the U.S. population was foreign born, significantly less than at the turn of the previous century, despite popular perception to the contrary.

riod, requiring farms to be divided into smaller and smaller plots. Peasant farmers "were left barely clinging to their fields and hence vulnerable to any agricultural setback."[40] The economic situation for Italian farmers was further complicated by the globalization of the era, as grain from the American Great Plains began to enter the European markets at cheaper prices, while the growth of the citrus industry in Florida and California meant less demand internationally for Italian oranges.[41]

Unable to support themselves and their families as farmers as they once had, many Italian peasants set sail in cramped steamships for America. They established themselves primarily in New York and quickly sent money and letters back home to Italy, which "spread the news of opportunities and inspired prospective emigrants."[42] By the turn of the century, many regions of Italy were experiencing "America fever," with immigrants leaving every day for the promises of a better life in the United States; one mayor of a southern Italian town during this era greeted visitors "in the name of the five thousand inhabitants of this town, three thousand of whom are in America and the other two thousand preparing to go."[43]

While the Italians came primarily for economic reasons, Russian Jews came to New York fleeing political and religious discrimination. In 1882, following the assassination of Czar Alexander II, the passage of the May Laws made life nearly impossible for people of Jewish descent and faith. They were barred from living anywhere except in the large cities of a particular region of the country, and strict quotas limited their access to education. Government-approved anti-Semitic violence became increasingly common. Facing such repression, and the economic challenges that accompanied it, Jews began leaving for America, which had the reputation as "a free country for the Jews."[44]

Predictably, these new waves of immigrants spurred a new nativist backlash. The Immigration Restriction League, founded by recent Harvard graduates in 1894, became one of the most effective voices opposed to the new immigration, relying heavily on supposedly scientific theories that argued that the new immigrants were biologically inferior to, and thus less capable of assimilation than, the races that had populated America in the previous centuries.[45] Many Americans accepted this rhetoric, as well as continued rhetoric based on religious grounds, and they began to actively lobby their political leaders for increased restrictions on immigration.

In democratic fashion, political leaders responded to the nativist concerns of the voting electorate, gradually adding piecemeal restrictions on who could enter the United States and initiating a federal bureaucracy to control and monitor immigration. In 1911, under pressure from the Immigration Restriction League and other nativist groups, a commission of the U.S. government published a report, named after the commission's chair, Senator William Dillingham. The Dillingham Commission report suggested that racial distinctions made the "new" immigrants biologically inferior to the old, and thus less likely to become good Americans.[46] For example, the Commission found that "certain kinds of criminality are inherent in the Italian race" and that "the high rate of illiteracy among new immigrants was due to inherent racial tendencies."[47] The Commission thus recommended "restriction as demanded by economic, moral and social considerations."[48]

After several years of debate, Congress responded to these recommendations by passing a literacy requirement for immigrants in 1917 and also excluding additional Asian immigrants to the United States.[49] Though World War I slowed immigration levels from Europe substantially, public opinion toward immigrants continued to be harsh, and demand for further restrictions led to temporary restrictions on immigration that were passed in 1921 and 1922, leading up to permanent restrictions passed in 1924 that would redefine immigration to the United States of America.

The Quota System: 1924-1965

The Immigration Act of 1924 marked a turning point in U.S. immigration history. The new law tightly restricted immigration, setting strict quotas for immigrants based on their nationality. The new law allowed the admittance into the United States of no more than 2 percent of the foreign population from a given country that existed in the United

States in 1890. The 1890 census data was used, rather than the recently completed 1920 census, precisely because the older census predated the most recent wave of immigration, meaning the earlier baseline date would more tightly limit the immigration of new Italian and Jewish immigrants. The effect was to cap new immigration at about 180,000 people, the vast majority of whom would come from northern European countries such as England, France and Germany.[50] The "new immigrants" from southern and eastern Europe, as well as Asians, were effectively shut out.

Notably, the quota system did not apply to immigrants from the Western Hemisphere, so Mexican and Canadian immigrants were still allowed to immigrate outside of numerical restrictions. This exception came about at the insistence of legislators from the western and southwestern states, who argued that their regions depended on Mexican agricultural labor.[51]

The act also introduced, for the first time on a permanent basis, the requirement of a visa to enter the United States of America.[52] Whereas previous generations of immigrants could simply board a steamship and show up in the New World without securing permission from the United States government beforehand, immigrants have henceforth needed the permission of the U.S. State Department in their home country before they would be allowed to legally enter the United States.

The importance of this new rule should not be understated. While it sounds reasonable to expect that today's immigrants come legally, the way that my ancestors did, the rules have changed entirely.* For those of us whose ancestors came prior to the 1920s, without the requirement of a visa, to proudly note that our ancestors came *legally* to the United States is quite like a basketball coach bragging that his team scored 100 points in a game while a baseball coach's team scored only six—the boast is illogical, because the rules are completely different.

---

*The next chapter provides a summary of the rules governing who can immigrate to the United States under current immigration and nationality law.

The Bracero Program: 1942-1964

While immigration from most countries dwindled after the drastic change in policy in 1924, immigrants from Mexico continued to come north in increasing numbers in response to an increasing need for labor. The agricultural industry, in particular, depended on migrant laborers.

Beginning in 1942, when World War II led to shortages in the labor market, the U.S. and Mexican governments agreed to implement a specific guest worker program known as the *bracero* program, which lasted in various forms until 1964, with as many as 400,000 Mexican agricultural laborers entering in some years.[53] Bracero workers were supposed to be temporary nonimmigrants, but many stayed in the United States illegally rather than returning to Mexico at the end of the season. The program was criticized both by organized labor, who felt that the Mexican laborers were stealing jobs from American citizens, and by those who were concerned that the Mexican workers themselves were being exploited. Braceros, who worked under contract, complained of "violations of wage agreements, substandard living quarters, exorbitant charges for food and clothing, and racist discrimination."[54] The lobbying efforts of the agricultural interests, though, proved strong, and the program was consistently renewed until 1964.

When the bracero program was finally disbanded, it was, at least in part, due to the concerns raised by Cesar Chavez, a union organizer who was concerned that the bracero program undermined the rights of workers—both the braceros themselves and those in the United States who could not compete with their cheap, contracted labor. Chavez, who cofounded the United Farm Workers union, would become a revered leader in the Mexican American community.

The 1965 Reforms

As the bracero program officially ended, a new era was dawning in immigration law. The quota system that began in 1924 had been, with slight modifications, the immigration law of the land for approximately forty years, though not without criticism. President Harry Truman

The Church and Immigration History

Just like the American public at large, American churches have espoused differing and ever-changing opinions on immigration. Protestant Christians were among those most opposed to the waves of Irish and German immigrants who arrived in the mid-nineteenth century, because they saw their Roman Catholic faith as a threat.[55]

In contrast, Protestant church leaders were, with some exceptions, among the foremost defenders of the Chinese immigrants on the West Coast during the late nineteenth century, with Presbyterian, Methodist and Baptist clergymen beginning churches among the new immigrants. They also displayed "stubborn courage in their advocacy of the Chinese," opposing local and national policies designed to exclude the Chinese, even when this meant battling public opinion.[56]

As the second great wave of European immigration commenced in the 1880s, with Italian Catholics and Russian Jews in particular pouring into New York City, most Protestants, while still skeptical of Catholicism, advocated welcoming the newcomers and attempting to convert them, with very few considering the political solution of restrictions on immigration.[57] That perspective gradually changed, though, and by the 1890s most prominent Protestants were advocating some level of immigration restriction.[58]

Interestingly, the general sentiment among Protestant believers reversed course again, quite dramatically, in the first decade of the twentieth century. Historian Lawrence B. Davis suggests that the evolution in attitude was the result of increased personal acquaintance with the vilified new immigrants: "one might speak disparagingly of foreigners in the abstract," Davis writes, paraphrasing a Baptist pastor of the era, "but would regard them as brothers upon personal confrontation."[59] The change came about as Christian men and, in particular, women, heeded the call of evangelical leaders such as Howard Grose, who in a series of popular books extolled the arrival of the "incoming millions" as "an opportunity" to "carry the gospel to [foreigners] in our own land" and provided a number of practical suggestions for caring for one's immigrant neighbors, such as helping them to learn English.[60]

The change in perspective toward immigrants affected Protestant attitudes toward immigration policy, as well. Though many had been fervently calling for immigration restrictions around the turn of the century, by the 1920s, many Protestant denominations vocally renounced the restrictions based on national origin that became law in 1924.[61]

Forty years later, though, when Congress was reconsidering the national origins quota system of immigration restriction, evangelicals, speaking through the National Association of Evangelicals,* opposed the opening of immigration policy proposed by John F. Kennedy.[62] Ironically, as evangelical historian Douglas Sweeney notes, the passage of the 1965 immigration reform has been a boon for evangelicalism, as Asian and Hispanic immigrants "have quietly contributed several million new adherents to the evangelical movement."[63]

Today, as throughout American history, American churches are divided over the question of immigration. We will look more closely at how churches are responding to the immigration issue, and to immigrants themselves, in chapter nine.

---

*The National Association of Evangelicals (NAE) represents a number of evangelical denominations and churches and is the parent organization of World Relief, our employer and a partner in the publication of this book. While World Relief was in existence at the time of the NAE's statement, it was not involved in ministry to refugees and immigrants until the 1970s. It seems that, as was the case with the generation of American evangelicals who lived a century ago, a closer proximity to immigrants and refugees may have changed our perspective on immigration policy.

called the 1924 law and subsequent variations of the law based on the same national-origins premise "a slur on the patriotism, the capacity, and the decency of a large part of our citizenry," but the will of the Congress prevailed over Truman's criticisms, and the law remained generally in place.[64]

It was not until President John F. Kennedy's administration, in the 1960s, that the quota system would be effectively challenged. As the civil rights era was bringing questions of racial and ethnic discrimination to the forefront of the public discussion, the blatantly racial nature of the existing law was called into question.[65] Kennedy argued, in a book on the topic of immigration, that the United States should have an immigration policy that was generous, fair and flexible, allowing the nation to "turn to the world, and to our own past, with clean hands and a clear conscience."[66] To Kennedy, this meant a system based on a series of preferences, based primarily on family relationships and job skills.

When Kennedy was assassinated in 1963, President Lyndon Johnson, who had supported the status quo as a senator, voiced his support for his predecessor's reform plan.[67] After much debate and some significant modifications—including the insertion of a numerical limit on immigrants from the Western Hemisphere, which had never before existed—the bill was finally approved by the Congress and then signed by President Johnson. In a speech given after signing the bill, in the shadow of the Statue of Liberty in New York Harbor, President Johnson stated, "The days of unlimited immigration are past. But those who do come will come because of what they are, and not because of the land from which they sprung."[68]

Though there have been significant modifications—some of which have been generous toward new immigrants and some of which have added further restrictions, usually in response to the public sentiment of the era—our current immigration system, which is described in the next chapter, is still modeled after the 1965 law. As Johnson noted, the bill certainly did not bring us back to the era of unrestricted immigration that existed through our country's first century of existence. The 1965 law did, though, dramatically change who was entering: though it may not have been the intention of the bill's supporters, the 1965 bill opened up immigration for people from Asia, Africa and other parts of the world beyond just Europe. At the same time, it subjected many Mexicans and other Latin Americans, who had historically crossed the border without numerical limit, to new legal bars to their entry. The 1965 law permanently changed the nature of immigration to America, resolving some problems with the previous immigration system while creating new problems, many of which we, as a nation, are wrestling with today.

Conclusion

Whether we trace our roots to the early western European colonists, to the Africans who were forced to migrate prior to the abolition of the slave trade, to the southern and eastern Europeans who journeyed through Ellis Island, to the more recent waves of immigrants from Latin America and Asia, or to some combination of the above, each of us has an individual immigrant history. Like the Israelites, whose ancestors were immigrants in Egypt, we each have a story that can—and, Scripture suggests, should—inform the manner in which we treat immigrants entering our country today.

As we have seen, though immigrants themselves still come to the United States for many of the same reasons that immigrants have come since the colonial period, immigration laws and policies have changed drastically. In the next chapter, we will examine how immigration law works today, which goes a long way toward explaining why there are so many undocumented people living and working in violation of the law.

IMMIGRATING THE LEGAL WAY

OUR IMMIGRATION SYSTEM TODAY

American citizenship is priceless and it ought to be done the legal way just like my ancestors did.
U.S. Representative James Sensenbrenner, Republican of Wisconsin, debating immigration policies in 2006, on CBS News' *Face the Nation*

One of the greatest points of confusion for many native-born U.S. citizens, such as those whose ancestors came through Ellis Island, is why *illegal* immigration has become so common. It is reasonable to expect that immigrants wishing to start a new life in the United States go about the proper legal channels to reside here. Much of the frustration revolves around why 11 to 12 million people decided to enter the country illegally (or to overstay a temporary visa).

Misconceptions persist about how our immigration system works today. Many believe that people stay undocumented to avoid paying taxes, preferring to be paid in cash under the table. It simply is not right, they argue, for people to receive government services, like education and emergency healthcare, when they refuse to pay their taxes like everyone else.

Others think the undocumented are simply unwilling to fill out the proper forms to obtain a green card and a Social Security number. Once, at a training session on citizenship and immigration law for social workers, a well-meaning social worker, whose clients were mostly immigrants, expressed his bewilderment at the apparent unwillingness of many of his Mexican clients to get a Social Security card. His Polish clients, he said, go to the Social Security office as soon as they arrive, but many Mexicans just never go. He was under the impression they never acquired a valid Social Security card because of sloth. He was genuinely surprised to learn that they were almost certainly ineligible to apply for a Social Security card, since they had not been legally admitted to live and work in the United States, while his Polish clients were apparently lawful residents, with valid green cards or work authorization.

Still others are vaguely aware of the legal processes necessary to obtain a green card—knowing this involves filling out various forms available from the government, which are then adjudicated by the United States Citizenship and Immigration Service (formerly the Immigration and Naturalization Service)—and recognize that, as with any bureaucracy, this process will likely take some time. Some suppose that immigrants who come illegally have chosen to forego this legal process because they are simply too impatient to wait their turn in line.

If the issue were really (as anti-illegal-immigration activists often suggest) that people who are undocumented refuse to go through the legal channels and wait their turn, or are lazy, it would be entirely reasonable to think them outrageous for demanding to be subsequently rewarded for having entered (or overstayed) illegally. If this were really the situation, Christians, who are directed by Scripture to be welcoming and hospitable to the stranger but who do not want to be taken advantage of, might therefore prefer to reserve their hospitality exclusively for legal immigrants.

The reality, though, is that immigration today is not so simple, and most undocumented immigrants are undocumented not because they choose to remain undocumented, but because there is no process for them to enter legally or obtain legal status. As we saw in the previous chapter, the immigration policies in our country have changed drastically since the era of Ellis Island, when 98 percent of immigrants who arrived were admitted into the United States, usually after just a few hours of processing and without need of a visa.[1] In those days, while the journey to the United States was often a harrowing voyage by ship and required great bravery and risk, it was very easy to immigrate "the legal way." In fact, it would have been difficult to find a way to immigrate that was illegal.

Now, though we might encourage undocumented immigrants to wait their turn in line, there is very often no line in which they can begin to stand. They can repeatedly line up at the U.S. consulate, pay a substantial fee, and apply for a visa, but for the majority, especially those without substantial education or financial resources, they will leave the consulate disappointed, finding there is not even any line in which they can wait.

Immigration Statuses

If we are to understand the current immigration problem, we need to start by understanding how our country's immigration system works today, which is the root of why we have so many undocumented immigrants living among us.

In general, there are three basic statuses that a foreigner residing in the United States can have: legal nonimmigrant, Lawful Permanent Resident, or U.S. citizen.* Most foreigners who do not have one of these statuses are undocumented, meaning they have no legal status and could be legally deported solely on that basis.

Nonimmigrants. Foreigners on a nonimmigrant visa are admitted into the United States on a temporary basis, usually either as tourists, business travelers, temporary workers or students. These nonimmigrants have come to stay for a limited period, and their home is still in the country from which they came. Depending on the specific details of their visas, they may or may not be allowed to work during their time in the United States. If they are not authorized to work but do so anyway, they could risk deportation.

Visitor visas are typically granted at the U.S. consulate in a foreign country. The visa is sealed into the foreign passport, and in most cases the visitor will then be allowed to enter the United States. To be granted a

---

*Technically, refugees cannot apply to become Lawful Permanent Residents until one year after their arrival in the United States, so until then they could be considered as having a fourth category of legal status. In practical terms, almost all refugees eventually become Lawful Permanent Residents, so their refugee status is an interim classification.

visa, the U.S. government must determine that the potential visitor meets all of the admissibility requirements set forth in the Immigration and Nationality Act, which is the federal law that governs immigration. These requirements include prohibitions against people with certain infectious diseases, people who have committed certain crimes and people who are expected to be a "public charge" (costing the country money), among other requirements.[2] Even with a visa, visitors can be refused entrance when they arrive if they meet one or more of the grounds of inadmissibility.

Nonimmigrant visas generally have a specific expiration date. If a person stays in the United States beyond that time, and has not arranged to change their status, she or he becomes undocumented. In fact, approximately 45 percent of the estimated 11 to 12 million people who are undocumented came on a valid visitor visa but overstayed.[3] These visa "overstayers" come from every country in the world. For obvious geographic reasons, undocumented immigrants from countries other than Mexico, Canada and Central America are more likely to have entered on a visitor visa and overstayed than to have crossed a border illegally.

It is precisely because so many temporary visitors overstay their visas, often with that intention in mind even before they leave their home country, that it can be very difficult to obtain a visitor visa. The U.S. government is wary about granting a visa to anyone whom it deems likely to overstay. So, it is nearly impossible for many of the world's poor to obtain even a visitor visa, because the potential for economic advancement is so strong by staying in the United States that consular officials consider them too high a risk. Conversely, most western Europeans, who live in and have steady employment in countries where the economic standards are roughly equivalent to those in the United States, can enter the United States without difficulty as nonimmigrant visitors. In fact, for certain countries, the visa requirement is waived.

In some cases, visitors who were admitted to the United States on a temporary basis can apply to adjust their status to that of a Lawful Permanent Resident, even if they have already overstayed. For example, a student who falls in love with and marries a U.S. citizen while studying at a university in the United States would in most cases be eligible to adjust status and obtain a green card without ever leaving the country. In other cases, the only option is for individuals to leave the United States and process their petition for Lawful Permanent Resident status through the U.S. consulate in their home country, which often causes further complications.

Lawful Permanent Residents. Lawful Permanent Residents possess a "green card" that identifies them as having been legally admitted to live permanently in the United States.* They have the right to live and work, and their status never expires, although their green cards currently need to be renewed every ten years.

To be granted a green card, a potential immigrant must meet all of the same requirements of admissibility as a visitor or anyone else who wants to enter the United States as a noncitizen, in addition to other requirements. Once admitted, a green card holder still could be deported, for example, if the immigrant commits certain crimes, claims to be a U.S. citizen or votes illegally, stays outside the United States for too long, or is suspected of threatening the national security of the United States.[4]

Lawful Permanent Residents have the right to petition for certain family members—spouses or unmarried children of any age—to immigrate to the United States as Lawful Permanent Residents, although they will need to wait—sometimes for a very long time—for a visa to become available.

Lawful Permanent Residents can apply to become U.S. citizens after having resided in the U.S. lawfully for four years and nine months, if they meet all other requirements for naturalization, including passing a test in English (with limited exceptions) of U.S. history, civics and government,

---

*The green card itself is officially known as a Permanent Resident Card; the current green cards are actually pinkish-tan. Each green card bears the resident's picture, name, birth date, date of admission as a Lawful Permanent Resident, and "A Number," or Alien Registration Number, which the United States Citizenship and Immigration Service uses to identify them. The misnomer "green card" comes from an early version of the Permanent Resident Card, which was indeed green.

and pay a fee, currently $675. Lawful Permanent Residents married to a U.S. citizen may apply earlier, after two years and nine months.

U.S. citizens. U.S. Citizens include naturalized citizens, who must first have been Lawful Permanent Residents, pass a test, demonstrate that they are of Good Moral Character (as vaguely defined by immigration law), swear an oath of allegiance to the United States and meet certain other requirements. In recent years, about 650,000 Lawful Permanent Residents per year have naturalized.[5]

Other U.S. citizens, of course, receive that title simply by being born in the United States (whatever the immigration status of their parents), based on the fourteenth amendment of the Constitution. Still others acquire U.S. citizenship at birth abroad, if one or both parents are U.S. citizens, while others derive citizenship if a parent naturalizes before their eighteenth birthday.

U.S. citizens, by whichever of these means they acquire that title, have several rights that Lawful Permanent Residents do not. These rights include the right (and responsibility) to vote, the right to run for public office, the right to travel with a U.S. passport, the right to apply for certain jobs, and the right to petition for additional family members (children of any age, married or unmarried, as well as spouses, parents and siblings) to immigrate as Lawful Permanent Residents.

The undocumented. Most of those who are present in the United States and do not fit into any of the previous three categories are undocumented.* We discussed in chapter two exactly who these people are, what motivates them to come, and how they live. While some undocumented migrants have no intention of living permanently in the United States or eventually becoming U.S. citizens, many others yearn for the legal status offered by a green card—and with that the freedom from fear of deportation, the confidence to demand fair labor conditions, and particularly, the

---

*There are a few other categories of legal statuses, such as those paroled into the United States (mostly from a few specific countries, such as Cuba), refugees or asylees who have not yet adjusted their status to Lawful Permanent Resident, and certain individuals given temporary legal status, but these constitute a relatively small number of the total foreign-born population.

ability to travel back to their home country and be reunited, even temporarily, with family. Many of these immigrants want a green card, and eventually to be citizens, but the current system, in most cases, makes that difficult if not impossible.

Paths to Legal Status in the United States

There are literally millions of undocumented people living in the United States who yearn to be on the path to citizenship, but at this point, are not. Elena is a very typical example. She came to the United States for the first time in 1990. She came, like many others, because there were insufficient work opportunities in her home country. Elena graduated from high school in Guerrero, Mexico, in the mid-1980s. After working for a few years for very little pay as an accountant and spending too much of her income just on transportation to reach the difficult-to-find job, she decided to try to go north to the United States. She had relatives in the Chicago area who assured her that she could make a better life there for herself, and even more so for the family that Elena hoped to have one day. Many immigrants are willing to work a difficult job for their entire lifetimes in exchange for the hope offered for advancement for their children—who within one generation can, with lots of hard work and education, be very successful.

Elena thought about trying to obtain a visa, but with very little money she knew that she would be denied a tourist visa, as she would be suspected (rightly) of being a potential overstayer. She would have liked to have immigrated legally as a Lawful Permanent Resident, but there were no accessible legal options for her to immigrate. So, instead, she paid about $600 to a *coyote*, trekked three days across the desert without food and drink, and eventually arrived to the hospitality of her relatives in the suburbs of Chicago. With their help, she secured a false document to work and began flipping burgers at a fast-food restaurant within a month of arrival. She has since married and had two children—U.S. citizens by birth—but she still does not have a green card.

Within the four general processes by which a person can obtain a green card under current immigration law, Elena has no options. Those four options are employment, family, the diversity lottery, or a fear of persecution in the home country.

Employment-based immigration. Employers may petition for immigrants to come as permanent resident workers or temporary workers, filling positions within their companies, with the intention of meeting the labor demands of the U.S. economy. Within the permanent resident worker program, preference is given to immigrants with unique skills and high levels of education who meet a particular labor shortage within the United States. This path always requires an employer sponsor. The U.S. Department of Labor must also certify that the employment of the immigrant will not adversely affect the wages and working conditions of U.S. citizens. The employer thus obtains a labor certification from the government allowing them to hire the immigrant, who after thorough criminal background checks, would be admissible to the United States. This process usually requires the services of an immigration attorney, as extensive paperwork has to be filed by the hiring company.

Employment-based visas are also granted to investors who invest large amounts of money (at least $1 million dollars, at present) in the United States and employ U.S. citizens or Lawful Permanent Residents.[6] This provision has been criticized as selling green cards to the very wealthy, though the rationale is that these investors generate employment within the United States.

A minimum of 140,000 immigrants is allowed to enter the United States each year based on employment.[7] The majority of these visas are reserved for individuals who have "extraordinary" or "exceptional ability," for "outstanding professors and researchers," and for others "holding advanced degrees."[8] For example, some medical professionals—especially doctors and nurses—may be able to obtain a green card through employment-based channels. Special employment-based visas are also available for religious workers and a few other specific categories of workers.

The current employment-based immigration system has very little to offer, though, to the low-income, relatively-low-education migrant like my neighbor Elena, who came to the United States expecting, at least initially, to do what most Americans would consider menial labor.

Although Elena has now worked at fast-food restaurants for nearly fifteen years, and has seen her hourly wage rise from $3.75 to $8.75 as she has demonstrated her assiduousness, her employer would not be likely to expend the money necessary to pursue an employment-based visa, nor would it be likely to be granted, since Elena's high school education in Mexico does not meet the requirements for highly educated, skilled workers for which most employment visas are designated. Indeed, very few of those currently undocumented have any chance to receive a visa on the basis of employment, even if they could afford to initiate the application process.

Family-based immigration. Most immigrants who come to reside permanently in the United States immigrate on the basis of family relationships, with the intention of reuniting families. Each year a minimum of 226,000 immigrants are granted Lawful Permanent Residence based on a relationship to a U.S. citizen or a Lawful Permanent Resident.[9]

Lawful Permanent Residents have the right to petition for a spouse or for a son or daughter of any age, so long as the son or daughter is unmarried. Citizens can petition for spouses, sons or daughters (whether married or not), siblings, and parents (but not until the child/petitioner is at least twenty-one years old). In many cases, if a person is granted a visa on the basis of a family relationship, her or his spouse and children under age twenty-one are granted green cards as well.

However, although a person may have a qualifying relationship with a U.S. citizen or Lawful Permanent Resident, that person still must wait for a visa to be available. Visas are available immediately, without limit, for certain relatives of U.S. citizens (spouses, unmarried children under age twenty-one, and parents). They must simply file the proper form, pay the required fee, and wait just the time that the government agencies involved require to process and adjudicate the request, often about one year. Nevertheless, the immigrant relative must still qualify with all other eligibility rules to be granted Lawful Permanent Residence.

The situation is much more challenging for other family-based petitions. Visa availability is based on the particular relationship to the U.S. citizen or Lawful Permanent Resident, and then further affected by country quotas, as no single country is allowed more than 7 percent of the family-based visas for any given year.[10] The visa categories are divided on a preference system in which each preference is based on the status of the person petitioning in the United States (a U.S. citizen or U.S. Lawful Permanent Resident) and the relationship of the U.S. sponsor to the intending immigrant.

The *first preference* is for unmarried adult children of U.S. citizens; currently, the wait time for these people, from most countries, is approximately six years.[11] For immigrants from the Philippines, though, the wait time is more than fifteen years, and for those from Mexico, about sixteen years. If the unmarried child gets married between the time when the petition is filed and when the visa becomes available—a very good possibility, with wait times of up to sixteen years—he or she is no longer eligible under this preference and falls to the third preference category, increasing his or her wait time by about two years in most cases. (If the immigrant has a live-in girlfriend or boyfriend and has children but does not legally marry, he or she can maintain a spot in line—which has the not-so-family-friendly effect of discouraging marriage.)

The *second preference* includes spouses and children of Lawful Permanent Residents. For a Lawful Permanent Resident applying for his or her spouse or children under age twenty-one, the wait time for most countries is currently about five years.[12] Mexicans wait around six years. If a child turns twenty-one before the visa is available, he or she moves to the lower preference category of unmarried adult children of Lawful Permanent Residents (twenty-one or over), who generally have wait times of about nine years.* Mexicans and Filipinos again prove the exception: Mexican adult, unmarried children of a Lawful Permanent resident are currently waiting

---

*The Child Status Protection Act, which was passed into law a few years ago, sometimes preserves a person's "child" status beyond the twenty-first birthday through a series of complicated calculations, based on the reasoning that immigrants should not be penalized by the government's processing delays, as was often the case prior to the introduction of the new law.

Waiting Your Turn in Line:
The Current Family-Based Immigration Preference System

The following are examples of wait times for a visa to be available, based on family relationship, immigration status of the petitioner, and (in some cases) country of origin of the beneficiary*:

Spouse of a U.S. citizen (from any country): No wait time, beyond the six months to two years usually required to process all required paperwork

Spouse of a Lawful Permanent Resident from Canada: Five years

Minor child (unmarried) of a Lawful Permanent Resident from China: Five years

Brother or sister of a U.S. citizen from India: Eleven years

Unmarried adult child of a U.S. citizen from Mexico: Sixteen years

Brother or sister of a Lawful Permanent Resident: No option to immigrate

Unmarried adult child of a Lawful Permanent Resident from Iran: Nine years

Unmarried adult child of a Lawful Permanent Resident from Mexico: Sixteen years

Married adult child of a Lawful Permanent Resident: No option to immigrate

Parent of a U.S. citizen: No wait time, beyond the six months to two years required to process all required paperwork

Parent of a Lawful Permanent Resident: No option to immigrate

Brother or sister of a U.S. citizen from the Philippines: Twenty-two years

Unmarried adult child of a U.S. citizen from Italy: Six years

Married adult child of a U.S. citizen from Ghana: Eight years

Married adult child of a U.S. citizen from the Philippines: Seventeen years[13]

Having a visa available is just the first step: would-be immigrants could still be prohibited from immigrating for criminal problems, health problems, previous unlawful presence in the United States, and for many other reasons. They also could face problems if they change their status during the years that the petition is pending, such as if an adult child of a Lawful Permanent Resident decides to marry.

---

*These wait times are taken from the most recent U.S. Department of State Visa Bulletin, and wait times are rounded to the nearest year. The Visa Bulletin is updated monthly, and wait times may vary slightly from one month to another.

about sixteen years for a visa, while Filipinos are waiting about eleven years under this category. If they marry before the visa becomes available, they become ineligible to immigrate, as Lawful Permanent Residents do not have the right to petition for married children.

The wait times for the *third preference,* which is for married sons and daughters of U.S. citizens, are particularly long. The wait time is around eight years for those with family in most parts of the world, while for Mexicans it is currently about sixteen years and for Filipinos it is seventeen years.[14]

Finally, the *fourth preference* category, for brothers and sisters of U.S. citizens, is particularly startling. For immigrants in most countries of the world, the wait time for a sibling to come is about eleven years, with slightly longer waits for those from India and mainland China and much longer waits—thirteen and twenty-two years, respectively—for those from Mexico and the Philippines.[15]

Given these long wait times during which would-be immigrants are separated from their families, it is not entirely surprising that many, particularly from Mexico (who have merely to cross their northern border to arrive) choose to wait their turn for a visa while already living in the United States, albeit without the benefit of legal status. In some cases, they may be able to adjust their status from undocumented to Lawful Permanent Resident once the wait time is up. Yet in most cases they must return to their country of origin to claim their visa, often to find that their unlawful presence in the

Unites States has made them ineligible to immigrate for up to a decade.

The backlogs in the family-based immigration system, which are built into the law to limit immigration, are often further compounded by processing delays. The U.S. Citizenship and Immigration Service (USCIS), the agency within the Department of Homeland Security that processes all petitions for family members, adjudicates thousands of applications per month, but a lack of resources as well as inefficiencies in the system lead to the delays. These delays have become particularly burdensome in recent years, as the number of pending applications has risen exponentially from 540,688 in 1990 to about 6.08 million in 2003.[16] As a result, people can wait more than a year in many cases—and occasionally several years—for a correctly submitted petition to be considered.

The USCIS is funded almost entirely by the fees paid by immigrants themselves, rather than by taxpayer monies.[17] Thus, in order to have the resources to address these backlogs and other problems within the bureaucracy, the USCIS has increased fees charged to immigrants several times over the past several years. In 1998, for example, the fee for naturalization was $95; less than a decade later, the total fee was $675—an increase of 710 percent! Likewise, the fee for filing an Adjustment of Status (filing for a green card for someone already physically present in the United States, usually on a nonimmigrant visa) jumped from $130 to $930 in the same ten-year time period.[18] Even with these additional funds flowing into USCIS, though, the backlogs continue. Meanwhile, the increased fees present an additional burden for immigrants seeking legal status.

An understanding of the actual waits implied when we suggest that immigrants wait their turn and immigrate the legal way is helpful. It is equally important to acknowledge, though, that many (probably most) of the people who immigrate illegally to the United States did not even have the option to get in line, because they have no qualifying family member who is a U.S citizen or Lawful Permanent Resident. Elena is a good example. She chose to come to Illinois because she had family living there—a U.S.-citizen uncle and Lawful Permanent Resident cousins—but they did not have any right to petition for their niece or cousin, respectively. So Elena had no one to apply on her behalf for a family-based visa, and instead she came, as so many do, by crossing the border illegally.

Elena's son, who was born in the United States and is thus a U.S. citizen, will turn twenty-one in the next several years, at which point he would technically be eligible to petition for his mother. Under current law, though, this would not really benefit Elena, because she would have to return to Mexico to apply for the visa—no adjustment of status within the United States would be possible in her case, at least under current law—and the moment that she crosses the border, leaving the United States, she would trigger a ten-year bar to legal reentry, because of a tough law passed by Congress in 1996. In her circumstance, there is no waiver or exception available, so unless she wants to be separated from her children for ten years, she does not have a particularly good option.*

Diversity Immigration. Since most immigration to the United States is based on family relationships, the countries that already have the most immigrants living in the United States are also the countries that send the most new immigrants each year. For countries that have historically sent few immigrants to the United States, there are few naturalized U.S. citizens or Lawful Permanent Residents who can apply for family members to come, and immigration from these countries is very limited. To slightly adjust this imbalance, Congress instituted a new means of obtaining a green card in the early 1990s, known as a Diversity Visa. These visas, which are distributed randomly, can be applied for, free of charge, by anyone from an underrepresented country who has completed high school or has at least two years of work experience in a skilled profession. Potential visa recipients are selected by lottery, and then must demonstrate that they meet all other requirements for admission into the United States.

In recent years, 50,000 visas have been issued annually through the di-

---

*Some people in this situation may be eligible to apply for a waiver, which an officer has the discretion to approve or deny. To be eligible for a waiver in this case, though, a person would need to demonstrate that his or her absence would cause extreme hardship to a U.S.-citizen spouse or parent. Elena has neither, and the effect on her U.S.-citizen children is not considered under the law.

versity lottery. Indeed, it really is a lottery, as the odds of being selected for the 2009 lottery were one in 182, and the lottery receives more applications each year.[19] For the countries that already have the most immigrants (both with and without documents) in the United States, however—including Mexico, the Philippines, India, China, Canada, Haiti, El Salvador, England, South Korea and Poland, among others—the diversity lottery is not currently an option.[20] Elena, from Mexico, would thus have had no possibility of a diversity lottery visa, either.

Refugees and Asylees. Another way in which a person might obtain a green card is by entering the United States as a refugee or, on entering the United States, claiming and ultimately being granted asylum. Both refugees and asylees, according to the definition accepted by the United Nations and the United States, flee their home country based on "a well-founded fear of being persecuted for reasons of race, religion, nationality, membership in a particular social group, or political opinion."[21] Refugees are usually given this title in a country other than their own.

The United Nations High Commission for Refugees estimates there are currently nearly 10 million refugees in the world, of which only a small fraction of 1 percent are resettled in the United States.[22] Asylees are individuals who arrive in the United States as nonimmigrants but, once here, request asylum based on fear of returning to their home country. Both refugees admitted into the United States and those asylees whose cases are approved by the United States government are eventually granted green cards in most cases, allowing them to live permanently in the United States and, ultimately, to apply for citizenship. Refugees and asylees generally go through harrowing, tragic life circumstances to become a recognized refugee or asylee in the United States, but once they arrive it is usually not a complicated process to receive a green card.

The total number of refugees admitted annually varies each year, based on a maximum set by the President. President Bush set the maximum for the fiscal year 2009 at 80,000, though in recent years usually only about 55,000 refugees have been resettled annually.[23]

Most refugees in recent years have come from eastern Europe (particularly the former Yugoslavia and former Soviet Union), Africa (particularly Somalia, Sudan, Rwanda, Burundi, Sierra Leone and Liberia), the Middle East (Iran, Iraq and Afghanistan), Southeast Asia (especially Cambodia, Vietnam and, recently, Burma) and Cuba.[24]

Critics of U.S. refugee resettlement policy argue that, particularly in the Cold War era, refugee status was determined based on U.S. foreign policy more than on the genuine and legitimate fear of returning to the country of origin. For example, Presbyterian theologian Dana Wilbanks notes that many Salvadorans, Guatemalans and Nicaraguans faced legitimate persecution during the 1980s, at the hands of governments allied with the United States, that was more severe than the situation of some Cubans who were admitted at the time, whose government is of course at odds with the United States.[25] Yet during that time, a very small number of Salvadorans, Guatemalans and Nicaraguans were actually granted refugee or asylee status compared to the number of Cubans who were allowed to enter during that time.

The definition of refugee does not include those who flee their home country because of environmental or natural disasters—such as a famine, tsunami or earthquake—or those who flee dire economic circumstances, which would include many who come to the United States illegally each year, particularly from Mexico and Central America. Elena came to the United States because she could not find work to sustain herself in Mexico, but fleeing economic hardship is not a valid reason to be classified as a refugee under the U.S. system.

Conclusion

Almost all Lawful Permanent Residents and naturalized U.S. citizens living in the United States today received their status through one of these four manners.*[26] For those like Elena who are undocumented, though,

---

*The largest exception would be those who were previously undocumented but were granted Lawful Permanent Resident status through the Immigration Reform and Control Act, commonly known as the amnesty, which was signed by President Ronald Reagan in 1986.

none of these legal paths may be an option. For her, there was no hope of an employment-based visa, no qualifying relationship to apply for a family-based visa, no diversity lottery, and no persecution that would merit a plea for asylum or refugee status.

Millions of others were in similar situations and, like Elena, elected to come illegally or to overstay a temporary visa. For many others all over the world, particularly from countries where the economic situation among the lower classes is deteriorating, coming to the United States seems to be the only hope—just as it has been for immigrants throughout our country's history. Now, though, there is simply no legal way to im-migrate for the majority of those who would like to do so, even though those who can arrive anyway do not seem to have difficulty finding will-ing employers.

I (Matthew) lived for a while in Nicaragua, a country that sends its share of undocumented workers north to the United States. Nearly half its population lives in extreme poverty, on less than $1 per day. Many there see the United States—whose streets are rumored to be paved in gold, whose federal minimum wage of $6.55 (soon to be $7.25) per hour sounds to many like a fortune to be made, and whose extravagance is dis-played to the Nicaraguan people on the ubiquitous television—as the great hope for a better life for their families.

While in Nicaragua, I heard story after story of people who had tried in vain to secure a visa to go to the United States. When there was no avenue to apply for an immigrant visa, many would apply for a visitor visa, some-times with the intention of overstaying. In almost every case, they were denied the visa, but they still had to pay a $100 fee—more than a month's income for the average Nicaraguan—just for the privilege of the appoint-ment at the U.S. consulate.* For many Nicaraguans facing extreme pov-erty, unsure of where the next meal for them and their children will come from, spending their last $100 (or, more likely, borrowing $100 from a better-off relative) is like buying a lottery ticket, hoping they might beat

---

*The fee to apply for a nonimmigrant visa at foreign consulates has since increased beyond $100.

the odds and win the chance to live and work in the United States.

That immigrants should wait their turn and immigrate the legal way sounds entirely reasonable, but the realities of our present immigration system complicate this truism. The immigration system, many would agree, is broken. Just how we fix this broken system, though, is a question of heated controversy—in Washington and even in our churches. As Christians, our response to these challenging issues should be informed by Scripture, which guides us toward how God would have us think about immigration policy and about immigrants themselves. We turn to Scripture in the next chapter.

THINKING BIBLICALLY

ABOUT IMMIGRATION

Welcoming the stranger (the "immigrant," we could say today) is the most often repeated commandment in the Hebrew Scriptures, with the exception of the imperative to worship only the one God. And the love of neighbor (especially the more vulnerable neighbor) is doubtlessly the New Testament's constant command. . . . Whatever the cause of immigration today, there can be no doubt as to where the Church must stand when it comes to defending the immigrant.
Theologian Orlando O. Espín

For Christians who take very seriously the authority of Scripture, all of life should be viewed through the lens of what God tells us about himself and his world in the Bible. While the Bible does not provide a specific prescription for a U.S. immigration policy—or for any other particular policy decision—it certainly offers principles that guide us as we consider the immigration dilemma and seek to influence policy in a way that reflects God's love, compassion and justice.

In fact, immigration is a very common theme in the Scriptures. There are several words in the original Hebrew of the Old Testament rendered into English as *alien, stranger, sojourner* or *foreigner,* depending on the translation. The most common word, and that which best describes the immigrants whom we encounter—not just tourists traveling through, but strangers who establish themselves, at least for a time, in a foreign land— is the Hebrew word transliterated into English as *ger.* Based on textual, historical and archaeological evidence, scholars believe that *ger* (in the context of the Hebrew Scriptures) refers to "a person not native to the local area" and thus often without family or land; the same term is used to refer both to the Israelites when living (whether as welcomed guests or resented laborers) in Egypt as well as to non-Israelites living among the Israelites.[1] The noun *ger* alone appears ninety-two times just in the Old Testament. Throughout the text, we find stories of *ger* (sojourners or immigrants), as well as guidance and commands from God to his people about how to treat the alien living among us.

Immigrants and Immigration in Scripture

When we read the Bible as a sacred narrative of God's interaction with humanity, we find that immigrants and refugees play many of the most important roles in the story. Throughout Scripture God has used the movement of people to accomplish his greater purposes. Like immigrants and refugees today, the protagonists of the Old Testament left their homelands and migrated to other lands for a variety of reasons.

Abram, later Abraham, is introduced in Genesis 11 as an immigrant from Ur to Haran. Abram's journeys did not stop there: this Ur-born immigrant later journeyed on to Canaan, with a stay in Egypt as well. Abram's decision to leave Haran and bring his family to Canaan parallels the stories of many historical and contemporary immigrants, who leave the lands they know and cross borders in pursuit of a promise—in this case a divine promise that God would bless him, make of him a great nation and bless all nations through him (Gen 12:1-5). Indeed, Abram's courage in making the journey and his faith in God's promise mark one of the pivotal moments in the Old Testament narrative.

Abraham also serves as a model of hospitality toward foreigners. When three strangers—unbeknownst to Abraham, messengers from God—passed by Abraham's home, he was so eager to offer them food and drink that he ran out to greet them (Gen 18:1-6). As an immigrant himself, he understood the experience of being a stranger in a foreign land, and he was eager to make others feel welcome. Likewise, today's immigrants to the United States are often embraced by earlier immigrants, who have already learned English and sufficiently understood U.S. culture to help the new arrivals orient themselves.

A few generations later, Abraham's great grandson Joseph becomes a different sort of immigrant—one who leaves his homeland not by choice or in pursuit of a better life, but as one sold into slavery. Joseph's brothers, tired of their younger brother's haughtiness, sell him to slave traders and invent a story to explain his absence to their father. Historically, of course, millions of people have been forced into involuntary migration; Americans are particularly aware of the slave ships that brought Africans to the New World against their will. Most would be surprised to know, though, that there are likely more involuntary immigrants—people forced by violence, coercion or deception into crossing borders—today than there were at the height of the transatlantic slave trade.[2] Like Joseph, many of today's victims of human trafficking are betrayed by their family, who profit from their relatives' suffering.

Eventually, through a series of divinely directed events, Joseph's status was raised from slave to the second-most-powerful person in Egypt, and God used him in powerful ways to save both his own family *and* his host country, Egypt. Joseph's experience, as theologian Justo González notes, reminds us that immigrants can make important contributions to the country that receives them.[3]

In God's plan, Joseph was ultimately reconciled to his family, who then took up residence in Egypt and lived there as foreigners for several generations. As the Israelites multiplied in Egypt, though, their growing numbers began to concern the native-born Egyptians, who began to oppress them, forcing them into slave labor. Likewise, many immigrants arrive eager to work in the United States, only to be mistreated, paid less than they were promised, or subjected to unsafe working conditions.

The book of Exodus explains how God used an unconfident man named Moses to lead his people out of Israel, fleeing a tyrannical government that had decreed death for all Israelite male infants. The Israelites, under Moses' leadership, became refugees, fleeing persecution in Egypt and escaping, with God's help, to a new land where, like many refugees today, they found new challenges. God ultimately used Moses to bring his people out of Egypt, so they could live in a "good and spacious land, a land flowing with milk and honey" (Ex 3:8).

Not all of the migrants in Scripture were *from* Israel: as the Israelites became established, there was also immigration *into* Israel. A woman named Ruth, from the land of Moab, married a foreigner in her home country and then, after her husband's death, decided to follow her mother-in-law, Naomi, to the foreign land of Judah. Ruth was like many immigrants today, who leave their homeland for the sake of family unity. God used Ruth's migration to Israel, and her subsequent marriage to Boaz, to form part of the lineage of Jesus, the Messiah.

Ruth's great grandson, David, was thus born as a descendant of an immigrant. In God's perfect plan, that did not stop him from becoming Israel's greatest king. Likewise, many of the great heroes of American history have been immigrants or second- or third-generation immigrants. Before becoming king, David also crossed borders himself, fleeing the wrath of King Saul and seeking asylum from King Achish of Gath, in the territory of the Philistines; David established himself there in Gath, along with his family (1 Sam 21:10; 27:3).

Eventually, of course, David returned to his homeland and became king. Several generations later, though, the people of Israel and Judah, led astray by various kings of less integrity than David, were carried off into exile. After a while some, like Nehemiah, were allowed to return to their homeland and begin to rebuild. Nehemiah, who had been serving in the Persian government of King Artaxerxes, was granted permission to travel to Jerusalem and rebuild the city walls. Because of his commitment to God and to his people, he was eager to go do the work he believed God was calling him to do.

Just as immigrants and refugees are important actors in the Hebrew Scriptures, they feature prominently in the New Testament too. The most notable refugee was Jesus himself, who fled, the Gospel of Matthew tells us, with his father and mother to go to Egypt, legitimately fearing King Herod would kill them if they remained in Judea (Mt 2:14). In another sense, of course, Jesus was a divine immigrant, leaving the glories of heaven to live among us and save us on earth (Phil 2:6-8).

Persecution was also the impetus for the great scattering of the earliest Christians in Jerusalem as described in Acts. When Stephen was martyred for his strong defense of the gospel, "a great persecution broke out against the church at Jerusalem, and all except the apostles were scattered" (Acts 8:1). God used this dispersion of Christ-followers to spread the gospel throughout Judea and well beyond. For example, Philip went south toward Gaza and encountered an Ethiopian pilgrim who accepted the good news and presumably brought it back to Africa (Acts 8:26-30).

Furthermore, Scripture suggests that all of us, as followers of Christ, whatever our nationality, have become aliens in this world, as our allegiances are to lie not primarily with any nation state but with the kingdom of God. Paul reminds the believers at Philippi that their citizenship is in heaven, while both Peter and the author of Hebrews refer to believers as "aliens and strangers" in the world (Phil 3:20; 1 Pet 2:11; Heb 11:13).

God used migration throughout Scripture to accomplish his purposes and bring his people to a greater understanding of his will for creation. God, who used migration so vividly throughout the Bible, works today to move his people from one place to another.

The Biblical Mandate to Care for Immigrants

Since so many of the characters of the biblical story were migrants of one sort or another, it is not surprising that God gives us a great deal of guidance about interacting with immigrants.

God reminds the Israelites early on of their own history as aliens in a foreign land, commanding them that, given their own experience, they should welcome the immigrant among them. In Leviticus 19:33-34, God commands the Israelites, "When an alien lives with you in your land, do not mistreat him. The alien living with you must be treated as one of your native born. Love him as yourself, for you were aliens in Egypt. I am the LORD your God." In fact, Israel's very identity was tied to how they treated the foreign born, as it reflected Israel's trust in God to provide and their willingness to follow his commandments. The words of Exodus 12:49, repeated throughout the Pentateuch many times, make clear: "The same law applies to the native-born and to the alien living among you."

At the same time, immigrants are recognized as being particularly vulnerable, and God therefore commands the Israelites to take special concern for them. The term usually translated as *alien* or *sojourner* appears repeatedly in conjunction with two other categories of people of special concern to God: the fatherless and the widow. For example, Deuteronomy 10:18 says that God "defends the cause of the fatherless and the widow, and loves the alien, giving him food and clothing." Psalm 146:9 echoes this concern: "The LORD watches over the alien and sustains the fatherless and the widow, but he frustrates the ways of the wicked." The same linkage extends throughout the Old Testament, such as in Ezekiel, where the evil rulers of Israel are condemned for having "oppressed the alien and mistreated the fatherless and the widow," and in Zechariah, where we are commanded, "Do not oppress the widow or the fatherless, the alien or the poor" (Ezek 22:7; Zech 7:10).

Given God's special concern, the Israelites are commanded in Deuteronomy 24 to make special provisions for immigrants, as well as for orphans and widows:

> When you are harvesting in your field and you overlook a sheaf, do not go back to get it. Leave it for the alien, the fatherless and the widow, so that the LORD your God may bless you in all the work of your hands. When you beat the olives from your trees, do not go over the branches a second time. Leave what remains for the alien, the fatherless and the widow. When you harvest the grapes in your vineyard, do not go over the vines again. Leave what remains for the alien, the fatherless and the widow. (Deut 24:19-21)

Likewise, the Israelites are commanded in Deuteronomy 14 to participate in a special triennial tithe, when they set aside a portion of their harvest so that the aliens, along with the Levites, the orphans and the widows, may have a feast (Deut 14:28-29).

Many of these biblical imperatives also warn that those who disregard

God's instructions—who do not specially care for the alien and others who are vulnerable—will face God's judgment. The prophet Malachi lumps those who deny justice to immigrants with sorcerers and adulterers:

> "I will be quick to testify against sorcerers, adulterers and perjurers, against those who defraud laborers of their wages, who oppress the widows and the fatherless, and deprive aliens of justice, but do not fear me," says the LORD Almighty. (Mal 3:5)

Moses also reminds the Israelites right before they enter the Promised Land:

> Do not take advantage of a hired man who is poor and needy, whether he is a brother Israelite or an alien living in one of your towns. Pay him his wages each day before sunset, because he is poor and is counting on it. Otherwise he may cry to the LORD against you, and you will be guilty of sin. (Deut 24:14-15)

The Hebrew Scriptures, particularly the books of the Law, are full of instructions on how to treat immigrants. Old Testament scholar Daniel Carroll R. notes that such frequent and specific injunctions in the Mosaic law toward care for the sojourner are unique in that the law codes of other nations in the ancient Near East "are almost totally silent" about how to treat immigrants.[4] While these instructions (along with the rest of the law) were directed to the people of Israel as rules to structure their society, and few American Christians believe that we should adapt the entire law as given to Moses (with its sacrificial system and dietary guidelines) directly to U.S. policies, the many commandments to care for the immigrant demonstrate that God has a special concern for immigrants, a concern that, as God's people, we are commanded to share. Our concern for the foreign born in our own society will have personal manifestations, but should also inform our positions as we consider immigration policy.

While the New Testament speaks less frequently about immigrants, the same ethic of concern for the alien and stranger is consistent. The author of Hebrews advises us to care for and welcome strangers with hospitality, because in doing so, we may be entertaining angels unaware (Heb 13:2). Likewise, Jesus told his disciples that whenever they welcomed and invited in a lowly stranger, they welcomed him (and, alternately, whenever they shut the stranger out, they shut him out as well—and would be judged harshly) (Mt 25:31-46).

Caring for immigrants is a central theme in Scripture. We have reviewed just a sampling of the many passages woven throughout the text that tell us we are to take special concern for immigrants. God does not suggest that we welcome immigrants; he commands it—not once or twice, but over and over again.

No Longer Foreigners and Aliens, but Fellow Citizens

Scripture teaches that each of us who comes from outside the bloodline of Israel has something in common with immigrants today. Paul tells the Gentiles of the church at Ephesus that, because of their nationality, they were previously "separate from Christ, excluded from citizenship in Israel and foreigners to the covenants of the promise, without hope and without God in the world" (Eph 2:12). The promises of God in the Old Testament, which we celebrate in our worship songs, were *not* initially directed at us (the Gentiles), but to the Jewish people whom God had specially chosen. Simply for reason of the location of their birth—which, of course, they had not chosen, any more than someone today chooses to be born in Mexico, Poland or Vietnam rather than in the United States, Canada or western Europe—most of the world was without hope and without access to the God of Israel, the one true God. Like most Asian immigrants in the United States until 1952 and like any undocumented immigrant today, we who are Gentiles were once barred from citizenship.

Thanks be to God, though, this was not his final plan; by his grace, we have now been naturalized into God's kingdom and adopted into his family through the blood of Jesus Christ (Eph 2:13). What is more, Christ has personally

destroyed the barrier, the dividing wall of hostility [between Jews and Gentiles] by abolishing in his flesh the law with its commandments and regulations. His purpose was to create in himself one new man out of the two, thus making peace, and in this one body to reconcile both of them to God through the cross, by which he put to death their hostility. (Eph 2:14-16)

The parallel to our current immigration situation, of course, is inexact—to be naturalized into the United States is almost unmentionably insignificant in contrast to becoming a citizen of God's kingdom—but many immigrants today know keenly what it means to have a law standing between them and really belonging as citizens. Even as many immigrants gratefully find their citizenship in heaven (through Christ, not through the law of the Old Testament) they yearn for a change to laws in the United States that do not allow them to admit their infraction of undocumented presence and proceed to become fully integrated members of our society. We, who now "are no longer foreigners and aliens, but fellow citizens with God's people and members of God's household," might remember the grace that we have received on a cosmic scale and, corporately, seek appropriate ways to extend to those who seek it the much smaller grace of being allowed to pursue citizenship in the United States. While we need not necessarily advocate open borders—there is an appropriate role for the government in monitoring and controlling those who enter our country—we ought to have a strong bias toward generosity in light of the enormous blessings that we have received.

Furthermore, we do well to note that by bringing Jews and Gentiles together as one person—though not, the apostle Paul makes clear, by requiring Gentiles to become as the Jews in every way—God creates a single body, his church (Acts 15:10; 1 Cor 12:27). Each part of Christ's body—Jew and Gentile, Asian, African, Hispanic, Native American, Caucasian and every other group of people—must be reconciled to one another and to God to effectively be the unified body that God has called us to be, doing his work in the world.

Who Is My Neighbor?

Perhaps the simplest reason that we, as Christians, should care for the immigrant is that she or he is our neighbor—both figuratively and, increasingly, for many Americans, literally. When a legal scholar asked Jesus what the most important command of Scripture was, Jesus indicated that there are two commands that sum up all of the Law and the Prophets: to love the Lord with all of our heart, soul, and mind, and to love our neighbor as ourselves (Mt 22:35-40).

Our natural tendency when we read this commandment is to apply the narrowest possible definition of a "neighbor," seeking to justify ourselves. In this, we are like the legal scholar, who pressed Jesus for a more precise, probably limited, legal definition. Were the definition of a neighbor narrowly limited, we could shirk the responsibility to love immigrants by arguing that they are of a different culture, ethnicity and language, and by avoiding living where immigrants might move in next door. Of course, Jesus proceeded to tell the inquisitive lawyer the parable of the Good Samaritan, where we find that our neighbor might be a person of an entirely different (and maybe even disliked) culture, far away from his homeland, with serious needs (Lk 10:25-37).

However we approach immigration policy, we must first approach immigrants themselves as neighbors—with love. The love to which we are called is a conscientious decision based on commitment and trust, not simply a warm feeling or emotion.

In our experience, and in the historical experience of previous generations of American Christians, this sort of love becomes much easier when you actually meet and get to know the immigrants in your community and begin to realize that, for all your differences, you also have a great deal in common—probably a taste for good food, a concern for your families and very often a common Christian faith.*

As we begin to interact with immigrants personally, we will inevitably confront questions of immigration policy that have enormous effects on

---

*We will explore more in chapter nine how the immigrant church is growing in the United States.

our new neighbors. To love our neighbors does not necessarily resolve any number of legitimate questions about how to construct a national immigration policy—we will turn to some of the most common concerns in the next chapter—but it ought to be our guiding principle both in personal interactions and as we think about structural issues that affect our immigrant neighbors.

CONCERNS ABOUT IMMIGRATION

We send troops thousands of miles away to fight terrorists, but we refuse to put them on our own border to keep them out. We will never be able to win in the clash of civilizations, if we don't know who we are. If Western civilization succumbs to the siren song of multiculturalism, I believe we're finished.

U.S. Representative Tom Tancredo, Republican of Colorado, at a Family Research Council event in April 2006

While Scripture gives many explicit commands to care for immigrants and strangers, there are also principles in Scripture, as well as extrabiblical concerns, that may cause us to be cautious. In our own interactions with other believers about immigration (whether as an invited speaker at a church or just around the table at a family gathering), we have heard many arguments *against* a more generous immigration policy. Among others, we have heard that accepting more immigrants might detract from care for the poor already in our country; that more immigrants may have a deteriorating impact on God's creation; that welcoming immigrants may be inconsistent with protecting our national security; that allowing some immigrants in will create an unstoppable chain of immigrants; and that immigrants negatively affect our culture. Others have no problem with legal immigration, but are particularly concerned about illegal immigration and the tension between welcoming the immigrant and submitting to the governmental authorities God has placed over us.

Immigration and Caring For the Poor *Already* Among You

Many Christians are concerned that allowing more immigrants to enter legally may have a negative impact on those U.S. citizens who are already living in poverty. Throughout the Bible, there is a consistent and indisputable mandate on God's people to take special concern for the poor and oppressed.[1] While immigrants come from all economic and education levels, just as they come from all countries, many immigrants enter the United States at the bottom levels of the economic ladder and accept low-wage jobs. By allowing immigrants to come and join the poor already here, some Christians feel we are neglecting a primary responsibility to those poor born in our country.

For example, Christian scholar Carol Swain argues that allowing more low-skill and low-education immigrant workers into the United States depresses wages for historically disadvantaged groups of U.S. citizens—particularly African Americans, Native Americans and Hispanics who have been living in the United States for many generations.[2]

Indeed, basic economics suggests that if fewer workers are available for a given job, the wages will rise, whereas if there is a plethora of labor, the wages will go down. It may be disingenuous of an upper middle-class, white-collar worker to complain that immigrant laborers are "stealing our jobs." But for a low-income, single woman, finishing her GED while raising two children and expecting a third, it is reasonable to think that she might make an extra dollar or two per hour at her fast food restaurant if her Mexican coworkers were still in Mexico (though she and everyone else might also then pay more for their meal, as well).

Swain argues that our first priority should be to care—and ensure employment—for the poor among us, not those outside of our borders. James Edwards, a Christian and an adjunct fellow at the conservative Hudson Institute, agrees, arguing, "Scripture indicates certain priorities of our obligations."[3] He notes 1 Timothy 5:8, where Paul advises Timothy that we have a responsibility to care for our own family members, and that the person who fails to do so is "worse than an unbeliever."

The context of the passage, though, is referring to the care of widows—

and the greater point is not that we should look out just for our own, but that we should look out for our own and then, as the church, look out for others as well. Whether or not this passage can fairly be applied to suggest that our first responsibility is to those who share our citizenship (as opposed to those who are our relatives, as in the text) is not the point, Paul's point is that the church should care for *all* widows in need. We should likewise be concerned about *all* those in need of work, whether born in the United States or born elsewhere. Our responsibility does not stop at our national boundary.

We might be right to condemn other nations for not providing a livable wage for their citizens, just as Paul criticizes those who were not caring for widows within their own family. However, Paul never suggests that if a widow's family is not caring for her that she should be left hungry; quite the contrary, he insists that the church should care for those widows "who are really in need"—who have no families or whose families have abrogated their responsibility to them (1 Tim 5:3). In the same way, to the extent that we can do so, we should not close work opportunities to those who desperately want a job to support their families.

Furthermore, we ought to consider that, while foreign governments, particularly the more corrupt ones, may bear much of the responsibility for unemployment and underemployment in their countries, economic and political policy decisions in the United States and other wealthy countries can also have dramatic, and certainly not always positive, effects on the economic conditions in the Global South. For example, the passage of the North American Free Trade Agreement (NAFTA) in 1994, which eliminated most tariffs and trade barriers between the United States, Canada and Mexico, may have helped many Mexicans reach the middle class, was economically devastating for others, particularly small corn farmers who could not compete with subsidized U.S. corn; many abandoned their farms and moved to the city or went north to find work in the United States.[4] In cases where U.S. policy decisions have negative consequences for the poor in other places, perhaps the responsibility to care for our own that Paul writes about might refer to many immigrants too, especially when their economic malaise is the result of U.S. economic policies.

Practically speaking, it is also true that the United States already has a low unemployment rate, with many jobs available, particularly in low-wage sectors such as hospitality, agriculture and landscaping. There are definitely people in need of work, particularly in historically disadvantaged groups that tend to achieve lower levels of education, and our nation—both through the church and through governmental policy—ought to be striving to help each person into a dignifying job that allows her or him to support a family. Nevertheless, corporations complain that they currently have a great need of laborers, which immigrants (with and without legal status) have been happy to fill.[5]

Dan Pilcher of the Colorado Association of Commerce and Industry says that the businesses in his state have been struggling since the state legislature passed tough new laws targeting unauthorized employment. "Workers have gone to other states," he says, creating "a real labor shortage in agriculture, construction and hospitality. Our economic output as a state is suffering."[6] Without immigrants eager to fill these jobs (or, as is the case in Colorado and some other states, now unable to fill such jobs because of newly-enforced employment authorization laws), most of these jobs would not go to a U.S. citizen for a higher wage. Instead, the jobs move to another state or, in an era of globalization, simply go to another country for a much lower wage than what the corporation had been paying (both to immigrant *and* citizen workers) in the United States.

We ought then to redouble our efforts to care for the poor born in the United States, but we should not allow the persistence of poverty within the United States to close off our borders and our hearts to those abroad.

Immigration and Creation Care

Another concern over immigration from a biblical perspective is that further immigration to the United States could have a negative impact on the natural environment.[7] As Christians, we are called to be stewards of God's creation, and evangelical Christians are increasingly taking this mandate seriously.[8] Scripture declares, "the earth is the Lord's, and everything in it" (Ps 24:1). As stewards of the land, we will give an account for how we have cared for God's creation.

Immigration might relate to our care for creation because individuals who live in the United States, on average, contribute much more than people from most other countries to environmental problems such as pollution and climate change. For example, the emissions of carbon dioxide each year for each American is about 5.6 metric tons, whereas a Mexican's emissions are not even one fifth of that amount and an Indian's are less than one tenth.[9] This difference in environmental impact is a result of our standard of living and the amount of energy that we use: those elements of life in the United States that make immigration so appealing also mean we contribute more to environmental problems than countries where poverty is the norm. It also means, of course, that it would not be sustainable for God's creation to have the entire world's population living in (and using as much energy as the average person in) the United States. The critique of immigration from an environmentalist perspective is that each immigrant to the United States is likely to be one more person switching from the sustainable emissions levels of most Global South countries to the unsustainable levels of the United States.

For a Christian who is really concerned about caring for God's creation, though, we ought to look at our own contribution to environmental problems before looking at others', heeding Jesus' advice to remove the plank from our own eyes before removing the speck from our brother's eye (Lk 6:42). First Corinthians 10:24 tells us, "Nobody should seek his own good, but the good of others." If we are to take this command seriously, we should lower our own level of contribution to environmental problems to that of those of the Global South before we limit their admission into our country because of their potential contribution to these problems.

Immigration and Homeland Security

Particularly after the terrorist attacks of September 11, 2001, another significant concern with immigration is that we may be allowing terrorists to enter our country, putting us at risk for further attacks.

It is entirely right that we take appropriate caution to avoid further attacks. Certainly it is within the rights of every country to keep out those who intend to do harm, and there is some biblical basis for this idea as well. The Israelite tribes of Gad and Reuben, for example, established fortified cities east of the Jordan River specifically to protect their families, and Nehemiah's great wall-building project was certainly designed, at least in part, to protect Jerusalem (Num 32:17).

Without contesting the idea that we should keep terrorists and criminals from entering the United States, however, we cannot presume that most immigrants are terrorists and criminals. The vast majority of immigrants are well-meaning people seeking a better life, and we certainly should not exclude everyone on the grounds of seeking protection; indeed, in a globalized society, we could not conceivably do so.

A wise response, then, would be to carefully monitor who comes into the country. We can do so to an extent by criminal records checks, as we already do. The irony of our present system, though, is that by restricting immigration tightly and making it nearly impossible for many people to immigrate legally, millions have entered without inspection. With so many immigrants crossing the borders every day, even a beefed up border enforcement can apprehend only a fraction of those who try to enter. If there were a reasonable legal procedure that immigrants could follow to enter the country, most—except those who might have something to hide in the inspection process—would not risk their lives to enter illegally through a desert. Border enforcement agents could then much more effectively monitor and inspect people who enter the United States and ensure those who cross are doing so legally and not to harm the United States. Most immigrants themselves are not opposed to securing our borders—they want to be secure, too—but we cannot do so unless we expand the legal process for entry *with* inspection. As long as the pull of employment in the United States matches the push of economic hardship in other countries, migration will not stop, no matter how challenging and hazardous we make the process for entry.

We must also address the undocumented immigrants in our country today. Having such a large undocumented population in a country that prides itself on the rule of law is indefensible and has led to a feeling of ill will against immigration in general. An opportunity for the undocumented to regularize their status, so that we know who they are, would free up resources, allowing law enforcement officials to target those intending to harm us rather than those here working to provide for their families.

Immigration, Identity and Cultural Homogeneity

Another concern over immigration that one hears increasingly, even among Christians, is that we need to keep immigrants out because they are "polluting our culture."[10] They do not, it is said, share our American values. Immigrants—people from other countries and cultures, by definition—are of course going to look, talk and to a certain extent live differently from people of the majority culture of the United States, especially when they have just arrived. While many come already speaking some English—and English as a Second Language (ESL) classes are full throughout the country—other immigrants take decades to master the language, and others, especially those who arrive at older ages, never learn to communicate in English.[11] Many Americans are frustrated by the increasing prevalence of Spanish and other non-English languages that they hear in the streets of their communities, at the supermarket, on the radio and even in their churches. Out of this frustration has grown an increasingly popular movement to declare English the official language of the United States.

Others argue that immigration is a problem because immigrants will change the cultural and ethnic makeup of the United States, which has since its founding been a nation with a majority of light-skinned people descended from European countries. For example, Patrick Buchanan, a former Republican and later Reform Party presidential candidate, has throughout his career advocated harsh restrictions on immigration because he believes that the cultures descended from the original European settlers of North America are superior to (and are now being contaminated by) "third world" cultures, whose people he considers unlikely to assimilate in the United States.[12] In a 1984 column, Buchanan stated bluntly that "the central objection to the present flood of illegals is they are not English-speaking white people from Western Europe, they are Spanish-speaking brown and black people from Mexico, Central America and the Caribbean," and his rhetoric has not changed substantially over the decades.[13]

While most would probably distance themselves from Buchanan's language, many Americans—including many Christians—share his concern that large-scale immigration is destroying the homogeneity of our culture. It is notable, though, that not even Buchanan—a Roman Catholic who was connected to the Christian Coalition during his rise to fame in the early 1990s—bases his arguments in Scripture, as such ideas are not found in the Bible.

Scripture is very clear that, under Christ, we who are his followers, whatever our cultural background, are united as one body—the church—and that each part is dependent on every other (1 Cor 12:12-27). "There is neither Jew nor Greek, slave nor free, male nor female, for [we, as Christ's followers,] are all one in Christ Jesus" (Gal 3:28). While in the Old Testament God commanded the Israelites not to intermix with their neighboring cultures—so that they would not be led astray by their false religions (which is exactly what they proceeded to do)—in the New Testament, all barriers based on ethnicity or culture were broken down, as Peter learned when God, in a dream, commanded him to break Jewish purity rules by dining and sharing the gospel with a Gentile, Cornelius. After the experience, Peter concludes "God does not show favoritism, but accepts men from every nation who fear him and do what is right" (Acts 10:34-35). We are called to the same standard. As beneficiaries of Christ's reconciliatory work, the church is called to a "ministry of reconciliation," bringing people of different backgrounds and cultures together around Jesus Christ, not dividing ourselves by race or country of origin (2 Cor 5:18).

If we are to think biblically about immigration, then, we need to disavow arguments based on claims of racial or cultural superiority. To the extent that all of us might harbor some of these feelings and ideas, we need to recognize that they may be rooted in our upbringing, our experiences, or the media we watch, read and listen to, but that these ideas do *not* come from the Bible. While it may be natural to prefer our own native language, foods and customs, and even to be frustrated as the culture we know is changing all around us with the influence of immigrants and refugees living among us, we must recognize there is no scriptural justification to claim superiority or to exclude others on this basis. Quite the contrary, the bulk of the biblical record on the treatment of immigrants, as we have seen, commands us to welcome and take a special concern for foreigners entering our land. Rather than saying that immigrants do not share our values, it is our responsibility to demonstrate in action what our values are to our new neighbors.

All of us as people carry a common and important need to know who we are. We cultivate this sense of identity through our genealogy, our schools, churches and communities, our families and often the state and country in which we live. Thus, when something new or different changes the environment in which our very identity is rooted, it is natural to resist, because we are afraid of change and its possible implications.

What happens, for example, when the neighborhoods in which we grew up start to change and people who speak a different language or look different move into our communities? How do we react when we go to the store and the person taking our money speaks with an accent and looks different from us? Or when a local restaurant serving hamburgers and chicken fingers turns into an ethnic restaurant?

The issue of immigration confronts our deepest fears of who we are and who we should be. As Christians, we can choose to respond in fear, or we can choose to embrace our identity in Christ and allow our citizenship in heaven (Eph 2:18-20, 22) to affect how we view and treat others.

We can look at how immigration changed the national identity of Egypt during the time of Joseph and see two starkly different examples of how the Egyptians treated the foreign born. In Genesis, we see Pharaoh welcoming Joseph's family with open arms as many people were fleeing famine in their homeland. The Egyptians, under Joseph's leadership, had carefully stored enough food to respond to the disaster at hand. Pharaoh not only eagerly opened up his stores, he also gave them the best piece of land in the area and went above and beyond what was expected of him to meet the needs of this migrant family. The Israelites acquired property in Egypt and were fruitful and increased greatly in number (Gen 47:27).

After the death of Jacob and Joseph, we see the Egyptians' attitudes toward the Israelites change dramatically, in a situation that has many parallels to the current immigration situation in the United States. In Exodus 1, we find that the Egyptians have forgotten the role of Joseph and his immigrant people in Egyptian history (Ex 1:8). They became concerned about the growing number of Israelites affecting their national identity (Ex 1:9), national security (Ex 1:10), and the country's economic situation (Ex 1:11). Eventually, the governing authorities began to make decisions about who would stay and who would go, decreeing that all Israelite girls should be allowed to live while all Israelite boys should be thrown into the Nile River (Ex 1:22).[14] In the following chapter, we see how one Israelite family responded to this situation. Like many undocumented immigrants in the United States, Moses' family was motivated by love and high hopes for their children (Ex 2:2) and so resorted to working around the law that proclaimed their children to be worthless, in order to save the life of their child (Ex 2:7-8).[15]

The changes in Egyptian immigration policy from the time of Joseph to the time of Moses are quite stark. What had transformed Egypt from a blessed land that recognized the contributions of its Israelite migrants and offered its best to them, to one that enslaved the Israelites and sought to kill off a generation of their male descendants? We can see throughout Exodus that Pharaoh developed a hardened heart and acted out of fear. He thought that if he did not oppress the Israelites that they would eventually outnumber the Egyptians and perhaps overpower his people: they were a threat.

We can learn much in our current situation from the scriptural description of the Egyptian case. We as Christians must not be driven by a spirit of fear that produces a hardness of heart, but rather we must extend grace and a welcoming spirit to the immigrants that God places in our communities, even if it makes us uncomfortable. We can be sure in extending this grace to our neighbors that God will be pleased, because we are recognizing that the prosperity God has given us is not ours alone.

Our responses to various issues are often influenced by our personal experience, cultural upbringings and mental attitudes and assumptions. As Christians, however, we are called to lay all of this at Jesus' feet and allow him to refine us to think as he wills (2 Cor 10:5).

"Anchor Babies" and "Chain Migration"—Immigration and Families

Two of the most common concerns about the current immigration situation relate to families and children. Many are concerned that immigrants illegally enter the United States simply to have children born in the United States who, as U.S. citizens by birth, will be able to help their parents. Building on the same concern, many are concerned that the family-based nature of our immigration laws allows one individual who gains (or is born into) legal status to sponsor an uncontrollable number of new immigrants.

The principle of birthright citizenship was enshrined in the U.S. Constitution in 1868 as the Fourteenth Amendment: "All persons born or naturalized in the United States, and subject to the jurisdiction thereof, are citizens of the United States and of the State wherein they reside."[16] This principle granted full equality and rights to those who are born in the United States and prevented any future tier of "second-class citizenship."

The idea of birthright citizenship, however, has been scrutinized in recent years because many purport that children born in the United States to undocumented immigrant parents should not automatically acquire U.S. citizenship and all its benefits. Some suspect that immigrants, who have no other way to gain legal status in the United States, cross the border so they can have "anchor babies," who will then be able to secure U.S.

rights and benefits for the entire family. Many people support repealing or re-interpreting the Fourteenth Amendment so as to eliminate birthright citizenship and deter future flows of illegal immigration.

In reality, the birthright citizenship guaranteed by the Fourteenth Amendment does not provide any direct benefit to the U.S.-born citizen's parents. Most undocumented people bear children in the normal process of living their lives here in the United States—not because they think their child is going to help them gain legal status. Having a U.S.-citizen child does not entitle the parent to any extra benefits, allow her or him to gain legal status in the U.S. immediately, or prevent deportation.

A U.S.-citizen child *can* file for the parent when that child turns twenty-one years old, but few people would have a child only to perhaps gain legal status twenty-one years later. Furthermore, under current law, if the parents entered the United States illegally to give birth (as opposed to entering on a visa), and do not have any other U.S.-citizen or Lawful Permanent Resident relatives (such as their own parent or a spouse), their U.S.-born child's petition would probably do them no good, as they would need to leave the United States to be eligible for the visa through their child, and they would be ineligible for any waiver of a ten-year bar to their reentry for having been unlawfully present in the country for so long.[17] Thus, the parent would not benefit directly or immediately from having a U.S.-citizen baby, even though the baby would have U.S. citizenship and could receive government services and benefits like any other citizen. The ultimate question may not be whether an "anchor baby" should be able to benefit the parents, but whether the baby should gain the benefits of being born a U.S. citizen.

Ending birthright citizenship would leave thousands of children without citizenship or nationality, rendering them stateless, as many countries do not provide citizenship to children born abroad to a citizen parent. They would be without alternatives or means to return to the country of their parents, while the undocumented adult parents would not gain any direct benefit. Approximately 3.1 million children in the United States have at least one parent present illegally.[18] Children born in the United

States to an undocumented parent have not broken any law themselves, yet they would bear the brunt for the infraction of illegal presence by not being granted citizenship. The effect on vulnerable populations, like asylum-seekers and victims of trafficking, would also be significant, as many asylum-seekers and victims of trafficking often do not have documentation before they flee persecution or forced servitude.

Immigrants do not come to the United States specifically to birth children here, but rather to improve their economic lot by working. In the normal course of their lives, of course, many do fall in love and have children. Eliminating birthright citizenship would thus neither discourage them from coming nor encourage those already here to leave, but would rather create a second-tier of human beings within our country, with huge numbers of children in legal limbo. There are better ways to address illegal immigration than attempting to amend the Fourteenth Amendment or ending birthright citizenship. To alter the basis for U.S. citizenship would inherently change our national identity and ultimately limit the diversity of the U.S. population.

Many critics of our current immigration policy are also concerned that our immigration system leads to "chain migration," purportedly allowing immigrants to sponsor an uncontrollable number of family members, who in turn sponsor further family members, increasing the number of immigrants exponentially. In reality, only immigrants who have already gained legal permanent residency or U.S. citizenship can sponsor relatives. Since there are already highly restrictive caps on family reunification visas, and all admitted family members must qualify under one of the categories approved by Congress, there is no opportunity for such "chain migration" to occur. Only children, spouses, parents and siblings qualify for such sponsorship—cousins, aunts, uncles, grandparents, in-laws and other extended family members cannot come to the United States through the family system.[19] In addition, in order to sponsor a family member, U.S. citizens or Lawful Permanent Residents must prove they have a stable income and commit to financially support their family members, to ensure they will not rely on taxpayer-funded social services.

Family members cannot sponsor their relatives overseas unless they commit to (and prove their ability to) maintain their relative at a standard of living no less than 125 percent of the federal poverty level. Given these many limitations on family sponsorship, it is not surprising that, on average, immigrants only sponsor an average of 1.2 family members.[20]

The alternative—further limiting the ability for families to be reunited through immigration laws, as many would like to do—is problematic from a Christian perspective. In fact, we believe that the current family-based immigration system, plagued by backlogs of years and sometimes decades, needs to be repaired. God endowed every human being with the need for himself and the need for each other. God instituted the family saying, "it is not good for the man to be alone" (Gen 2:18).

God instituted the family unit, and he uses it as the building block of an ordered and procreative society through which people can grow and experience his love. Throughout the Bible, we see the family as an integral structure through which God carries out his purposes. God, our *Abba* Father, works through the family to bring us to a closer understanding of his love for us. When God promised Abraham to make a great nation out of his children, he did not promise to do so through political influence or economic power. Instead, he was able to establish a great nation through family, telling Abraham, "I will establish my covenant as an everlasting covenant between me and you and your descendants after you for the generations to come, to be your God and the God of your descendants after you" (Gen 17:7).

In the story of Ruth, her loyalty to her mother-in-law is integral to God carrying out his plan—not only to show Naomi his faithfulness to her in her old age but also to bring Boaz and Ruth together. Ruth then bore a son, Obed, who was the father of Jesse, the father of David. Throughout the Bible, families were often multigenerational, comprised of clans and tribes with extended relatives. Immigrant families, who often treat extended family members such as cousins, nieces and nephews as immediate family members, give us a more biblical picture of family. By reuniting families in the United States, we open up more opportunities for God to work today as he has in the past and also create stronger, more stable communities.

As we consider who should come to the United States and who should not, family values and the societal benefit of intact families should be central to the debate. Rather than trying to minimize family-based immigration, we should quickly try to reunite families who have been waiting years for their applications to be processed and visas to become available. Any policy that undermines the ability of families to be together can only weaken our society. Immigration based on market needs will strengthen our economy, but immigration based on family will strengthen our social fabric and culture. Immigrant families are no different from native-born families in many respects. In fact, many immigrants, in our experience, have stronger family ties than native-born families, which adds to the vitality of the family unit here in the United States. Extended family has also helped immigrants adjust to their new unfamiliar environment by providing resources to care for children and start family businesses. The desire of some to limit the scope of immigration should not have to come at the expense of reunifying those immigrants who are already here, legally, with their family members. According to the Family Research Council, "The family is the great generator, and the intact family the greatest generator, of human capital."[21]

The Special Challenge of Illegal Immigration

The many concerns raised above aside, we believe it is evident from the many references to immigrants and immigration, aliens, sojourners and strangers in both the Old and New Testaments that God has very clearly commanded his people to welcome and care for foreigners. We can appropriately extrapolate that Christians seeking to influence a national immigration policy should push for laws that are welcoming to and specially concerned with immigrants and refugees, just as God decreed for the nation of Israel.

The present immigration dilemma, however, presents a special challenge, as Scripture's many references to immigrants never mention or consider their legal status—a concept which may not have applied during the biblical era, just as it did not apply during the early history of the United States, when there were practically no limits on immigration and when all immigrants were, as far the governing authority was concerned, legal. Indeed, many Christians would readily recognize that they should care for immigrants and refugees in a general sense, but they are troubled by the legal status issue and are not sure that they want to or should assist individuals whose presence in the United States is unlawful.

The current state of immigration helps to explain (if not necessarily justify) why so many people are in the United States without documents: the present laws make it impossible for most people to immigrate legally, while the economic or political situations in their home countries make it exceedingly difficult to stay put there.

Nevertheless, many Christians are uncomfortable with the idea of, and some even openly hostile toward, undocumented immigrants. Micah 6:8 commands us "to do justice, love mercy, and walk humbly with your God," but some Christians feel a tension between doing justice—which they might define as following and enforcing the law—and loving mercy—which might mean giving a break to those who have violated a law, especially without malicious intent in doing so.[22]

James Edwards, for example, recognizes sympathetically the situation that many migrants are in, but he argues, "even desperate circumstances don't make a lawless act moral."[23] He notes Proverbs 6:30-31, which says that, although most people would not blame a starving man for stealing some food, the thief is still responsible for the consequences of his crime.

Many others have pointed to Romans 13, which states emphatically, "everyone must submit himself to the governing authorities" since "the authorities that exist have been established by God" (Rom 13:1). The text continues to say that those who disobey the civil authority should expect judgment from that same authority, which "does not bear the sword for nothing" (Rom 13:4).

We seem to be faced with a dilemma, then: Scripture tells us to welcome and care for immigrants, without reference to legal status, but it also commands us to obey and respect the laws created by the governing authorities. Given this apparent paradox, it is understandable that Christians who take Scripture very seriously have diverging opinions on this topic.

The issue needs closer scrutiny, though. The words of Micah 6:8, translated above as a command to "do justice," are translated as "act justly" or "do justly" in alternate translations of the text (the New International Version and New King James Version, respectively). To many North American ears, to "do justice" implies law enforcement, whereas to "act justly" implies doing what is right and fair. We believe the latter understanding is closer to the justice that God calls us to.

In many situations throughout history, the laws of the civil authorities have not been just according to the principles that God gives to his people: the Egyptian government of Pharaoh held the Israelites as slaves, and many of the kings of Israel and Judah strayed from God's commands. There are many other examples throughout Scripture and throughout world history. We need not—and ought not—presume that the national law is necessarily just. Theologian John Howard Yoder notes that Romans 13 calls us to be subject to the law, but this does not necessarily mean unthinking consent and obedience to every law; he notes,

> The Christian who accepts his subjection to government retains his moral independence and judgment. The authority of government is not self-justifying. Whatever government exists is ordered by God; but the text does not say that whatever the government does or asks of its citizens is good.[24]

While we recognize that everyone must submit to the governing authorities, which God has established, we must simultaneously recognize that laws were created for the well-being of human beings and society. The question for us if we are to seek God's justice, then, is not only what the law is and is it being followed, but is the law itself just? Ultimately the laws must answer to God's higher law, which requires us to treat all human life with sanctity. All persons bear God's image and thus should be treated with the dignity and respect that we would afford our Savior. Valuing persons includes doing what we can to preserve them, to care for them, and to create fair systems that lead to healthy societies.[25] We must ask if our human-made laws create a just and better existence for those created in God's image. Ultimately, "we must obey God rather than men" (Acts 5:29).

For most Christians, this is intuitive; for example, the majority of evangelical Christians believe that our federal government's allowance of abortion, through the Supreme Court's 1973 decision in *Roe v. Wade,* is unjust.[26] While recognizing that we are called to be subject to the state—very few call for anarchy or violent revolution over this policy—many Christians feel strongly that to seek justice as God commands us means to seek within the law to make abortion illegal, through protest and lobbying. Similarly, the heroes of the civil rights movement violated unjust laws in order to end segregation. Likewise, many churces send missionaries to countries where it is illegal to preach the gospel.

When considering our nation's immigration laws, we should likewise ask: is the law just, or should we, as Christians living within a democratic system of government where advocating for change does not go against submission to the authorities, push to change the law? On one side, there is nothing inherently unjust about a nation having borders. Carol Swain, arguing for more stringent immigration policies, contends that "it's not unbiblical for a Christian to have a position that's in favor of maintaining national boundaries," as most would probably agree.[27] She cites Acts 17:26, which states that God has made "every nation of men to dwell on all the face of the earth, and has determined . . . the boundaries of their dwellings" (NKJV).

Stronger border security measures, however, are not inconsistent with a more generous immigration policy; they in fact reinforce one another. By having responsive legal avenues through which immigrants can enter our country, we will relieve pressure off the border and allow our law enforcement officials to focus on those who intend to harm our country, rather than on those who are entering to work or reunite with family. It takes a great deal of creative inference and conjecture to find anything in the biblical text that *mandates* that we restrict immigration.

The United States in fact has doubled spending on border security over the past decade, but illegal immigration has only increased since then—as have deaths associated with illegal crossings as migrants trying to avoid border patrols have moved further out into the desert to cross. In fact, it is estimated that over three thousand people have died trying to cross the border over the past decade. In one U.S. story that received prominent media attention in May of 2003, seventy-three undocumented immigrants climbed aboard a tractor trailer in which the driver was paid $7,500 to drive them from Harlingen, Texas, near the border of Mexico, to Houston, Texas, about 300 miles away. The truck's refrigeration unit was turned off and, after extended hours in the truck, nineteen immigrants died of asphyxiation, thirst and heat. Witnesses said the immigrants were frantically scratching at the insides of the tank, screaming for help, and even attempted to make an emergency call, but all to no avail. Border security is necessary for the sovereignty of our nation, but responsive legal avenues through which people can migrate back and forth are also essential to create an orderly system.

More generous immigration policies, particularly when further legal immigration is likely to benefit the economic situation and, therefore, the common good, should be pursued. While we need not necessarily condone any violations of the law, such as living in the United States illegally, we should recognize that our complex and inadequate immigration system has made it impossible for many of the hard-working people that our country needs to enter or remain in the country legally or to be reunited with family members.

Since we live in a democracy—where laws can be changed, usually in response to public pressure—the dilemma of wanting to welcome immigrants while also expecting people to follow the law is not insurmountable: we can overcome this dilemma by changing the law so that many of those who today come illegally would be able to enter legally. In this sense, we are showing compassion to those who wish to immigrate—while not encouraging them to violate a law by entering without a visa. We are not advocating limitless immigration or open borders, but we do believe that those who desire to migrate to the United States to work in a job that is eager to have them should be allowed to enter legally, and should be welcomed by churches as they arrive.

We are left with the question of what to do with those already present unlawfully, who have violated the laws of the United States by entering without inspection or by overstaying their visas. It is a fallacy to suppose that we have only two options—total amnesty* or harsh consequences such as deportation. While the idea of amnesty is not necessarily inconsistent with the Christian faith—as pastors Rob Bugh and Al Guerra have noted, a hope in "divine amnesty" is central to our faith, particularly for those of us who believe that salvation is by grace alone—it is also reasonable to expect that there be a consequence for having violated the law.[28] Nonetheless, these consequences can be compassionate and understanding, such as a reasonable fine and putting those who have entered unlawfully behind those who have been waiting for years (or decades) to receive a visa in the line for Lawful Permanent Residency.

The issue for many undocumented immigrants is that there is no restorative measure to address the infraction of entering illegally or overstaying a visa. We should look to the Bible to help inform our decisions about justice, restitution, redemption, restoration and integration into our communities. Most immigrants are hard-working, God-fearing individuals. If provided the opportunity, they would want to admit wrongdoing and come out of the shadows as law-abiding, contributing members of our society. They should be provided an opportunity to admit their unlawful behavior of maintaining undocumented presence in the United States, but the punishment should correlate reasonably with the offense committed. The biblical concept of restoration into full fellowship within the church context (2 Cor 2:5-8; Gal 6:1) is something we might also do

---

*We would define amnesty as forgiving, forgetting or overlooking a past offense, as opposed to bearing a punishment or penalty for the offense.

well to apply as a society, aiming to integrate those who are here as undocumented individuals into our communities.

We must strive to promote justice where it is due. Justice in the Scriptures is based on a just and righteous God who commands his people to reflect his character. Human laws, thus, must reflect divine law and justice. Justice, however, is not limited to legal benefits, like fair processes and procedures and access to courts, but also includes socioeconomic benefits like access to food, water, shelter and land. Isaiah cries out against the economic injustice of Israel when he says, "Woe to you who add house to house and join field to field till no space is left and you live alone in the land" (Is 5:8). Amos also denounces the Israelites who "trample on the poor and force him to give you grain" (Amos 5:11). God demands that his people share the wealth that he has given them, or else face harsh judgment. We as Christians must consider what we have been given in light of God's command to share his blessings with others. This idea of distributive justice can inform how we are to treat the immigrants among us.

Justice is not just a temporary alleviation of difficult circumstances, but it requires both a deliverance from the unjust situation at hand and a change in the structures that perpetuate injustice. This idea of procedural justice can inform how we are to think about the legal status of immigrants and the immigration system today. Throughout Scripture, justice means the delivery of God's people from slavery (Mic 6:4) and from captivity (Jer 51:10). A country's ability to regulate its borders and the movement of people is not unjust; it is necessary. We cannot, however, continue to ignore a large segment of our population that exists in the shadows of our society. Requiring immigrants who are in the country illegally to admit their infraction against the law and become fully restored members of our communities—while reforming the immigration system to allow for orderly, future flows—will ensure that we do not create a society where the economy and social ties attract immigrant workers without providing a legal avenue for them to come. As Ronald Sider of Evangelicals for Social Action argues,

The goal of justice is not only the recovery of the integrity of the legal system. It is also the restoration of the community as a place where all live together in wholeness. Opportunity for everyone to have access to the material resources necessary for life in community is basic to the biblical concept of justice.[29]

The biblical concept of restoration is not only an extension of grace but also instills in the recipient a responsibility to live by the rule of law. This reciprocal action obligates the immigrant to live within a set of norms and culture while the extension of grace allows for his or her full restoration into society.[30]

In chapter eight, we will look at some of the proposals that have come out of Congress in the past several years, and we will gauge how these proposals balance a concern for justice—making it clear that the laws should be respected—with compassion, recognizing that people are coming out of desperate situations and may not have wanted to break the law, but to support their families. First, though, having considered many of the criticisms of immigration, we will consider the value that immigrants bring to our society.

THE VALUE OF IMMIGRATION

TO THE UNITED STATES

Immigration is one of the major reasons why the U.S. economy is so robust, diverse, dynamic and resilient. This is not to minimize the negative impacts immigration can have on particular workers, families or communities. But, in general, U.S. policy should be supportive of, rather than resistant to, immigration.

Economist John Stapleford

Looking up at a square building in the middle of dusty Tijuana, Mexico, I (Jenny) tentatively stepped through the squeaky wrought-iron gates. There I was welcomed by a warm, Brazilian Catholic priest who was running a shelter for migrants recently deported from the United States. I sat down to dinner at the shelter with a young man named Guillermo who had been living in Northern California for over eight years and who is the father of a three-year-old girl, born in the United States. While driving back home after a long day of work, Guillermo was pulled over at a traffic signal for a broken headlight, summarily detained, and then deported back to Mexico without having said goodbye to his daughter in person one last time. Since he arrived in Mexico, Guillermo had been communicating with his daughter every few weeks over the phone. "She always asks me where I am, but what can I say? How do I begin to tell her where I am or what happened to me? She won't understand. I can never go back. I don't know if I'll ever see her again," he said quietly, pushing his fork into a bowl of salad. When asked what he will do next, he says, "I will probably go back to my home [in Mexico], but I don't know if I will be able to find a job." Guillermo's daughter is now being cared for by Guillermo's father and wife who are still living in California.

Thousands of immigrants like Guillermo find themselves seeking economic opportunity in the United States. In Guillermo's case, he had worked picking grapes in Northern California for three years, working eight hours a day in the hot California sun for $6 an hour. Though his wages were low compared to what most Americans earn, they were more than he could have earned for the same work in Mexico, allowing him to provide his family with a better life. At the same time, his employer profits from his hard labor, and the many Americans who buy inexpensive fruit at their local supermarket benefit from his work.

Not everyone thinks the presence, and labor, of immigrants like Guillermo is so beneficial, though. At a recent town hall meeting in rural Iowa, for example, a group of over 100 concerned citizens gathered to talk about immigration and its impact on their community. Over the past decade or so, many jobs that were once done by native Iowans, particularly in agricultural and manufacturing industries, have been filled by Mexicans and Central Americans. Naturally, these new residents also had changed the town in many ways, bringing with them their language, their culture, and their children, who attended the town's public schools. Citizens were uneasy about the arrival of new immigrants who seemed to be taking away jobs and resources. A man stood up and declared, "We can't have people who are not going to pay taxes that we just don't know here." Another stood up and opined, "Our schools shouldn't be educating these kids who shouldn't be here anyway." In a community traditionally receptive to immigration, there was growing concern of the negative impact it was having on the community.

There are competing stories being told all over the United States as to the costs and benefits of immigration for the country. What effects do people like Guillermo, who come to the United States to pick our produce for a low hourly wage, have on the overall economy? Does immigration hurt the American worker? Are foreign workers even needed? What about the costs of providing services—education, healthcare and other public services—to these people? Can our country afford to welcome so many immigrants? Could we afford not to have them here?

From a Christian perspective, these questions ought not to be primary: the scriptural witness is that we are to care for the immigrant stranger living among us, without any caveat that exempts us from this responsibility if it is not in our individual or national economic interest. Furthermore, immigrants contribute much to our society that is not easily quantified, and we err if we reduce the immigration dilemma to one of mere mathematics. God created and delights in cultural diversity, and immigrants have added richly to our communities through their different cultures. Nevertheless, economic considerations are among the most common concerns raised in the ongoing immigration debate in our country, and they need to be addressed. In this chapter, we will look at the balance of costs and benefits that immigration implies both to the United States and to immigrant-sending countries, as well as consider the global dynamics fueling migration—not just in the United States but also around the world.

The Economic Impact of Immigration

Since the time of the Puritans, who emigrated from northern Europe seeking religious freedom in the West, immigration has defined the United States as a country and added to the richness and vitality of America today. Many of the immigrants in the United States today were driven by the same dreams and hope for prosperity that attracted the founders of our country to a new land. Now that the United States is a stable, settled country, however, is immigration still beneficial to the United States? And if so, how many more immigrants can the United States sustain?

From the founding of our country until now, peaks in immigration have often happened during periods of fundamental economic change in the country, playing a key role in helping us through these economic transitions.[1] At the height of the great wave of immigration around the turn of the twentieth century, the United States was turning from an agricultural society into a manufacturing economy, and many immigrants fled poverty and came to the United States to work in newly formed industries. The same questions about whether immigration was beneficial to the United States were asked then, and immigration restrictions eventually followed as the general public increasingly felt that immigration was not in their economic interest. In hindsight, even though income was not always equally distributed in the short term, we now know that the long-term economic impact of immigration during that time period was generally positive.[2] For example, the wages of residents increased over that time, and local employment of residents also increased despite heavy immigration.

Now, at the beginning of the twenty-first century, we live in an age of globalization, where the world is becoming increasingly interconnected. The United States is transforming from a manufacturing society to an information-based society, and immigration can help the United States adapt. The U.S. economy is expected to grow at a rate of 2.8 percent from 2006 to 2016.[3] In this period of relatively steady U.S. economic growth, we will see an increase in need for workers in the labor force. From 1980 to 2000, a majority of the growth in the labor force came from an increase in native-born workers between twenty-five and fifty-four years old, mostly women and baby boomers entering the labor market. Between now and 2020, however, no net increase in the native-born workforce between the ages of twenty-five and fifty-four is expected. In fact, older individuals (ages fifty-five years and older) in the labor force are expected to grow at five times the rate of the overall labor force.[4]

The combination of the aging of the baby boomer generation, of which an estimated 77 million are expected to retire in the next few years, and low U.S. fertility rates will not only slow the labor force growth but will also increase the ratio of retired people to working people. A greater number of retired dependents will thus need to be supported by a worker who can pay into the Social Security and healthcare systems. Even if new native-born workers replace the retiring native-born workers in their jobs, there will not be enough native-born workers to fill the new jobs created by a growing economy. To fill in the gaps, older workers will either need to continue to work, or more immigrants will need to join the labor force.

Not only is the U.S. workforce aging, the native-born worker is also becoming more educated. In 1960, for example, half of all American men dropped out of high school, presumably to seek work in an unskilled labor field, whereas less then 10 percent of American men do so now. Yet, half of the 50.7 million new jobs likely to be created between 2006 and 2016 will require no more than a high school education.[5] The construction industry, for example, is the only goods-producing sector, excluding agriculture, that is expected to have positive employment growth from 2006 until 2016, adding 780,000 jobs. In an industry in which up to 20 percent of the work force is comprised of undocumented immigrants, yet in which half of all builders say they consistently have a shortage of labor, the industry will need to continue to meet the demand to build more while finding workers to do the job. According to Hugh Morton, a board member of the National Association of Home Builders,

> Illegal immigrants have . . . supplemented American workers and provided the labor for an expanding housing market, particularly in the growing Sunbelt states. Builders who were struggling to find quality roofers, concrete finishers . . . etc., found the immigrant trade contractors a godsend.[6]

The restaurant industry, the largest employer in the United States besides the federal government, is projected to grow at a rate of 16 percent through 2017, adding 2 million jobs to the 12.8 million jobs already existent. In an industry dominated by younger workers, whose overall number is expected to decrease in coming years, immigrants can play a key role in fueling economic growth in this sector as well. The industries expected to grow the most in the next ten years are ones in which human labor cannot be mechanized by greater technology or shipped overseas to another company, but require work to be done here in the United States.

Given the need for an ever-increasing labor market, almost all economists agree that immigration (whether legal or illegal) provides and will continue to provide a net benefit to the economy of the United States. In fact, according to a survey by the *Wall Street Journal*, forty-four out of forty-six economists surveyed thought that illegal immigration was beneficial to the economy.[7] Most economists agree that "on balance, immigration is good for the country. Immigrants provide scarce labor, which lowers prices in much the same way global trade does. And overall, the newcomers modestly raise Americans' per capita income."[8] As is often the case in economics, though, a phenomenon that carries an overall net benefit may incur costs and benefits disproportionate to particular subgroups.

Are Immigrants a Drain on Public Resources?

One of the disproportionate effects of immigration is on governmental expenses, with federal, state and local governments affected unequally by immigration. As we have already explained, most immigrants *are* paying taxes—taken out of their payroll checks for Social Security, Medicare and income tax, as well as sales tax and property taxes—thus their presence involves an input of funds into the governmental coffers. At the same time, of course, immigrants' presence results in expenses for the state: even though immigrants are ineligible for most public benefits, their children (regardless of status) are eligible for public primary and secondary education, they will still be treated in an emergency at the hospital even if they are unable to pay, and they still use police, fire and other municipal services. Researchers Michael Fix and Jeffrey Passel have found, in a survey of various studies conducted at various levels of government throughout the United States, that

> most national studies suggest that immigrants are not an overall fiscal burden on the native population. At the state level the picture is mixed, resulting in part from the differing responsibilities assumed by different state governments. At the local level, analyses . . . have invariably found immigrants to be a net fiscal burden.[9]

In fact, a study by Stephen Moore, an economist at the libertarian-leaning Cato Institute, suggests that the average immigrant (legal immigrants, refugees and undocumented immigrants) pays about $80,000 more in taxes than he or she receives in benefits over a lifetime. That net benefit to the government, though, is the result of paying $105,000 more over a lifetime than the benefits received to the *federal* government, while receiving $25,000 in benefits more than what is paid to *state* and *local* governments.[10]

While the economic benefits of having immigrant labor are most obvious at the national level, local communities often spend resources supporting the workforce and not feeling the benefits of immigrants. The federal government has recognized this mismatch of resources and flow of benefits, and Congress has introduced measures to direct national resources to help states deal with the costs of undocumented immigration, but the disparity persists. Nevertheless, immigrants have a generally positive economic effect on public resources and the national economy.

What Is the Impact on Native Workers?

Another common economic concern is that immigrants take jobs from native-born U.S. citizens. Research by leading immigration economist George Borjas concludes that immigration has had a negative impact on low-skilled native workers specifically. Since such workers, who often have not had access to quality education, tend to be among the poorest in our society, they merit particular concern. Borjas has argued that, as the supply of immigrants to fill unskilled labor jobs increases, it drives down wages of the native-born unskilled workers, following the basic law of supply and demand. In a recent study Borjas conducted that focused specifically on illegal Mexican immigration to the United States, he found that in the 1980s and 1990s, the influx of undocumented immigrants accounted for a decrease in wages of 8.2 percent for native-born high school dropouts.[11] Like most economists, Borjas acknowledges that there is a net benefit overall for the entire native-born population of about $10 billion per year, or about 0.1 percent of the Gross Domestic Product for the entire population, but he argues that the overall net gains to the U.S. economy from immigration are negligible compared to the losses suffered by a particularly vulnerable segment of the native workforce: low-skilled native workers.[12]

Many economists, however, have poked holes into Borjas's findings, saying that Borjas focuses narrowly on certain economics trends without examining other economic forces that minimize the negative effects of immigration on the U.S. economy. For example, while Borjas contends that undocumented immigrants depress the wages of unskilled native-born workers, he does not consider that some of these businesses that employ immigrants would otherwise not exist in the United States if it were not for immigrant labor, since they would be undercut by cheaper imports from abroad. These businesses would either close out completely or move their operations elsewhere. For example, strawberry pickers in California are not necessarily competing against native workers but against pickers in Mexico and other countries. One farmer, Steve Sarconi, who owns Valley Harvesting and Packing in California, said he invested $1 million in research on mechanization and found that machines could still not tell good crops from bad crops. "I'm as American red-blooded as it gets," he states, "but I'm tired of fighting the fight on the immigration issue."[13] He eventually moved his operations to Mexico because the workforce was more reliable and he did not have to worry about immigration raids.

Immigrants contribute to the economy not just as workers but as consumers as well. Their presence creates new markets (such as for grocery stores specializing in Mexican, Polish or Korean foods) and expands existing markets. Immigrants often fuel local businesses and invest in the communities in which they live, buying houses, clothes and food. In many parts of the country, a fast-food restaurant, for example, is very likely to employ immigrant workers, but immigrants also likely make up many of its customers. In this way, immigrants supply their labor to the market but also, by their purchases, add to the demand for more workers. If entering immigrants increase the supply of workers at the same time there is an increase in the demand for workers, wages do not decrease as much as expected.[14]

The possibly slight negative impact of immigrants on native, low-skilled workers should not be glossed over. Instead, policymakers have a responsibility to make sure that immigrants who are here in the shadows are regularized in a system so U.S. workers can compete fairly. Having immigrant workers is not necessarily what hurts native-born workers: what may hurt native workers in some cases is the fact that these workers are here illegally. Having undocumented immigrants, who do not have equal rights and protection under the law, allows employers an unfair competitive advantage in hiring cheap immigrant labor over native workers. Often, this can lead to the exploitation of workers by unscrupulous employers.

In the tomato industry in Florida, for example, an estimated 80 percent of the migrant workers are undocumented.[15] Working ten to twelve hours a day handpicking tomatoes, they earn about forty-five cents for every thirty-two-pound bucket. On a typical day, these migrant workers carry and unload two tons of tomatoes in hot, humid weather. According to the Department of Justice, there have been some cases of slavery among these farm workers, where migrants are underpaid and kept in chained trailers at night. This is an injustice. Recognizing the economic benefits of having immigrant workers in the economy needs to be coupled with providing legal status and rights for these workers, such as the rights to switch jobs or to join a union. By having a workforce where everybody is legal, workers, both native born and immigrant, are better off.

Competition or Complements?

Many have argued that immigrants compete with American workers and take their jobs. In many situations, though, immigrants complement native workers, rather than competing with them. Immigrants often are entrepreneurs and start up businesses that would otherwise not exist, offering services in communities, employing other workers and overall increasing the Gross Domestic Product (GDP) of the U.S. economy.

It is easy to blame immigrants when unemployment is on the rise in the United States. When we see our economy declining, certain companies laying off thousands of workers and the dollar getting weaker, we point to what we see as the obvious change—immigrants in a previously homogeneous society—and think that they, rather than unseen economic forces, are causing our maladies. Many factors other than immigration, though, may cause a decline in wages, such as trade policy, the advance of technology and the erosion of the minimum wage's buying power.[16] Immigrants often respond to these changes in the economy rather than cause them.

Many people incorrectly assume that there are a fixed number of jobs in the economy. This is simply not true. The U.S. labor market has an incredible ability to absorb new workers. Immigrants do not further split up the economic pie; they enlarge it.[17] Immigrants often do not have the same skill sets as native-born workers. Rather than taking jobs from the native workforce, they create their own job opportunities and fill jobs in which they have a specific skill set. Immigrants thus choose different occupations in which they have a specialized skill set rather than copy the work of U.S. workers. For example, the foreign born constitute 54 percent of tailors in the United States and 44 percent of plaster-stucco masons. However, they make up less than 1 percent of crane operators and less than 1 percent of sewer-pipe cleaners.[18]

Even within the same professions, complementary differences allow for more business opportunities. For example, Chinese cooks differ from American cooks in their traditional fare, while Italian tailors and American tailors will sew clothes differently according to their trade. This idea of complementarity also allows Americans to earn more in the occupations they currently have. For example, a doctor who hires an immigrant landscaping business to take care of his lawn can then spend more time at the hospital taking care of patients. More construction workers also means more jobs and higher wages for architects, plumbers, electricians and contractors, since their work is dependent on new construction projects, which in turn is dependent on the availability of contruction workers.

New York City is a prime example of a community where immigrants are adding richly to its economic vitality. According to Mayor Michael Bloomberg,

New York City alone is home to more than three million immigrants, who make up nearly 40 percent of our entire population. About 500,000 came to our City—and continue to come—illegally. . . . Although they broke the law by illegally crossing our borders or overstaying their visas, our City's economy would be a shell of itself had they not, and it would collapse if they were deported. The same holds true for the nation.[19]

Entrepreneurship has made the United States an economic powerhouse and will continue to help the country quickly adapt to changing market conditions. The United States benefits from the entrepreneurial spirit, hard work ethic and innovation of immigrants who often find themselves unable to prosper in their homelands, due to the lack of infrastructure or robust financial markets, but who flourish with the opportunities in a relatively stable U.S. economy. The very fact that immigrants move from their homes characterizes their willingness to take risks to succeed in the United States.

Immigrant entrepreneurs have founded thousands of businesses, from engineering companies and cleaning services to restaurants and medical practices, and these businesses often revitalize neighborhoods that were dying off. Sergey Brin, the founder of Google, Inc., came to the United States from Russia with his family when they felt they could not fully thrive in a society that regularly discriminated against Jews. Once here, Sergey advanced through his classes and went on to a doctoral program at Stanford University, though he eventually quit the program to start his business out of someone's garage. Google, Inc. is now a multibillion-dollar company and has made Sergey Brin very wealthy, but he also has a desire to give back to the community.

> In terms of being remembered, I think I want to make the world a better place. One is through Google, the company, in terms of giving people access to information. I'm sure I will do other endeavors in terms of technologies and businesses. The second is just through philanthropy. I don't have a significant amount of wealth beyond

that on paper right now, but I hope that I have the opportunity to direct resources to the right places.[20]

John Tu, another immigrant entrepreneur from Taiwan, founded Kingston Technology in Fountain Valley, California, with fellow Taiwanese immigrant David Sun. Tu sold the company for $1 billion and gave $100 million of the sale's proceeds to his American employees. Gary McDonald, a Kingston employee, said, "Kingston's success came from a philosophy of treating employees, suppliers and customers like family, this being based upon the Asian family values of trust, loyalty and mutual support practiced by John and David."[21]

Immigrants often arrive in the United States without the educational and financial characteristics that would necessarily portend success once here. Their initial starting place in life, however, should not discount their ability to succeed in the future. Dr. Alfred Quinones-Hinojosa, a neurosurgeon at Johns Hopkins University, was an undocumented immigrant who picked tomatoes in the fields of California, where the farmer's son would look down on him with disdain. He worked his way through school and eventually went to Harvard Medical School where he gave his class's commencement speech. "The last thing I was thinking was that I was going to break the law," he says. "I felt what my father felt, not being able to put food on the table for my family, but I had a dream."[22]

High-Tech Jobs

As Sergey's, John's and Alfred's stories illustrate, immigrants are not just concentrated in low-skilled jobs; but also in high-skilled jobs. One-third of immigrants do not have a high school degree, but one-quarter have a college degree or higher.[23] This heavy concentration at opposite ends of the employment spectrum reflects the growing polarization of the U.S. labor market, with job growth concentrated most heavily at opposite ends of the spectrum for low-wage (or low-education) labor and high-wage (or high-education) labor at the expense of middle-wage labor, due in part to computerization of work.[24] The education and skill set of immigrants will thus fill jobs in industries that are expected to create the most jobs in the future. For example, more than 20 percent of workers in the computers and mathematics industries—industries among those expected to grow most rapidly from 2006 to 2016—are currently foreign born.[25]

With state-of-the-art research facilities and some of the best educational institutions in the world, the United States has been the destination of choice for the world's best scientists and researchers. Overall in 2000, 17 percent of science and engineering workers with bachelor's degrees were foreign born, 29 percent with master's degrees were foreign born, and 38 percent with doctoral degrees were foreign born.[26] The contributions of immigrants to the advancement of science and technology in the United States are unmistakable. Yahoo, Google and Sun Microsystems were all founded by immigrants who came to the United States to live the American dream. Jerry Yang, the Taiwanese immigrant who founded Yahoo, Inc., has said

> Yahoo would not be an American company today if the United States had not welcomed my family and me almost 30 years ago. We must do all that we can to ensure that the door is open for the next generation of top entrepreneurs, engineers, and scientists from around the world to come to the U.S. and thrive.[27]

Between 1990 and 2004, over one-third of U.S. scientists who have received Nobel Prizes have been foreign born.[28] A recent study found that immigrants started 25 percent of venture-backed U.S. public companies over the past fifteen years. These companies have a market value of $500 billion and created 400,000 jobs worldwide, attesting to the ability of immigrants to create enormous wealth and employment opportunities not just in the United States but also throughout the world.[29]

Currently, there are tight caps on the number of visas granted annually to high-skilled workers. Microsoft Corporation has said that thousands of core technology positions go unfilled every year because of these caps. This has inhibited the productivity of Microsoft so much that its chairman, Bill Gates, has proposed eliminating caps on these

A Benefit or Loss for the Sending Country?

Brain drain, or the emigration of high-skilled workers from low- and middle-income countries, is often cited as one of the negative effects of immigration, especially on developing countries that invest large amounts of their resources into training and educating their work force, only to have them leave to work in another country. In Ghana, for example, half of all medical school graduates emigrate within five years of graduation. This large exodus of health care workers to more developed countries like the United States and Canada has been a major barrier to delivering quality health care at the community level.[31] Where there is a dearth of doctors and nurses, local community health workers are often stepping in and providing the needed medical care.

In other countries, however, the emigration of skilled labor can be seen as a consequence of "brain overflow," as well-educated workers lack job opportunities in their communities after graduation and migrate to countries that will best utilize their skills. In some cases, "replacement migration" has occurred, when professionals from surrounding countries have filled in the vacancies left by the emigrating native workforce. In South Africa, for example, doctors from Tanzania, Kenya and Nigeria have replaced South African doctors who moved to the United Kingdom or other more developed countries. To further ease the effects of "brain drain," the United Kingdom has developed policies to not actively recruit health care workers from developing countries.

Skilled migration is also not always a permanent loss to the sending countries. Large, growing networks of transnational links and increased communication flows can provide opportunities for professionals in more developed countries to share their knowledge and skills with those in their home countries.

visas altogether.[30] Intel Corporation and Motorola have also struggled to find enough U.S. workers with advanced degrees in the sciences to fill positions in their businesses. Instead, these companies have invested heavily in research centers in India and China.

India and China are slowly gaining on the United States competitive edge and they are graduating more students with higher degrees in science and engineering than the United States. The European Union has also stepped up efforts to streamline its education systems, and it now offers more courses in English and has launched campaigns to attract international students. The European Union is now granting more doctoral degrees than American universities, suggesting an erosion in the preeminence of the United States as a leader in research and technology.[32]

Critics argue that, rather than importing workers, the United States should focus on training its native-born population to pursue higher degrees of education or specialization in specific computer and technology-related fields. This is a challenge that should be met with gusto, and the latest trends suggest there has been a renewed interest in the science, math and engineering fields. From 1999 to 2005, enrollment of U.S. citizens and permanent residents in graduate science and engineering programs has increased steadily, after a period of relative decline throughout the 1990s.[33] In an era of increasing global competition, however, immigrants and their skills can help the United States maintain a competitive edge over other countries by complementing the native workforce while spurring growth in key fields that have allowed the United States to lead in technological advances.

High-skilled immigrants whose successes are easy to identify and quantify play an important role in maintaining our economy, but so, too, do low-skilled immigrants who also come to work in lesser-known and lesser-paying jobs. Low-skilled immigrants, who often labor in difficult conditions picking our produce, landscaping our lawns, and cleaning our homes and offices, have added dynamically to the U.S. economic landscape and are a part of who we are as America. Their intrinsic worth should not be measured by their capital output, though this may be the world's standard. Rather, we should recognize that they, like high-skilled immigrants and native-born workers, bear the image of God and should be treated with the dignity and respect we would afford our Savior.

Remittances

If skilled migration may have some negative costs on the sending country, remittances, or monies that immigrants send back to their countries of origin, are a strong benefit for many sending countries. Remittances can also have a significant effect on development in many contexts. Most (about 90 percent) of the money that immigrants earn is circulated back into the local economy where they live.[34] Yet in 2006, Latin American immigrants in the United States still managed to send about $45 billion back to their countries of origin.[35] In Mexico, where 17.6 percent of their population is unable to buy basic food for a healthy diet, remittances have a direct and immediate impact on the ability of families to meet basic nutritional needs.[36] In other countries like Haiti and Honduras, where remittances constitute over 20 percent of their Gross Domestic Product, they have also been shown to reduce poverty and inequality.[37] In fact, a recent, comprehensive study of seventy-one developing countries found that a 10 percent increase in per capita remittances leads to a 3.5 percent decline in the share of people living in poverty.[38]

Remittances not only supplement income but also allow families to make investments that can serve them in the longer term. Mexico, for example, does not have a well-developed financial infrastructure to provide credit and financing to help people purchase a home. Having a steady income of American dollars saved up can help a family eventually purchase their own home. "Households use international migration as a tool to overcome failed or missing markets at home," explains Douglas Massey, an expert on migration at Princeton University.[39] The government of Mexico also provides matching funds for remittances used for home investments.

While remittances should not be a substitute for long-term development policy, they can in the short term help alleviate the immediate effects of poverty in the home countries of immigrants who currently work in the United States. Immigrants who work in the United States thus keep the U.S. economy strong but also add enormously to the wealth of their families and community members back in their countries of origin.

Global Dynamics of Immigration

The turn of the twenty-first century is marked by a world in which globalization has taken front and center stage. Many argue about the costs and benefits of globalization, but, undoubtedly, free trade and open markets have been touted by most of the industrialized world as engines of strong economies worldwide. A greater flow of goods and capital stream across national boundaries as countries grow more specialized in producing certain goods and services. The increasing global interconnectedness also inevitably leads to an increase in the movement of people who follow these trade flows, whether within countries from rural to urban areas, or between countries as people migrate to find better economic opportunities abroad.

The movement of people has marked human existence since creation. The International Organization for Migration (IOM), the leading intergovernmental organization in the field of migration, estimates that there are approximately 192 million migrants in the world today, or about 3 percent of the world's population.* The percentage of migrants in the world today versus the total world population has not changed significantly since the mid-1900s.[40] What has changed in the last fifty years is that a greater number of migrants are now concentrated in the more developed regions of the world.[41] In 1960, Europe, North America, Australia and Japan hosted about 3.4 percent of the world's migrant population. These developed regions now host about 9.5 percent of the world's migrant population.

This should not be surprising. In the past few decades, the inequality between the developed and developing countries has increased dramatically. It is estimated that the top 10 percent of adults, by income, now own 85 percent of global household wealth.[42] People who live in North America, Europe and high-income Asian Pacific countries collectively hold almost 90 percent of total adult wealth.[43] Immigrants in the developing world who are unable to earn enough to feed their families, cannot find

---

*Migrants are defined as people who live outside their country of birth.

jobs, or do not have infrastructures in their local economies to build assets thus often feel compelled to migrate to these more developed regions of the world, often temporarily, to improve their economic lot. With approximately 12.5 percent of our population being foreign born, the United States is hardly alone in having what is perceived to be a large percentage of migrants in the total population. Switzerland (22 percent), Australia (20 percent) and Canada (18 percent) all have a greater share of the foreign-born as a percentage of their populations than does the United States. In fact, in Europe, immigration is equally if not more heatedly debated, as they have traditionally been a more homogeneous society.

In addition to the growing inequality and demographic differences between developed and developing countries, regional economic liberalization trade agreements have increased the interdependence among countries, spurring migration between countries that are now more openly engaged in the free trade of goods and services. In the United States, where approximately 56 percent of the undocumented and 31 percent of the total foreign-born population are from Mexico, trade policies like the North American Free Trade Agreement (NAFTA) were expected to "stop" illegal immigration by developing a more robust Mexican economy. In actuality, illegal immigration has increased since its implementation. NAFTA opened up Mexico's market to American imports and displaced many Mexican farmers who, for years, had worked in the agrarian economy but, now unable to compete with American imports, found themselves migrating north. Migration is often spurred not only by a lack of economic development but also is due to the onset of development itself. According to Princeton University sociology professor Douglas Massey, "The shift from a peasant or command economy to a market system entails a radical transformation of social structures at all levels; a revolutionary shift that displaces people from traditional ways of life and creates a mobile population on the lookout for alternative ways of making a living."[44]

The forces that drive people to migrate are not just affecting the United States, but many countries throughout the world, especially Europe, and they are often outside the control of government. For sure, structural changes and development are needed in the immigrant-sending countries so migrants do not feel the need to migrate. Still, national migration policies that do not reflect the global reality of economic and social forces will not stop people from coming to the United States who are driven by overriding factors such as job availability or reunion with family. Migration to the United States is also inextricably linked to conditions in countries of origin. Restrictive immigration policies may in fact drive people to take more clandestine routes to get to their destination of choice. Thousands of migrants cross the treacherous seas of the Mediterranean every year to find work in European countries, and many die along the way, just as many die crossing the deserts of the American Southwest.

The Value of Cultural Diversity

Immigration in and of itself is not a panacea to all of our country's economic needs. Nor should immigrants be given value only if they can add an economic benefit to our country. Greater questions must be asked about who we are and what we want to become as a country that may be inherently more important when crafting immigration policy than any economic considerations. Indeed as Christians, we must be wary of valuing persons solely on the contributions they can make to our affluence. We should also recognize the personal and cultural contributions they can make to our country. If our measuring stick of success is affluence, we become blinded to or devalue the blessings God has poured on us in other forms.[45]

Immigrants add to the diversity of the United States, and God works within cultural differences to bring people to understand who he is. Walking into a church where the beat of African drums reverberates or attending a Hispanic church where songs are sung in Spanish continually pushes our creative imagination to see God, who is infinite and real to people from the world over. According to Richard Mouw, "God intended from the beginning that human beings would 'fill the earth' with the processes, patterns and products of cultural formation."[46] Indeed, our ability to unify through diversity can demonstrate the power of the gospel to transcend cultural differences and national identity. From the beginning of creation, God intended humanity to fill the earth and subdue it (Gen 1:28).[47] When people gathered in Babel to "make a name for ourselves and not be scattered over the face of the whole earth," God intervened and created different languages (Gen 11:4). It was an act of judgment but also of grace, as a way for the people to return to God's original plan.[48]

In the New Testament, Jesus commanded that his disciples be his witnesses "in Jerusalem, and in all Judea and Samaria, and to the end of the earth" (Acts 1:8). At Pentecost, the Holy Spirit empowered Jesus' disciples to preach the gospel to people from all nations as the wonders of God were declared in the languages of the nations that were gathered. Pentecost signaled to the world God's purpose in reconciling every tribe, language, people and nation to himself, and he enables us to do so with the power of the Holy Spirit.

Ethnic diversity can help us connect with communities who often experience God in different ways. In fact, throughout the Bible, we see how God used his servants whose different ethnicities were central to accomplishing their purpose here on earth. Moses was a tricultural Hebrew-Egyptian-Midianite who empathized with the suffering of his fellow Israelites but was able to speak before Pharaoh because of his Egyptian upbringing. Paul was a Jewish-Roman citizen whom God used to evangelize Gentiles who were previously unclean.

Beyond the diversity that, as Christians, we are guided to value, immigrants also benefit the United States by positively influencing our culture. Immigrants often traditionally come from countries with a strong emphasis on community and family life. Many Asian families live in multigenerational homes, for example, where the grandparents do not live in retirement homes, but take care of children and are cared for by their own children. Many Latino cultures also treat their extended family of cousins, uncles and aunts as members of their immediate families. Immigrants teach younger generations about the reward of hard work and delayed gratification. Refugees also teach us about the fragility of life and the ability of the human spirit to overcome tremendous obstacles in order to survive. Their testimonies of persecution and suffering allow us to glimpse into the reality of the world around us, and their sheer courage inspires us. Immigrants embody the ideals that have made this country great and remind us that the American dream can still be reached.

Cultural diversity also enhances art and beauty in our midst. Immigrant artists have added tremendously to our music, dance, art and food. Immigrants often find the challenges of displacement can be expressed through art.[49] Latin music expands our sense of rhythm and movement. In ethnic neighborhoods of a Little Italy or Chinatown, restaurants offer delicious foods that bring the world to our palate. Also many famous immigrants, while working in the United States, have added richly to the world. Fashion designers Oscar de la Renta and Carolina Herrera were both born in Latin America but now work in the United States. Elizabeth Taylor, Arnold Schwarzenegger, Salma Hayek and Michael J. Fox are all immigrants who have entertained us through movies and television. Yo-Yo Ma and Placido Domingo enrich us with their musical talent. Yao Ming, Patrick Ewing and Martina Navratilova have excelled in their respective sports. Madeleine Albright and Henry Kissinger speak fondly about how their immigrant upbringings shaped their foreign policy.

Alexis de Tocqueville, in his book *Democracy in America,* recognized early in our country's history the virtues that made America great, among them the spirit of equality embodied in the Declaration of Independence that "all men are created equal and are endowed by their Creator with certain unalienable rights." John F. Kennedy eloquently states in his book *A Nation of Immigrants* that

> immigration is by definition a gesture of faith in social mobility. [Immigration] gave every old American a standard by which to judge how far he had come and every new American a realization of how far he might go. It reminded every American, old and new, that change is the essence of life, and that American society is a process, not a conclusion.[50]

History teaches us that, over the generations, immigrants have integrated into American society, adopting American values, beliefs and habits. There are waiting lists for English as a Second Language (ESL) classes across the country today. Second- and third-generation immigrants often intermarry at higher rates than earlier ethnic groups, and by the second generation, most immigrants are speaking English, improving job status and, consequently, paying more in taxes.[51] We have seen in our country's history that the ability of our country to transcend racial differences and reconstruct our collective national identity, while initially difficult, has made us stronger. These new identities reaffirm our country's commitment to the motto stamped on every U.S. coin, *E Pluribus Unum,* or "out of many, one." Through the unique talents, values and personalities that immigrants bring with them to the United States, immigrants add value to our country in ways that economic measures might miss.

What Is Our Limit?

Economists agree that immigration is a net good for the U.S. economy, and immigrants also benefit our society in other ways. But if we believe, as most economists do, that legal immigration should be increased, what should be the limits to immigration? What is the capacity of the United States to absorb a large number of immigrants? We have seen through our history that the economic forces of supply and demand, where immigrant workers fill jobs in the United States, as well as social factors like family reunification, often override immigration enforcement. At the turn of the century and up until now, immigration has generally been a boon that has allowed the United States to thrive economically, even though immigration initially tested the social capacity of communities to receive newcomers. Our government must create responsible, balanced policies that reflect larger market forces so immigration flows can be managed in a manner that both economically and socially benefits the United States.

We as Christians, though, must also answer this question outside of strict market considerations. Our tendency may be to think that we should welcome immigrants only so long as they benefit our financial situation, but this attitude is hard to reconcile with Scripture. Often, we have seen God stretch his capacity and generosity toward us. A speech by Cardinal Roger Mahoney, the Archbishop of Los Angeles, guides us toward a larger understanding of God's resources and economy. "As Christians," he states, "there are no prior commitments that can overrule, or trump, this biblical tradition of compassion for the stranger, the alien, and the worker."[52] He notes how the word "economy" comes from the Greek *oikonomia,* which is the "full flourishing of everyone who is a part of God's economy, household or community." The church's position is thus grounded in the etymology of the word, which emerged in early Christian history to describe a household—God's household—which is ordered and open to those who long to sit at the table. To this end, the human person should not serve the economy, but the economy should serve the human person.

Immigration has been and will continue to be a part of the American story. But we must choose how to respond to the immigrants in our communities, whether with disdain and fear or with a warm welcome and trust that God will provide for all. As Christians, we are foremost citizens in God's kingdom, and everything we have is "on loan" to us here. The best of the United States may be shown in how we treat the immigrants among us.

While our faith need not lead us to support a policy of open borders, and there ought to be reasonable limitations on who is allowed to enter the United States, both the economic needs of our country and the guidelines of our faith lead us to a more generous, welcoming immigration policy, where immigrant laborers are able to enter the United States legally. Yet, as of this writing, there has been no substantial change in immigration policy. In the next chapter, we will look at the politics behind the immigration issue that have stalled any real reform thus far.

THE POLITICS AND POLICIES

OF IMMIGRATION REFORM

Where we can reunite families, we should. Where we can bring in more foreign-born workers with the skills our economy needs, we should. . . . The time to fix our broken immigration system is now. It is critical that as we embark on this enormous venture to update our immigration system, it is fully reflective of the powerful tradition of immigration in this country and fully reflective of our values and ideals.

Barack Obama Presidential Campaign, 2008, on the campaign website

As president, I will secure the border. I will restore the trust Americans should have in the basic competency of their government. A secure border is an essential element of our national security. But a secure border will contribute to addressing our immigration problem most effectively if we also recognize that America will always be that "shining city upon a hill," a beacon of hope and opportunity for those seeking a better life built on hard work and optimism.

John McCain Presidential Campaign, 2008, on the campaign website

Immigration has become one of the most politically volatile issues in the past few years, but this should not come as a surprise. Immigration has always been a hot issue on the campaign trail as well as in local and national debates. In the most recent presidential election, we saw the immigration issue become a political hot potato as presidential candidates found themselves backtracking on positions they had taken on the issue years before and fumbling over their responses to questions about granting particular privileges to undocumented immigrants, such as driver's licenses and access to medical care, that they probably had not given much thought to in the beginning of their campaigns.

Now, at the start of a new administration, the president will have to tackle the issue in a bipartisan fashion if any significant change is to happen, but the sensitivities surrounding immigration continue and will need to be considered for any forward movement on the issue. Politics tends to whittle large, complex policy issues down to catch phrases and defensive posturing. An understanding of the political playing field our leaders in Congress have to navigate every day will help us understand our role in engaging with them to produce the best immigration policy possible.

While the Bible does not directly tell us which policy to support, there are general biblical principles and practical considerations that can guide us as we call on our elected leaders to create a more just, compassionate immigration system. Foremost is the biblical principle to welcome the foreigner among us. Biblical scholar Daniel Carroll R., in his book *Christians at the Border*, argues that our hospitality on a personal level should be carried through into our public policy:

> Hospitality functions primarily at the personal and familial level and on an informal basis. Its practice could suggest that a people have an openhandedness about them. A test of this possibility is to examine their laws and the structures of their society to ascertain whether the moral qualities of welcome and kindness toward the outsider find formal expression. Do they impact how the society actually operates?[1]

As we Christians carefully consider our role in the public sphere, the politics and jargon can sidetrack us from seeing that there may be more similarities than differences in the positions between "restrictionists" and those who want a broader, more open policy. For example, most people agree that the border must be secured and regulated so that those with proper documents—but not those without—can continue to move back and forth legally. Most people who want a more open immigration policy still support secure, regulated borders, while those who wish to deal with border security first often do not want to deport everyone here, though they may be more cautious about the consequences of legalizing the undocumented. In understanding these dynamics, we can begin to forge a civil, thoughtful middle ground on immigration reform that will create a safe space in which our leaders in Congress and the new Obama administration can begin to fix the immigration system.

Comprehensive Immigration Reform

When President George W. Bush took office in January 2001, he vowed to make immigration reform one of his top priorities. As the border-state governor of Texas, he realized the importance of building better relations with Mexico and other countries in the Western Hemisphere. He also had personal friendships with immigrants and sought to lead the country in viewing them as he did, as people who were seeking better opportunities in the United States. He once famously remarked that "family values do not stop at the Rio Grande River,"[2] an approach that became a cornerstone to his compassionate conservatism philosophy. In his 2004 address to Congress, he specifically asked for a temporary worker program, which he maintained would benefit the economy, and said he opposed amnesty.

President Bush's position created space for Congress to consider broader immigration reform. In 2005, as Congress started to actively do that, Comprehensive Immigration Reform (CIR) emerged as the moderate basis for any immigration reform bill. CIR holds that to truly solve the issues around immigration, legislation could not just focus on one element (such as border security) but had to be comprehensive, addressing root causes of the broken system and the reality of a large undocumented population in the country. By addressing those already here (the undocumented), pathways for immigrants to come in the future (both family- and employment-based), plus border security, Comprehensive Immigration Reform encompassed all major areas of immigration.

Many in the faith community came together to support Comprehensive Immigration Reform as defined by the following four principles:

1. Border protection policies consistent with humanitarian values.
Everyone agrees that the current situation at the border, with many people entering without any inspection, is not a good, long-term situation. In protecting the border, though, we also believe in treating all individuals with dignity and respect. Our borders with both Canada and Mexico need to be secure while still allowing the legal flow of goods, services and people to happen daily. Border security measures must be carefully considered for their effectiveness in increasing our national security and not be used to overly penalize immigrants or simply provide us with a false sense of security.

2. Reforms in family-based immigration to reduce backlogs. Due to processing backlogs and visa numerical limits, many families here legally are separated from loved ones for long periods. Legal permanent residents, for example, who file for their spouses often face waits of over five years to be reunited. Families thus often face the difficult choice of being separated from their loved ones for a long time or entering the United States without legal status to be with their loved ones. By reforming the family-based system to reduce waiting times for separated families, we allow those who have waited fairly in line to reunite with their families as expeditiously as possible.

3. Creation of legal avenues for workers and their families. As we have seen, the current system makes it very difficult, and often impossible, for those who wish to migrate to the United States to enter the country and work in a safe, legal and orderly manner with their rights fully protected. Immigrants who wish to come to the United States to work—whether in high-skill fields like medicine or technology or in low-skill industries like agriculture, hospitality or construction, and everything in between—should be provided legal avenues to do so in any immigration reform legislation. By creating a system in which employers in the United States who need foreign workers can hire them legally, we provide viable options for both the employer and employee to gain the benefits of migration and significantly reduce the motivation for migrants to cross borders illegally.

4. Earned legalization of undocumented immigrants. We could not try to fix a system without addressing what to do with 12 million undocumented people living in the shadows of our society. This current situation mocks the idea of the rule of law and clearly requires reform, but we also recognize that most of the undocumented are hard-working, contributing members of our society. Immigration reform thus must include an opportunity for immigrants who are already contributing to this country to get right with the law by regularizing their status after satisfying reasonable criteria, and over time to pursue an option to become Lawful Permanent Residents and eventually U.S. citizens. A path to legal status would provide undocumented immigrants with a chance to admit their infraction against the law, pay an appropriate fine as a consequence, and proceed to become fully restored, integrated members of our society if they wish to stay here. This would not be an "amnesty" because immigrants would have to earn their right to stay in the United States.*

In addition to these four principles, immigration reform legislation should provide appropriate tools for employers to accurately and reliably verify the legal status of their workers, which is not possible with the current, flawed system. Also, the U.S. immigration system must be couched in a larger, overall strategy to tackle the root causes of poverty in immigrant-sending countries. Immigration is affected by trade pacts, economic development policies and financial flows. While economic development aid and strategies will not necessarily stop immigration to the United States, the function of a legal U.S. immigration system must work in close tandem with trade and development policies so the system can work and reflect the values that have made America an economically stable, welcoming country. It is crucial that all these aspects of immigration reform be addressed together in legislation, as individual parts alone will fail to solve the immigration dilemma.

There are also two other pieces of legislation that are often considered

---

*The question of "amnesty," which has become a shibboleth in the recent immigration debate, is discussed in greater detail later in the chapter. (See page 148.)

part of the immigration debate, sometimes tacked on as a part of Comprehensive Immigration Reform. The first is the DREAM (Development, Relief, and Education for Alien Minors) Act, which would allow young, undocumented immigrants who came to the United States at an early age (brought by their parents, not of their own volition) to obtain legal status if they graduate from high school and attend college or serve in the military. A second bill, AgJOBS (the Agricultural Job Opportunities, Benefits, and Security Act), would provide temporary legal status to undocumented agricultural workers, assist employers in finding agricultural labor and protect the laborers from exploitation.

The principles of Comprehensive Immigration Reform were incorporated into various bills introduced in Congress in the past several years. Other bills, however, did not incorporate Comprehensive Immigration Reform principles but were "enforcement-only" bills focusing on border security and interior enforcement alone.

HR 4437

One of the most controversial enforcement-only bills was HR 4437, The Border Protection, Anti-Terrorism, and Illegal Immigration Control Act of 2005. Representative James Sensenbrenner, chair of the House Judiciary Committee at the time, introduced it right before Congress was about to recess. This bill took a very hard line on the immigration question, harshly penalizing undocumented immigrants and those who assist them, with the aim of limiting further illegal immigration (but without expanding legal options for entry). With less than two weeks from the date of introduction to the date of passage in the House of Representatives, HR 4437 passed the House by a vote of 239-182, catching many immigration advocates off guard, and was deemed "the Christmas gift that nobody wanted."

Politicians are usually on the defensive because of the general recognition that our immigration laws are just not working. Members of Congress carefully heed what their constituents are saying, or even what they *perceive* to be the sentiment in their district or state, on a certain issue. On immigration, a broken border and lack of enforcement have often been cited as the main reasons for such a large undocumented population. Thus, much legislation considered in Congress has focused only on securing the border and increasing penalties for undocumented immigrants, and it has not focused on reforming the immigration visa system.

Enforcement-only bills can seem like measured, effective ways to "control" immigration. However, immigration is not simply a border security problem but a systemic problem that needs to be tackled holistically to be effectively resolved. Border security agents have also attested to the fact that they cannot do their job unless there are legal avenues through which immigrants can enter to relieve pressure off the border. According to David Aguilar, chief of the Office of Border Patrol, "To most effectively secure our border, we must reform our immigration system to relieve this pressure. We need comprehensive immigration reform."[3] As discussed earlier, a large percentage of immigrants have entered the United States legally but have overstayed a visa or are caught up in processing backlogs. Thus, by focusing on border security alone, without addressing larger legal avenues by which immigrants can enter and leave the United States, border enforcement will not be truly effective. Immigrants usually cross the border illegally because there are no legal means to do so.

HR 4437 had various provisions to secure the U.S. borders and increase penalties against terrorist and criminal aliens but did not reform the visa system in any way or provide a guest worker program. On close examination, many enforcement-only bills would not necessarily make us more secure, but they would be overly punitive to immigrants.

For example, the bill would have made unlawful presence in the country a felony, which would automatically make an immigrant deportable and detainable by law (currently, unlawful presence in the United States is considered a civil offense).[4] These were drastic measures for unlawful presence in the United States. Having millions of people whose only offense was to break an immigration law hauled off to jail is not a punishment in line with the offense committed, and it could have separated families and placed a heavy burden on our communities where there are large immigrant populations.

The bill would also have built 700 miles of double-layered fencing along the 2,000-mile U.S.-Mexico border. While we must continue to secure the border, through border patrols and effective technology, building a fence along the border of the United States and Mexico should be measured carefully in its effectiveness to stop illegal immigration. A fence would have separated populations that have long thrived on living between two communities. The United States has spent the past fifty years symbolically and literally tearing down walls between countries, whether it was the Berlin Wall or the Iron Curtain. To erect a wall now between two countries not at war would send the wrong message to our neighbors south of the border and to the rest of the world. Just as important, it would probably not work: past wall-building efforts have only redirected border crossings from large urban areas to the dangerous deserts of the American Southwest, without decreasing the overall number of illegal border crossings. A wall would funnel money toward a nineteenth-century solution to a twenty-first-century problem.

The section of HR 4437 that galvanized the debate was the section that also criminalized anyone who "assists" an undocumented person to "remain in the United States . . . knowing or in reckless disregard of the fact that such person is an alien who lacks lawful authority to reside in or remain in the United States."[5] While the language was intended to target human smugglers who assist undocumented immigrants, any charity or church organization, technically, could have been swept up in this broad definition and criminalized, subject to up to five years in jail—the same punishment as the person who was here illegally. HR 4437 was probably the single-most galvanizing force for immigrants, immigrant advocates, religious groups and others who used the bill to build a strong, central message for comprehensive reform.

In response to the passage of HR 4437 out of the House, Cardinal Mahoney of the Roman Catholic Archdiocese of Los Angeles, the largest in the United States, said he would call on his priests to engage in "civil disobedience" in opposing it. He said "current law does not require social service agencies to obtain evidence of legal status before rendering aid, nor should it. Denying aid to a fellow human being violates a law with a higher authority than Congress—the law of God."[6] The *New York Times* published an editorial on March 3, 2006, titled "The Gospel vs. HR 4437," which stated, "Cardinal Mahoney's defiance adds a moral dimension to what has largely been a debate about politics and economics."[7] In September 2006, Dr. Richard Land of the Southern Baptist Ethics & Religious Liberty Commission compared HR 4437 to the fugitive slave laws of the 1800s, which penalized pastors for assisting slaves in their underground journey north.[8]

Politics are often moved by large grassroots efforts, and this bill created the single, largest impetus for those who want Congress to take a more comprehensive approach. What had seemingly been a numbers game—11 to 12 million undocumented immigrants in our country today—became a human story with immigrants who had been largely living in the shadows of our country having the courage to show their faces in a united call for a more equitable situation. From the last week of March to the beginning of May 2006, millions of people participated in rallies in more than 100 U.S. cities to call for a solution to the immigration crisis. Chicago, Los Angeles, New York and Dallas had between 300,000 to 500,000 protesters in each of their cities. With many chanting "*Si Se Puede*" (or "Yes, It Can Be Done!") and holding up signs declaring "We Are America," these largely peaceful protests were a symbolic measure of people from all walks of life who were no longer disengaged and mere observers in a process that was to determine their fate and future in this country.

This large movement of people demonstrated that change must come from the grassroots up, not from the top down. While there will always be a segment of the population that opposes more comprehensive reform, the moderate middle that generally supports comprehensive reform must be more active and engaged in this debate in order for our political leaders to act.

Comprehensive Immigration Reform Act of 2006

The Senate took a very different approach to immigration reform beginning in 2006. The Comprehensive Immigration Reform Act of 2006 (S.2611) led by Senators Edward Kennedy and John McCain was a stark contrast to the enforcement-only HR 4437. The bill was comprehensive by addressing family backlogs, a guest worker program and the undocumented in the country, in addition to border security.

It would have created a temporary worker program for up to 200,000 visas annually with a path to legal permanent residence for the workers and their families. Immediate relatives (spouses, parents and children of U.S. citizens) were exempt from the annual family-based visa cap of 480,000, which would have greatly reduced waiting times for families and would have provided more slots for immigrants in other family preference categories to come to the United States. (Currently, immediate relatives take up visa slots in the overall family immigration system.) The bill also would have almost doubled the number of visas granted to highly skilled workers. For border security, the bill would have increased border and other enforcement personnel, biometric data enhancements, and training on document fraud detection and identification for the border patrol. To enforce laws relating to immigrants already in the country, the bill would have authorized twenty additional detention facilities, increased penalties for not filing appropriate paperwork with the Department of Homeland Security (DHS), and mandated expedited removal (the immediate deportation of an immigrant without the opportunity to go before a judge) in certain situations. AgJOBS, with a focus on agricultural workers, and the DREAM Act, which would benefit undocumented children, were also incorporated in the bill.

The bill's legalization provision was probably the most contentious part. A proposed three-tier system divided the undocumented population into three groups to determine legal status. In general, those in the country longer than five years would have been eligible for legal status without having to leave the country. Those in the United States between two and five years would have been eligible to receive up to three years of work authorization in the United States but then would have been required to leave the country within a year in order to continue legal status in the United States. Those in the United States less than two years would not have gained any legal status but would have been required to depart the United States and apply abroad for a temporary worker visa.

During the debate, many senators did not want to grant legal status to anyone in the United States illegally unless he or she left the country and reentered legally. This appealed to the more conservative members of Congress who thought any bill not requiring undocumented immigrants to leave the country would be paramount to amnesty. Splitting up the undocumented population to determine eligibility for legal status was thus a compromise the Senate reached. The bill was a far cry from House bill HR 4437, but it was difficult to see how this bill could be implemented practically.

In the debate, the word *amnesty* has been used to castigate any chance of real reform. The root of the word *amnesty* comes from the Greek word *amnestia*, or forgetfulness. Webster's dictionary defines amnesty as "the act of an authority (as a government) by which pardon is granted to a large group of individuals."[9] None of the bills proposed in Congress over the past several years provide a path to legal status that would forget or pardon the infraction of unlawful presence in the United States.

To allow an undocumented person in the country today, who is working hard and obeying the law, the option to pursue legal status by getting to the back of the line; paying back taxes, immigration filing fees and a penalty fee for having violated the law; learning English and civics; and undergoing medical and background checks is not a blanket pardon. Instead, the undocumented persons would have to admit their infractions against the law, pay the penalties of those infractions and earn their right to be in the United States. These would be penalties appropriate to the offenses committed. Deporting individuals who have worked hard and paid taxes, and who often have children here, is unworkable as well as detrimental to the family unit. As Dr. Richard Land of the Southern Baptist Convention says, "To call any proposed requirement—that individuals must learn to read and write and speak English and go through a rigorous process in order to earn their way out of a lengthy period of 'probation' in order to apply for legal status—'amnesty' is to do violence to the English language."[10]

While the bills were being debated, many Senators received calls opposed to Comprehensive Immigration Reform at a rate of ten to one compared to calls supporting the bill. Restrictionist groups also started a campaign to send bricks to Senate offices with notes attached that said to build a wall along the southern border. While most of the calls received by congressional staffers opposed any legalization, polls consistently showed throughout early 2006 that Americans favored allowing illegal immigrants a path to citizenship. For example, a *Time* magazine/SRBI poll from January 2006 showed that about three out of every four Americans (76 percent) favored allowing illegal immigrants to earn U.S. citizenship if they learned English, had a job and paid taxes, and 73 percent favored a guest worker program.[11] A similar poll by the Tarrance Group and Lake Research Partners in March 2006 also found that 76 percent of Americans would support a way for illegal immigrants to become citizens if they worked, paid taxes and learned English.[12]

Many of the key senators in the immigration debate had an eye on the midterm elections of November 2006. They felt the pressure from groups in their home states to get tough on border security, so openly supporting a broader approach to immigration could have been politically negative.

Hispanic civil rights groups, business groups and labor groups were all engaged in pushing for comprehensive reform. Faith-based groups, including the U.S. Conference of Catholic Bishops, Jewish groups and Protestant groups, were integral in bringing a moral voice to the debate. Other groups like Human Rights First and the Rights Working Group highlighted in the bill enforcement provisions that would unduly harm refugees and asylum-seekers or curtail due-process rights for immigrants.

The restrictionist groups engaged in the legislative process, however, proved extremely effective at mobilizing their constituents to oppose any kind of comprehensive reform. These groups include FAIR, the Federation for American Immigration Reform, which advocates a "temporary moratorium on all immigration except spouses and minor children of

U.S. citizens and a limited number of refugees"[13] and Numbers USA, a group led by Roy Beck that supports lower admissions numbers.

The most vocal anti-immigrant individuals in the United States call U.S. congressional offices because immigration is often their top concern. When legislation that would grant legal status to any of the undocumented population is being voted on, those opposed to the legislation are usually the first to call and often do so in overwhelming numbers. The 76 percent of Americans who favor allowing undocumented immigrants some kind of legal status often do not view immigration as a top concern, even though they generally support Comprehensive Immigration Reform. Thus, while a large percentage of Americans support some legal status for undocumented immigrants, the restrictionist groups have been more active in expressing their views, shifting the debate to reflect their perspective, when the majority of Americans feel otherwise.

Many of the groups that supported comprehensive reform represented large constituencies and worked with congressional staffers to tweak the bill, but they often couldn't bring their constituencies to show their support for the bill, even though a large majority of Americans supported comprehensive reform. This showed that the immigration debate is a political, not a policy, debate.

In my (Jenny's) work on Capitol Hill, numerous congressional staffers have told me of the inundation of calls whenever any legislation arises that would provide legal status for undocumented immigrants in the country. When the debate is at its peak, one can walk into a congressional office in Washington, D.C., and hear the phone ringing off the hook. Staffers fielding the calls speak of how angry the callers often are. One Hispanic staffer in a Republican office said he was personally barraged with messages of hate as his boss was considering support of the bill. The staffer of a freshman Democrat, who had worked with the congressman for years at the state level but was first exposed to immigration on the national level when his boss took office, said he was amazed at how intense and vitriolic the calls were on this specific issue. He told me that many of the calls bordered on complete bigotry.

In the end, the House bill HR 4437 and the Senate bill S.2611 were never conferenced* together, and a new Congress had to be elected to take up the issue again. Right before the elections of 2006, however, Congress did pass the Secure Fence Act that was signed into law by President Bush on October 26, 2006. This act was a largely symbolic measure that *authorized* additional fencing along the southern border and the increased use of advanced technology, but did not *fund* it. This act, in effect, did not substantially add to border security measures already taking place but allowed members of Congress to go home for the elections with a legislative victory in their pocket that made them look tough on border security and illegal immigration.

Election Year, November 2006

The elections of November 2006 were key in determining whether having an anti-immigrant stance was politically expedient. The Senate had thirty-three of one hundred seats open for contest, and all the House seats were open for contest.

While immigration was just one issue on voters' minds going into the election season—the war in Iraq and a weak economy were also heavy on voters' minds—many candidates took a strongly restrictionist position on immigration, hoping this would win favor with voters. Most—though certainly not all—Democrats stood by their support for Comprehensive Immigration Reform, while Republicans were more mixed: some, among them John McCain, Sam Brownback and George Bush, maintained their support for Comprehensive Immigration Reform, but many other Republicans took strong anti-immigration positions. Many Republicans seemed to be banking on a positive electoral response to channeling what they perceived as public outrage over undocumented immigrants. They lambasted their opponents as supporters of "amnesty" and, in some cases, ran political advertisements that equated undocumented immigrants

---

*When the House and Senate have two versions of a similar bill, a conference committee meeting must be held, in which the differences between the two bills are resolved, before the bill can be sent to the president to be signed into law.

with Osama bin Laden and other terrorists.

On Election Day, it became clear that this strategy had not succeeded. In what was recognized as a Democratic sweep, not a single incumbent Democrat lost his or her seat to a Republican challenger. This was the first time since 1948 that the Republicans failed to pick up a single seat occupied by a Democrat, and it was the first time in over twelve years that the Democrats won a majority in Congress. The elections of 2006 were notable in that many candidates who ran on an anti-immigration platform lost in the elections: Arizona, a border state, was the ultimate testing ground. An incumbent Republican representative of Arizona's 5th District who made frequent appearances on cable television and wrote a book opposing any comprehensive immigration measures, lost his race to a Democrat. Another Republican representative from Arizona's 8th District, also lost in the race against a Democrat.

President Bush and his political strategists during his campaigns had specifically courted the Hispanic voting bloc, the fastest growing in the country today, and immigration was a key issue. The Republican presidential candidates received 21 percent of the Hispanic vote in 1996, 34 percent in 2000 and 40 percent in 2004.[14] In the 2006 congressional elections, however, only 30 percent of Hispanics voted for the GOP, a drop of 10 percentage points from the previous election cycle. According to the Pew Hispanic Center's national exit polls, there was an eleven-point swing in favor of the Democrats as compared with 2004, and Latinos were moving away from the GOP in significant numbers.[15] While immigration is only one of many concerns for Hispanic voters, the caustic rhetoric leveled against immigrants in many of the political campaigns did not produce overwhelming support from the conservative base as the candidates had hoped and, in fact, may have driven away more moderate and conservative Hispanic voters.

Political strategists generally have said that while railing against immigrants may seem politically easy in the short term, in the long term it is not politically favorable. While Hispanics made up only about 10 percent of the total voting bloc in the United States in 2006, they are only going to grow in influence as they gain the right to vote and register in higher numbers.[16] Immigration is not the only issue or even necessarily the top issue for Hispanic voters, who tend to be more conservative than average on issues concerning family and culture. As they grow in influence, they will look for a party that will embrace not only the issues they care about but who they are and the contributions they make as a people. According to the Rev. Samuel Rodriguez, president of the National Hispanic Christian Leadership Conference, "This is a watershed moment for the Republican Party. Hispanics are social conservatives. Their votes can determine the next 25 years of national elections. But all that is in jeopardy, based on what is happening."[17]

As a new 110th Democratic Congress was installed in early 2007, there was renewed hope to pass Comprehensive Immigration Reform. The razor-thin majority of the Democrats in the Senate and House, however, meant that any immigration reform legislation had to be a bipartisan effort.

Comprehensive Immigration Reform: 2007

As the Senate started contemplating immigration again, a few marked differences affected the course of the immigration debate in the new 110th Congress. The first was that the White House played a key role early on. It took on a new hands-on approach, drafting policies and principles it thought could be well received by both Republicans and Democrats. President Bush had made immigration reform one of his top priorities again, with his eye on pulling out a domestic policy victory to temper the growing public disfavor of the Iraq War. The president found himself in a rare situation where the White House and most of the Democrats in Congress had the same agenda—to pass Comprehensive Immigration Reform. Many political pundits tagged immigration as an issue that would test the political influence on Capitol Hill of a not-so-popular president. Many believed that this Senate bill was the last chance President Bush had to check off immigration reform on his list of domestic priorities and that, if it did not pass, there would not be another chance until a new president was in office.

Another important shift in 2007 was that Senator McCain, who was the key Republican counterpart in 2006 who had worked closely with Senator Kennedy to craft a Comprehensive Immigration Reform bill, went largely missing to focus on his presidential campaign. He had championed the issue of immigration on Capitol Hill, and he had the influence to bring both Republicans and Democrats to the table to support comprehensive reform. Filling the void left in McCain's absence was Arizona's other senator, Jon Kyl, a tough negotiator representing the more conservative side on immigration. Senator Kyl previously had not been as extensively involved in immigration but became more engaged to shape the debate on an issue he felt was primarily about national security.

Immigrant advocates had a big battle ahead. Even though the polls had shown that a majority of Americans supported a path to legal status for the undocumented who are here, the restrictionist groups were more adept at crafting their message against any such legislation and mobilizing their supporters to call Congress and weigh in. In the previous Congress, HR 4437 had served as a central rallying point around which a strong message for comprehensive reform could be crafted, but a year later, different groups took different positions as the debate proceeded on the Senate bill. The more engaged role of the White House and new members of Congress now more actively involved in the debate also meant advocates had to consider the electoral makeup of new representatives' districts as well as the new messages coming out of the White House.

House of Representatives' activity on immigration was limited as they looked to the Senate to lead. The Security Through Regularized Immigration and a Vibrant Economy (STRIVE) Act, HR 1645, introduced by Rep. Luis Gutierrez and Rep. Jeff Flake, was a starting point for comprehensive reform in the House but never gained much traction in the new Congress.

The new Senate also started work on the Comprehensive Immigration Reform Act of 2007. It included trigger provisions requiring more border patrol agents, an employment verification system, and the quick processing of applications before any temporary worker program or legalization program could be implemented. The bill would have increased penalties for illegal entry and crimes committed by immigrants, and it would have increased penalties for employers who knowingly hired undocumented workers. A new Y-1 visa program would have allowed guest workers to come to the United States for a maximum of two years, renewable twice, but only if the guest worker were to return home for a year between renewals. The bill also provided for a new Z-visa in which those who are undocumented in the United States could earn legal status after paying a fine of at least $1,500, undergoing background checks, and eventually demonstrating proficiency in English and civics. The bill also contained the DREAM Act and AgJOBS.

In this new bill, however, family reunification, which has been the central goal of U.S. immigration policy for the last fifty years, was overturned in favor of a merit-based system in which the most highly educated, English-speaking individuals would be able to immigrate. Whole preference categories for family-based and employment-based immigration would have been eliminated, and all immigrants would have had to instead compete on a merit-based system. Brothers, sisters and adult married children of U.S. citizens or Lawful Permanent Residents thus would no longer qualify to immigrate on the basis of that family relationship alone, but would need additional qualifications, like the ability to speak English and a high level of education, to immigrate.

While the bill included many of the core elements of Comprehensive Immigration Reform, many advocates were very concerned about these changes to the family-based immigration system. Through this new bill the White House appealed to their conservative base and members of Congress who were worried about "chain migration." By creating an immigration system in which the "most qualified" would enter, they aimed to attract those immigrants with bankable skills while cutting out extended family members who had no additional qualifications.

When crafting legislation, however, family reunification should continue to be at the core of the U.S. immigration system. Allowing someone to immigrate to the United States, yet denying family members the opportunity to join her or him, or causing waiting times of many years or decades, creates broken communities. Families are the cornerstone of our society, the God-given unit through which an individual can thrive and experience God's love. The growth and stability of family units—native-born or immigrant—should be a fundamental value for our society. Families in general create moral support and extend care during difficult economic or emotional times, decreasing dependence on government assistance. Close family relationships as a basis for immigration should qualify on that merit alone.

Polls during the debate showed that a large percentage of Americans supported the bill. For example, a *New York Times*/CBS News poll in May 2007 showed that 62 percent of Americans believed that illegal immigrants who have been in the United States for at least two years should be allowed to apply for legal status, versus 33 percent who believed they should be deported.[18] In addition, 66 percent of Americans also said they would favor a guest worker program, while 30 percent said they would oppose a guest worker program. A *USA Today*/Gallup poll taken in April 2007 also suggested that 78 percent of respondents felt that people in the country illegally should be given a chance at citizenship.[19] Even though a majority of Americans would have supported the most contentious aspects of the bill, the outpouring of calls to Congress from those who opposed the bill shut the phone lines down temporarily in the last days of the debate. One Republican senator, who switched his vote and opposed the bill at the last minute, explained his switch by saying, "I don't think the American people are ready for this bill." The bill failed to pass in the end by a vote of 46-53 on June 28, 2007. This vote effectively ended any chance of Comprehensive Immigration Reform until 2009 or later.

The Coming Years

In the wake of the summer 2007 failure of the Compromise Immigration Reform, many correctly predicted that the administration and Congress would not take up immigration reform until this new administration in 2009. In the presidential campaigns for 2008, immigration came up as a hot issue, with Republicans vowing to secure the border and grant no amnesty in order to pull in the support of the conservative base, and Democrats vocally supporting Comprehensive Immigration Reform to allow the 11 to 12 million undocumented here to come out of the shadows, likely with an eye on the Hispanic vote, which is seemingly up for grabs.

Since the failure of Congress to act in 2007, state and local governments have felt the need to address the issue of immigration. Forty-five states introduced 1,257 bills in the first quarter of 2008.[20] While a small portion of these ordinances and legislation were immigrant-friendly, the overwhelming majority were mostly aimed at reducing benefits for undocumented immigrants and limiting their ability to drive, find housing and work.

In the 2008 elections, after the primaries, immigration was hardly mentioned by either Barack Obama or John McCain as it was considered detrimental to both candidates. Hispanics, however, who were heavily courted by Bush in his 2000 and 2004 campaigns, registered in historic numbers in order to vote in the 2008 elections. With 2 million more Hispanics who voted in 2008 than in 2004, they supported Obama by 67 percent versus 31 percent for McCain. They played a key role in giving Obama the victory in swing states like Florida, Colorado, Nevada and New Mexico, all of which were previously red Republican states but flipped to blue Democratic states. Florida, for example, was won by Bush in 2004 with 56 percent of the Latino vote, but Obama won this state with 57 percent of the Hispanic vote. In New Mexico, Obama would not have won without the Hispanic vote. The 2008 elections once again affirmed the importance of the Hispanic vote and showed that minorities (including African Americans and Asian Americans), in general, went with the Democratic party.

Just as in 2006, a number of anti-immigrant candidates lost to pro–Comprehensive Immigration Reform candidates in key battleground congressional races; pro-immigrant candidates defeated anti-immigrant candidates in nineteen out of twenty-one races tracked. In addition, nine members of the House of Representatives who lost their seats were members of the House Immigration Reform Caucus, which takes a hard-line stance on immigration.

As President Obama begins his administration, he will have to tackle major issues like the economy, the wars in Iraq and Afghanistan, and energy independence, issues which may be easier to get bipartisan support for than immigration. However, the need for a national, comprehensive plan to address the immigration dilemma is more urgent than ever. The failure of national reform has meant that states will try in piecemeal fashion to address this issue at a local level when immigration has to be addressed nationally. In addition, the overwhelming majority of Hispanics who voted for Obama in the 2008 elections means he will need to respond with leadership in addressing one of the major concerns of the Hispanic community: immigration reform. With a new president, and a Congress that has a different composition from 2007, our leaders have the opportunity and the responsibility to take action on immigration reform.

Politics is the art of compromise, and Republicans and Democrats must work together in a spirit of give and take in order to pass immigration reform. The debate in Congress over the past few years has shown that our leaders will need to hear from those who support a more comprehensive approach in order to balance out and hopefully surpass the voices of those who oppose a more comprehensive approach and are a minority in the debate.

In reading this book, you have taken the first step toward understanding the reality of the current situation and considering the biblical commands to welcome the stranger. However, with understanding must come action. Grassroots movements mobilized by truth and faith can bear tremendous fruit in advancing just and compassionate policies. While the issue can easily become mired in soundbites, Christians have an obligation to speak out to our elected leaders in Congress, to ensure that immigrants are not dehumanized and our Christian principles are taken into consideration when forming legislation. We need to call on our leaders to look at the issue with compassion, not fear. Having our leaders in government develop workable solutions will help us move beyond the rhetoric to see transformed, whole communities where immigrants are recognized as vital and integrated members of our churches and communities. Immigration indeed has shaped the American church landscape, and the next chapter will explore the church's role in the debate.

THE CHURCH AND

IMMIGRATION TODAY

We are called by God to aid the vulnerable. Therefore, we must see the alien and the stranger as individuals made in the image of God, the object of Christ's love and as people of intrinsic worth who are in need of our affirmation and support.

A Resolution of the General Conference of the Evangelical Free Church of America, adopted in 1996

The Immanuel Fellowship Church in Frisco, Colorado, was founded in 1999 with a congregation of about twelve families, and their purpose was specifically to minister to the growing Hispanic population in this small resort town an hour west of Denver. The church has now grown to a weekly attendance of eighty to ninety people and has weekly house church meetings, outreach events and regular praise sessions. Judy and Mike Phillips, the founding couple of the church, had lived in Mexico for years and developed a heart for Hispanic people, which led to their decision to plant a church in their hometown. "These are the hardest-working people you'll find around, and their integrity and willingness to give back to the community in appreciation for being able to live in the United States is unparalleled." The church also faces some unique challenges, however, because two-thirds of those in the church on any particular Sunday are undocumented.

Another small church, near Atlanta, Georgia, has traditionally had a primarily Anglo congregation, but recently, a number of undocumented immigrants have begun attending their service. The pastor of the church called World Relief to ask for assistance in developing programs to help these undocumented immigrants. "I don't know what we can do as a church," he stated. "We are called to minister to them but they live in constant fear. What can we do?"

In churches across the United States, immigrants, many of them undocumented, are showing up for Sunday service, sometimes singing more vibrantly than the members who have been in the church for years. Their vibrant faith is infusing new energy into the church. Immigrants often already come from a rich faith tradition in their home countries and, once here, find themselves comfortable sitting in the pews of our churches and participating in worship. Others, who wander into churches searching for some sense of community and friendship in this new country, encounter God here for the first time in a personal way and then become active members of local churches.

Welcoming the stranger has unlocked a historic ministry opportunity for the church. In churches' face-to-face encounters with immigrants, the "rule of law" becomes less of an issue as churches seek to minister to the spiritual and physical needs of immigrants. The sojourner or stranger, once considered on the "margins" of society, now through the church can be invited in to experience the fullness of worship together as one body. Churches are realizing through a diverse body of Christ that worship is a celebration of God himself, who made every tribe, language, people and nation to worship him.

Ministry to Immigrants

Ministry to immigrants is a key part of many church ministries and a missional aspect of how they interpret the gospel. Many denominations have already engaged in serving the refugee and immigrant populations in the United States through organizations that focus specifically on refugee and immigration services. For example, Church World Service (affiliated with the National Council of Churches), Episcopal Migration Ministries, Lutheran Immigration and Refugee Service, and World Relief (the humanitarian arm of the National Association of Evangelicals) all have refugee resettlement programs and immigration services, and they also engage in advocacy for just refugee and immigration policies. The Migration and Refugee Service of the U.S. Conference of Catholic Bishops is the largest refugee resettlement agency in the United States. Catholic Charities USA provides immigration legal services to thousands of immigrants throughout the country while Justice for Immigrants is a national campaign launched to mobilize the Catholic grassroots on immigration reform. These faith-based organizations live out daily what it means to "welcome the stranger," and their experiences working with immigrants often inform their positions on immigration and refugee policies.

Part of ministering to immigrants is based on a reciprocal relationship: we find that, in giving, we also receive, and are ourselves transformed through that relationship. Volunteers who have given their time to these organizations often say they receive more than they are ever able to give.

Jan Moore volunteers with World Relief as an English as a Second Language (ESL) teacher in Fort Worth, Texas. She has dreamt of becoming a missionary to those in other countries ever since she was eight years old, but family life and her job kept her from realizing this dream. When Jan started volunteering with World Relief, she had many doubts, but God fulfilled Jan's dream of becoming a missionary by bringing people from around the world to her own backyard. "Words cannot express how wonderfully blessed I am to share in the lives of this [immigrant] family . . . how special they have made me feel," she says. These volunteers realize that by participating and stepping out in faith, God works with their own gifts and desires to further his kingdom.

Churches and volunteers involved in immigrant ministries often realize that the personal testimonies of immigrants and refugees speak to how God works in the world around us. In the early 1980s, a Cambodian refugee, Nancy, was supposed to arrive in Fort Worth, Texas, after a year of living in a refugee camp. After surviving Cambodian dictator Pol Pot's brutal regime, she was finally going to start her life again in a new country. When the church that had planned to host Nancy had to back out at the last minute, World Relief staff decided to ask another Cambodian woman, Bo, who was resettled recently to Fort Worth, to host this new refugee for a few days. When the World Relief caseworker picked up Nancy at the airport and pulled up to Bo's house, Bo was waiting outside to greet Nancy. Nancy stepped out of the car, looked up and realized that Bo, her new host, was actually a long-lost sister whom she thought was killed over two years ago. They embraced, cried and marveled that they were each alive. Nancy and Bo's story is an extraordinary demonstration of God's divine hand in the movement of people and how we can often bear witness to his work in the lives of those who migrate.

Churches in the United States that traditionally send missionaries abroad, many to Mexico and other Latin American countries, are now experiencing an unprecedented opportunity to share God's love and the gospel message with folks from those countries—not abroad, but on their own doorsteps. The global mission impact a church can have with a small budget is now unparalleled due to immigration to the United States. The Evangelical Free Church of America, in fact, sees as much if not more evangelistic fruit among immigrant churches compared to missions efforts overseas. Ministering to the foreign born in the local community has brought a tangible option to engage a church member in a church's mission vision beyond just prayer and financial support.

Immigrant Church Growth

Besides providing support to refugees and immigrants through direct service programs, denominations are strategizing on how to reach immigrant communities to become a part of their churches. The Presbyterian Church USA, for example, developed a "Racial Ethnic and Immigrant Church Growth Strategy" during its General Assembly meeting in 1999, which focused on the "universal love of God and its power to transform people of every race, culture and class into a community living together as the household of God." This meant not dissolving the differences of the various cultures into the dominant culture but working within these cultures to empower people to preach the good news.[1]

The Southern Baptist Convention (SBC), the largest denomination in the United States, behind the Catholic Church, with 16 million members, has also realized the historic opportunity to minister to immigrants, some of whom come from previously unreached people groups. In the 1990s, ethnic minorities constituted about 4 percent of the constituency of the SBC, but now ethnic minorities constitute about 20 percent of its membership. Former SBC President Paige Patterson says "I believe . . . that the future of the Southern Baptist Convention has to be a multiracial, multiethnic future, or quite frankly, it has no future."[2] The Southern Baptist International Mission Board's president, Jerry Rankin, states,

> More and more, we are finding that the people groups of the world, which are the focus of our international mission efforts, are also represented among our own population in the United States. Partnering with the North American Mission Board to identify and reach these ethnic-linguistic pockets at home will not only stimulate an evangelistic outreach here that might otherwise be overlooked, it has the potential of evangelizing unreached people groups overseas.[3]

In 2007, the SBC planted 1,458 new congregations, half of which were ethnic and African American congregations.[4] These churches are raising up new leaders who speak many languages and are of many cultures, some of whom may one day return to their countries of origin to spread the good news.

The biggest gains in membership in recent years within the Church of the Nazarene denomination have come through an increase of immigrant and nonwhite people groups within their churches. According to Jerry Porter, the denomination's General Superintendent, "We marvel at what God has done in recent years through the US/Canada church among the immigrant population."[5] The Christian Reformed Church (CRC) of North America has also seen growth in ethnic minority churches throughout the country. In western Michigan alone, where the CRC headquarters is located, the number of ethnic minority Christian Reformed Church congregations has doubled since 1991.[6]

The Church of God is another evangelical denomination experiencing growth through immigrants, particularly Hispanics, arriving in the United States. Abundant Life Church in San Antonio, Texas, led by pastor Eliezer Bonilla, has grown from 350 members five years ago to 1,600 members now. The church has two services, in English and Spanish, every Sunday. Pastor Bonilla believes that the gospel compels him to reach out to everyone, regardless of legal status or ability to speak English. His church has experienced phenomenal growth because of the sense of community fostered as the first, second and third generations of immigrants take root in the area. "My church has served as a community center, where people tend to gravitate toward their own kind and find themselves getting connected into the church." The church has started a food bank in which they deliver food to undocumented immigrants in their church every week. "As a nation, we are being challenged. How will we practice what we stand for? This is a great moment to show the world that the most powerful nation can also act with mercy and a willingness to welcome the stranger."[7]

Charles Lambert, a consultant with the Church of God, says,

> The recent increase of growth for the Church of God has come through the start-up of Hispanic churches because of the strong immigration to the USA. While the Church of God is committed to ministering to anyone that attends a local church, including the undocumented immigrant, its strong growth comes from the 40 million Hispanics who are legally in the country. Perhaps this is God's hand of blessing for our faithful support of the Great Commission![8]

Not only are denominations seeing opportunities to grow their ethnic ministries, but also the immigrants themselves are forming their own churches to minister to others in their communities. Immigrant churches are growing exponentially, both in the United States and around the world. According to Todd Johnson, director of the Center for the Study of

Global Christianity at Gordon-Conwell Theological Seminary, the fastest growing evangelical churches are independent immigrant churches.[9] In twenty years, African, Asian and Latin American evangelicals will likely be at the forefront of global movements as well as their manifestations in the United States.

Ministering in Difficult Circumstances

As churches increasingly welcome immigrants as integral members of their congregations, they are also witnessing firsthand the consequences of a broken immigration system. Pastor Bonilla tells of when a member of his church, Joseph, opened the door of his home to immigration agents who knocked looking for somebody else. When Joseph said that there was nobody by that name in the house, they asked to see his papers. When he could not produce any, they arrested him and deported him from the United States, even though the agents had not originally gone to the house to look for him. He had lived in the United States for over six years and suddenly was forced to leave his wife and young U.S.-citizen child behind. There was nothing the church could do to stop the deportation.

Churches often have young members who are in the United States undocumented. Pastor Danny Kwon is the youth pastor of Yuong-Sang Korean Presbyterian Church in Horsham, Pennsylvania, which has over 3,000 members. One of the central missions of the church is to send missionaries throughout the world. Pastor Kwon has organized several missions trips for his youth group, but he finds that some of his students are unable to go because of their undocumented status in the United States. "It's not their fault they're here illegally," he says. "They often came here as young kids, but now they're stuck and often can't participate in normal activities like the rest of the kids in my youth group."[10] Instead, the church has organized domestic missions trips to help victims of Hurricane Katrina and even inner-city Philadelphia children. "Despite their undocumented status, they make a positive impact on society and are used by God for his work."

Churches often play a key role in immigrant integration, holistically addressing the spiritual and social needs of the immigrants in their communities. By offering those at the margins of mainstream society a safe space, community members can come together, encourage each other, and build each other up. Churches help negotiate the sometimes-strained relationship between mainstream society and the immigrant communities, and they assist in bridging the divide. By offering English classes, skills workshops and Bible studies, churches help immigrants navigate the larger community's often-inhospitable environment.

Restoration Church in Spartanburg, South Carolina, is a small Southern Baptist church that ministers to a mostly Hispanic congregation. Pastor Javier Gonzales, the senior pastor, says his church ministers to immigrants who are undocumented and that they are regular people who work hard, often twelve hours a day, and serve the community. He is frustrated when he sees Hispanics portrayed in a negative light, since many Hispanics he knows have served very honorably in various areas like military service in Vietnam and in Iraq and in a variety of capacities within the church.[11] The community in South Carolina has been generally welcoming to immigrants, he says, but at times when there has been tension, immigrants often just move to other communities that are more welcoming.

Pastor Samuel Aleman is pastor of another Hispanic church called Primera Iglesia Bautista Hispana de Metro Atlanta (or the First Baptist Hispanic Church of Metro Atlanta). He says there is much fear in the communities where he ministers. "All we can do is just pray and give them spiritual and moral support. We need to respect the rule of law, but they are here working and doing good things. There are two sides of the same coin, and the law has to reflect that."[12] Churches often try their best to integrate immigrants but realize that those here without legal status are stuck in a system where, under current law, no process of restitution exists to let them admit their wrong and become fully restored members of their communities. Churches instead can offer spiritual and moral support to immigrant individuals and families to help them feel welcome in society.

In the past few years, immigration raids have been separating families. On May 12, 2008, in one of the largest raids in U.S. history, at a meat processing plant in Postville, Iowa, immigration agents arrested over 300 immigrants, many of whom were the fathers and mothers of U.S.-citizen children. Sister Kathy Thill, a Catholic nun who helped immigrant families after the raid, said, "I am also a United States citizen who grew up believing that this is a democratic country in which the dignity of all people is respected and their rights protected. This is not the country I experienced this past week. Fear is rampant."[13]

Being a Prophetic Voice

The church has a place in the public square and can use its voice to guide our country in the right direction on immigration. The practice of "welcoming the stranger" has exposed many pastors to the real, human consequences of a broken system in which there are no restorative measures or opportunities for immigrants to become fully integrated members of our society. Church leaders are thus using their experiences and their moral authority to speak about immigration in a way that other leaders cannot.

A number of churches and denominations have spoken out strongly in favor of more generous, welcoming immigration policies, and have advocated for Comprehensive Immigration Reform among legislators in Washington, D.C. The Roman Catholic Church, for example, and many mainline Protestant denominations—such as the United Methodist Church, the Episcopal Church, the Presbyterian Church USA and the Evangelical Lutheran Church in America—have all released statements strongly supporting Comprehensive Immigration Reform.

Leaders of other religious traditions, as well, have joined with Christian leaders from various denominations to create the Interfaith Coalition for Comprehensive Immigration Reform. This coalition grew out of a June 2005 meeting in Baltimore, Maryland, where faith-based groups discussed the common theological basis for their respective positions on immigration, and they strategized on how best to relay that message to the broader community. The Interfaith Statement on Comprehensive

Immigration Reform was birthed out of this meeting and has gathered over 400 signatures in support of Comprehensive Immigration Reform from Catholic, evangelical, mainline Protestant, Jewish, Muslim, Buddhist and Mormon religious leaders and organizations. This statement says, "As faith-based leaders and organizations, we call attention to the moral dimensions of public policy and pursue policies that uphold the human dignity of each person, all of whom are made in the image of God. Our diverse faith traditions teach us to welcome our brothers and sisters with love and compassion."[14] The coalition was actively involved in pushing for Comprehensive Immigration Reform with Congress over the past several years and has gained recognition as the active voice of the religious community on the issue.

While religious groups in general have been among the strongest supporters of Comprehensive Immigration Reform, the evangelical community in the United States has been less unified, with many prominent evangelicals supporting immigration reform, while a few strongly oppose any solution that includes legalization for undocumented immigrants, and many others remain silent on the issue.

Evangelical leaders like Dr. Jack Hayford, president of the International Church of the Foursquare Gospel, is one of many evangelical leaders who believe there can be balance between the rule of law and compassionate action toward immigrants in our midst:

> Yes, America needs to vigilantly guard her borders, but equally true is her need to be generous with aliens who have taken haven here. Our dilemma can only be balanced by joining heart and mind by administering with God's justice an application of law tempered by generosity, and by exercising His patience and equitability toward foreigners already in our midst. And our greatest defense in an age of terror will be to avoid offending the One who commends compassion and who rules with mercy, knowing He will sustain in safety all who are humble in their exacting of law's just demands.[15]

Similarly, Chuck Colson, founder of Prison Fellowship, has urged

Christians considering the immigration debate to "see that the immigration debate generates light instead of heat. We must insist that the illegal-immigration issue be addressed without treating millions of Americans, many of whom died protecting our country, as a kind of fifth column."[16] Many prominent evangelical leaders have signed World Relief's statement in support of Comprehensive Immigration Reform, including Joel Hunter, senior pastor of Northland—A Church Distributed in Florida and former president of the Christian Coalition; William Hamel, president of the Evangelical Free Church of America and former chairman of the board of the National Association of Evangelicals; Peter Bergdorff, executive director of the Christian Reformed Church in North America; Ron Sider, president of Evangelicals for Social Action; Leith Anderson, pastor of Wooddale Church in Minnesota and president of the National Association of Evangelicals; and David Neff, editor of *Christianity Today*.

The Southern Baptist Convention also passed a resolution that affirms the call of the church to minister to the immigrant in its midst while also addressing larger policy issues, like the need for employer sanctions and border security. The Southern Baptist Convention's resolution in June 2006 urged the federal government to

> provide for the security of our nation by controlling and securing our borders, and . . . to enforce all immigration laws, including the laws directed at employers who knowingly hire illegal immigrants or who are unjustly paying these immigrants substandard wages or subjecting them to conditions that are contrary to the labor laws in our country.

They also state that

> we encourage Christian churches to act redemptively and reach out to meet the physical, emotional, and spiritual needs of all immigrants, to start English classes on a massive scale, and to encourage them toward the path of legal status and/or citizenship; and be it finally resolved that we encourage all Southern Baptists to make the

most of the tremendous opportunity for evangelism and join our Master on His mission to seek and save those who are lost (Luke 19:10) among the immigrant population to the end that these individuals might become both legal residents of the United States and loyal citizens of the Kingdom of God.[17]

Jim Wallis, founder of Sojourners, has also spoken forcefully about the need for Comprehensive Immigration Reform. Christians for Comprehensive Immigration Reform is a coalition of Christian leaders and organizations birthed out of Sojourners at the end of 2006. At key times in our national discourse when rhetoric against immigrants has become particularly caustic, this campaign has brought Christian leaders together to speak out on the need to treat immigrants with respect and dignity.

Hispanic evangelical leaders, in particular, whose communities are often most directly affected by the immigration debate, have provided a perspective that we are wise to heed. They have actively staked out a platform and challenged other evangelical groups to be more involved. Groups such as the National Coalition of Latino Clergy and Christian Leaders (CONLAMIC), Esperanza USA, and the National Hispanic Christian Leadership Conference have each made immigration one of their primary focuses. The leaders of these organizations have been particularly vocal about calling out some of the hateful rhetoric leveled against their communities and have actively worked with members of Congress and the administration to craft a just piece of immigration legislation. They have mobilized their constituent member churches and clergy to make a difference in the immigration debate by actively engaging the process.

The Iglesia Cristiana Misericordia, a Hispanic megachurch in Laredo, Texas, for example, held a National Immigrant Prayer Rally in which church members fasted, prayed and registered to vote in order to influence the immigration debate. Similarly, the Iglesia del Pueblo (the Church of the People) in Wheaton, Illinois, opened its doors and provided a lunch stop to a group of activists on a forty-mile march that culminated with a peaceful protest outside the office of a key congressional leader who had stalled efforts at Comprehensive Immigration Reform.

Engaging an issue that can be mired in numbers and rhetoric, Hispanic evangelical leaders have highlighted the impact of immigration on churches and the faith community, while also deftly raising the political cost to legislators drafting the immigration bills of alienating the Hispanic community. They consistently challenge and call out their fellow evangelical leaders, many of whom have been silent on the issue, to stand with them.

In an open letter, Reverend Luis Cortes, the president of Esperanza USA, calls on "our evangelical brothers and sisters to denounce unchristian policy reform and to stand for reform that reflects the values expressed in our history as followers of Christ," and he asks fellow evangelical leaders "to speak out on behalf of comprehensive immigration reform and support us in this struggle for a Christlike face to this problem."[18] Samuel Rodriguez of the National Hispanic Christian Leadership Conference has also asked

> why they [white evangelical leaders] came down in favor exclusively of enforcement without any mention of the compassionate side. So down the road, when the white evangelical community calls us and says, "We want to partner with you on marriage. We want to partner on family issues," my first question will be: "Where were you when 12 million of our brothers and sisters were about to be deported and 12 million families disenfranchised?"[19]

Similarly, many Asian American church communities have been advocating for reform to an immigration system that affects many of their members. For example, in a letter to Senator Dianne Feinstein in June 2007, a group of Korean American churches, businesses and community groups expressed concerns about guest worker programs that would not ultimately allow a path to citizenship, writing that "as a community composed of one out of five who is undocumented . . . we will oppose any deal that tears immigrant families apart, undermines basic rights and divides America by establishing a guest worker program that creates a permanent underclass of disposable, temporary workers with few rights."[20]

African American church leaders have also spoken favorably of immigration reform as they see the struggle for justice and equality as something they have themselves experienced. Many of their religious leaders have stood with the immigrant community and others in calling for immigration reform as a justice issue. Dr. John Perkins, the African American founder of the Christian Community Development Association, has said that, "I have made a commitment . . . to look to our Latino Christian leaders to help us to maneuver the steps we can take to make a difference for the 12 million men, women and children that are directly affected by our lawmaker's decisions in the coming days. At the heart of my conviction is God's mandate that we love the stranger and the foreigner."[21] Most African American churches and leaders recognize that immigrants should not be scapegoated for the economic ills of the country but that they are also part of the larger picture of yearning for justice and gaining access to a system that has often shut them out.

While many prominent evangelicals have supported immigration reform, a few have voiced a more restrictionist opinion on immigration. For example, Roberta Combs, president of the Christian Coalition of America, writes that in the "immigration debate, biblical references back American people's demand that national boundaries are to be honored and the rule of law must be respected." She cites Deuteronomy 27:18 ("Cursed is the one who moves his neighbor's landmark") as biblical grounds for her belief that to ignore or disrespect national boundaries is a sin. She also references Romans 13 to argue that undocumented immigrants have violated the God-ordained rule of the state, and thus should be punished.[22]

In between the many evangelical leaders and institutions who have voiced support for Comprehensive Immigration Reform and the few who are vocally opposed are many who are wary to take a firm position—or in some cases to say anything at all about the issue. For example, the largest umbrella group for evangelical denominations, the National Association of Evangelicals, issued a resolution on October 12, 2006, that supports border enforcement and calls on the church to act compassionately to the immigrants in their communities, but it does not advocate any specific policy:

It is appropriate for the borders of the United States to be secured in order for immigration to conform to the laws of the United States. Apart from issues related to governmental jurisdictions, we believe the gospel compels us to minister to all who live and work within our country. While we recognize the rights of nations to regulate their borders, we believe this responsibility should be exercised with a concern for the entire human family in a spirit of generosity and compassion (Deuteronomy 10:19, Leviticus 19:34). As evangelicals responsible to love our neighbors as ourselves (Matthew 22:39), we are called to show personal and corporate hospitality to those who seek a new life in our nation.[23]

Many other prominent evangelical organizations have opted to remain altogether silent—and thus presumably neutral—on the immigration question. The Family Research Council, the political arm of Focus on the Family, for example, conducted a poll among its membership in April 2006 and found that 90 percent of those polled said our country should forcibly deport the 11 to 12 million illegal aliens in the country today. Even though the poll demonstrated the preference of deportation, the Family Research Council has not yet officially supported any particular policy.

This fence-sitting may in many cases reflect concern that taking a particular position—even one that leadership might believe is biblically warranted—might upset parts of their core constituency. Indeed, there does seem to be a disconnect between the pulpit and the pews on the immigration question: while many prominent evangelicals have endorsed a more generous immigration policy, and very few have vocally opposed such a position, an April 2006 study found that 63 percent of white evangelicals see immigrants as a threat to U.S. customs and values, and 64 percent consider immigrants a burden on society—higher percentages than any other group surveyed, whether religious or secular.[24] While many evangelical leaders *have* spoken up—serving as a prophetic, biblical voice on the issue—they sometimes face strong opposition from ordinary, church-going evangelicals, and this clash has made other leaders wary to take a stronger stand in this debate.

Pastors who have been leaders on this issue have been changing the direction of this debate and will continue to do so through their public engagement. Only when evangelical Christians as a whole, however—not just selected leaders—agree on a unified, scriptural position on the immigration issue, one that welcomes the stranger and embraces both God's justice and his compassion, will our voice have a substantial effect on public policy.

Church: A Place for Reconciliation

While we can read about immigration and the ensuing debate, unless we reach out and interact with the immigrant communities ourselves, we will not be swayed by what we know secondhand. We have seen thus far that we, as a country, only grow stronger when we integrate, not marginalize, newcomers. The marginalization and subjugation of Native Americans by early European colonists continues to have effects today, as many Native Americans live on reservations and continuously struggle with the majority culture. The African American population in the United States is descended from people forced to come to the United States as slaves, and they have struggled for centuries to achieve their rights. It was not until the 1960s that the American people realized the injustice of having a "second tier" of human beings and finally passed laws that recognized the worth and dignity of every human today—and yet still discrimination and inequality persist.

We have an opportunity at this point in history to define the future as we decide how to interact with immigrant communities. We see a growing immigrant population, many of whom share our values and are attending our churches, open to hear the good news. We need to testify to the gospel in relationships with immigrants, and to be open to the possibility of our own transformation through these relationships.

Ultimately, the church must be the place of reconciliation in a broken world. It stands at a crossroads today and must determine its response to the growing diversity of people in the United States. The arrival of immigrants should open our eyes to opportunities for evangelism and ministry right here in our own backyards. As our communities and our nation change, with demographic shifts tugging at our own sense of identity, our initial reaction is often fear. We should not respond in fear, because we are first and foremost citizens of God's kingdom (Eph 2:19). God gives us the ability to adapt and respond to the immigrant situation to accomplish his greater purposes. If we identify with God's kingdom first, we often find that human distinctions fade in importance because "there is neither Jew nor Greek, slave nor free, male nor female, for you are all one in Christ Jesus" (Gal 3:28). Being in a position of discomfort may make us more vulnerable to see how God is working around us.

Correct obedience to God is submitting to what is essential to God's heart. Jesus paid the cost on the cross for every person and every ethnic group around the world to receive salvation. With his death on the cross, Christ purchased for God members "from every tribe and language and people and nation" (Rev 5:9). As Bill Nelson, a pastor with InterVarsity Christian Fellowship says, "Whenever there is an opportunity for the church to reach out to people in our communities, we must consider what it will take to further the Kingdom. If this means putting down the American flag and raising the Kingdom flag, that is what we should do."

Many churches and denominations are choosing to welcome and integrate immigrants into their faith communities. Religious leaders are using their moral authority and experience with the immigrant community to speak out on the need to fix the broken immigration system. Pastors and lay members are thus personally seeing God's providential workings in the migration of people. The American church's role in welcoming and speaking out on behalf of all people groups will be pivotal in providing a kingdom perspective on the immigration debate and moving us closer to the day Scripture promises, when "a great multitude that no one could count, from every nation, tribe, people and language, [will be] standing before the throne and in front of the Lamb" (Rev 7:9).

A CHRISTIAN RESPONSE

TO THE IMMIGRATION DILEMMA

Do not merely listen to the word, and so deceive yourselves. Do what it says.
James 1:22

The goal of this book has been to bring others in the church along on the journey, which we have both embarked on personally, of understanding the immigration issue, reflecting on how our Christian faith should inform our opinions, and analyzing the various ways that the church and the U.S. government have responded and are responding. We hope, though, that your own interaction with this important issue will not stop at understanding, information and analysis: we believe that this thinking ought to inspire appropriate and prayerful action.

Fortunately, there is a plethora of ways to respond: some big and some small, but all with the potential for significance. We can begin by bringing the immigration situation before God in prayer. From there, we move to action: we can serve our immigrant neighbors through volunteering, allowing us to know them personally and learn from them, as well as financially supporting ministries that facilitate such service. As we better understand the immigration issue through interaction with immigrant neighbors, we can help to educate others in our churches and communities. From there, we can advocate together on behalf of immigrants and refugees. Finally, if we wish to address the root issues behind migration, we will need to begin to address poverty, unemployment, conflict and environmental degradation in other parts of the world. This final chapter should help guide you in how to take the first steps toward a Christian response to the immigration issue.

We have argued that Scripture makes repeated and very clear calls on us to take special concern for the stranger, to love him or her as ourselves, and to welcome him or her as if serving Jesus himself. God commands us to obey, which is primary if we are to truly follow Christ. "There is no other road to faith or discipleship," Dietrich Bonhoeffer writes, except "obedience to the call of Jesus."[1] We dare not dismiss God's instructions to us, but rather should move from reflection to prayerful action.

Prayer

The biblical mandate to care for the foreign born requires action, but as Christians, we dare not attempt that action without prayer. "Prayer," Henri Nouwen writes, "must be our first concern [because] as disciples, we find not some but all of our strength, hope, courage, and confidence in God. . . . Prayer challenges us to be fully aware of the world in which we live and to present it with all its needs and pains to God. It is this compassionate prayer that calls for compassionate action."[2]

As we begin to know our immigrant neighbors, and to share in what they have suffered through the trauma of displacement and perhaps the challenges of their present situations, we can present that suffering to God in prayer, asking him, our Heavenly Father, to provide, protect and guide them.

We can also pray for policies that honor God and reflect his justice. None of us, individually, has the authority to change immigration laws, and, though we believe we are called to advocacy, the challenge of addressing structural issues can be daunting and frustrating. In prayer, we are reminded "that we can do nothing at all, but that God can do everything through us."[3] We are commanded specifically to pray for our political leaders. Paul exhorts Timothy "that requests, prayers, intercession and thanksgiving be made for everyone," but particularly "for kings and all those in authority" (1 Tim 2:1-2). Whether we voted for and support a particular president, senator or representative or not, we have the responsibility to pray for them, asking God to grant them wisdom as they make important decisions that affect millions of families.

We can also pray beyond the needs of the immigrants in our own communities and pray for the communities from which immigrants come, many of which face desperate poverty and conflict. As we do, God expands our love for these neighbors whom we do not personally know. Nouwen writes,

> In the intimacy of prayer, God reveals himself to us as the God who loves all members of the human family just as personally and uniquely as he loves us. Therefore, a growing intimacy with God deepens our sense of responsibility for others. It evokes in us an always increasing desire to bring the whole world with all its suffering and pains around the divine fire in our heart and to share the revitalizing heat with all who want to come.[4]

This love for others born in times of prayer is not a substitute for action but the fuel that sustains it. As we seek to live God's commands to care for the immigrant and refugee, we ought to begin with prayer and, without ceasing to pray, move into action.

Knowing, Learning from and Serving Our Immigrant Neighbors

We can begin to act by being involved in our own communities. Almost wherever you might live within the United States, you now probably have immigrants and refugee neighbors within your community, though you might not (yet) interact with them regularly. Our society is structured in such a way that you can live in the same community as thousands of immigrants and never know any of their names, with barriers of language, culture, race and economic status dividing us. Only when we begin to personally know our immigrant neighbors can we begin to contemplate the biblical mandate to love them. Psychologist Mary Pipher explains that, as we begin to interact personally with these individuals whom we had considered aliens, "that person stops being a stereotype and becomes a complex human being like oneself."⁵ The immigration policy debate then becomes less about statistics and more about human faces, about laws that have dramatic effects on families we know.

One of the best ways to begin to know the immigrants in our communities is to serve them. Volunteering can lead to beautifully reciprocal relationships; we can help a recently arrived immigrant to adjust to a new society, while they can help us to understand their cultures as well as our own through a new lens.

I (Matthew) have been blessed in many ways through my friendships with my immigrant and refugee neighbors. I often feel that I receive much more than I gain. I am able to help kids in my neighborhood with their homework—which is difficult for their parents, because their English is limited—but I am more than compensated when I am invited over for a delicious Mexican, Sudanese or Rwandan meal, not to mention the enjoyment of the company of good friends. In the process, I have also gained new insights into the immigrant experience, the countries and cultures that my neighbors have come from, and even into my own culture, which I can see a bit differently from an outsider's perspective.

A natural way to begin such reciprocal relationships is through volunteering. World Relief and many other organizations have a constant need for volunteers to help with English as a Second Language classes or tutoring, to care for the children of those in ESL classes, to assist newcomers in navigating the complexities of life in an entirely new culture, and above all just to serve as a friend. Appendix three provides a list of various Christian organizations serving refugees and immigrants throughout the United States, along with contact information for volunteer opportunities.

Giving

As with any ministry, those working with immigrants are often limited by financial resources. Many organizations and ministries that serve the poor are prohibited from serving undocumented immigrants, even if they would like to, because their funding sources—especially governmental grants—specifically state that funds should not be used to provide services to undocumented individuals. As a result, undocumented immigrants often have many serious needs but few places to turn for assistance.

Churches, though, and the individuals who make up the church, are not bound by limitations about whom they can serve. Churches and Christian ministries could be providing the practical assistance and social services that the government often cannot provide—if individual Christians were to invest the resources to serve these subclasses of our communities. Churches and organizations partnering with the church have a unique opportunity to provide these services in Christ's name. While some would rather not go near the controversial issue, we believe that, like the lepers of the New Testament era, undocumented immigrants are a stigmatized population whom God calls us to love and serve. We can do so, as the church, when we as individuals are willing to back up such work with a portion of the money God has entrusted to us.

Educating Our Churches and Communities

Churches will more readily heed the biblical call to care for immigrants—regardless of legal status—only with a substantial increase of education and awareness among individual followers of Christ. As we educate ourselves—through personal interaction with immigrants and refugees and through our own investigation into the issue—we can then help educate others in our churches and in our communities.*

There are many ways to do this. Churches could focus a Sunday school class or small group discussion on the issue of immigration from a Christian perspective; we have provided discussion questions in appendix one to help you use this book as a guide. You could also invite a speaker from an organization serving immigrants and refugees, or from an immigrant church in your community, to speak at a service or Sunday school class. Further, we can encourage immigrant involvement and leadership at all

---

*For those who would like to delve deeper into understanding immigrants and immigration, we have provided a list of additional resources in appendix five.

levels of our own local churches.

Churches could also begin new ministries to serve immigrants, such as English classes. Organizations like World Relief may be able to assist by providing technical support. Many churches have also begun to offer worship services in a second (or third, or fourth) language, or allow an immigrant church without a building to use their space.

One of the simplest ways to help educate others is simply by speaking up whenever we hear comments that we know to be untrue about immigrants. Nineteenth-century Baptist preacher Charles Spurgeon remarked, "a lie travels round the world while Truth is putting on her boots."[6] The truth never catches up unless we have the courage to gently and lovingly challenge false or prejudiced statements. When we hear, or receive by e-mail, a derogatory joke or rumor, we can remind our sisters and brothers in Christ that immigrants, whatever their legal status, are human beings made in the image of God.

Advocacy

While getting to know immigrants and refugees through service is an important start, compassion and justice run deeper than individual acts of service. Advocacy is crucial because transformation should be about the whole of society, by meeting immediate needs but also changing the structures in which society operates. Advocacy can be defined as being a voice for the voiceless, standing in the gap to present the realities of injustice around the world to those in positions of influence who can help change the situation.

Scripture specifically calls us to this task. Proverbs 31:8 commands us: "Speak up for those who cannot speak for themselves." It is a biblical imperative to advocate for justice, and most immigrants, who are not naturalized citizens, cannot vote and so speak up for themselves in our country. We see repeatedly throughout the Old and New Testaments that God's concern for the poor and for justice are central to his character. God loves justice, but he also *does* justice. From Moses and David to Isaiah and Esther, we see ordinary human beings being used by God to bring his vision of justice to the broken world around them, whether through changes in policy, social structure or attitudes toward certain groups of people.

We also realize that Jesus was the ultimate Advocate. We advocate because Jesus advocates for us daily, laying before God the sins of the world and acting as our intercessor (Heb 7:23-25; Rom 8:1). Jesus' life and ministry here on earth carried forward God's idea of justice from the Old Testament to the New Testament. He continually advocates on our behalf before God and covers over all our sins. Following Jesus' example, we should be intercessors on behalf of those who are the "least of these" (Mt 25:40). Christians must recover a spirit of social action and participate in God's great agenda, since we are called to advocate on behalf of humanity, particularly the poor and oppressed, knowing that God in the end has victory through Jesus' death on the cross.

Churches traditionally have been reluctant to engage in politics, and understandably so. There are certain principles, however, that can guide us as we engage our elected leaders to craft policies and legislation that reflect our values. In "For the Health of the Nation: An Evangelical Call to Civic Responsibility," the National Association of Evangelicals outlines the basis for evangelical engagement in government, stating,

> we engage in public life because God created our first parents in his image and gave them dominion over the earth (Gen. 1:27-28) . . . [and also] because Jesus is Lord over every area of life. Through him all things were created (Col. 1:16-17) and by him all things will be brought to fullness (Rom. 8:19-21). . . . [Thus,] as Christian citizens, we believe it is our calling to help government live up to its divine mandate to render justice (Rom. 13:1-7; 1 Pet. 2:13-17). . . . Our goal in civic engagement is to bless our neighbors by making good laws.[7]

Advocacy allows God's people to seek the fullness of the kingdom of God, keeping in mind that Christ has the final victory, so we can see God working his purposes out for the whole of his kingdom.

The following are a few ideas that you, your church, your school or communities can engage in to be a voice for immigrants:

- Find out the position of your local congressperson and senator on immigration issues. You can often find statements, congressional votes and other general information about their position on the issue on their website.

- Write a letter to your local congressperson stating how you feel about the immigration issue, or call them, highlighting the biblical basis for welcoming the stranger or highlighting some personal relationships you have with immigrants in your community. Appendix six will help you identify and contact your elected representatives.

- Schedule a meeting with your congressperson or a staff person to discuss your position on immigration issues. You can bring others who share a similar viewpoint as yours to the meeting and give their office some relevant information. Make sure you follow up on the meeting with a thank-you e-mail or letter!

- Write an editorial in your local newspaper about your personal experience with immigrants and how you feel they positively affect the United States.

- Identify church leaders in your community who support Comprehensive Immigration Reform and provide forums for them to speak about their position. You can create a statement of principles, have them write an editorial to the local newspaper or organize a press conference at a key time in your community.

- Have an "Immigrant Sunday" at your church: organize a panel discussion at your church on a Sunday and get members of your church to write in letters, postcards or e-mail messages to your local elected officials. You can arrange a panel of speakers and ask people to pray and fast on behalf of immigrants in your local community.

- Stay up to date on advocacy issues relating to immigrants and refugees by signing up for World Relief's advocacy updates. To join, simply e-mail: advocacy@wr.org.

Jesus asked in the Lord's Prayer that his Father's will be done "on earth as it is in heaven" (Mt 6:10). Injustice plagues us here on earth, but by seeking justice for those who do not have it, we are furthering God's kingdom.

Advocacy is vital, both practically and theologically, to the church's calling to bring about justice, speak out for truth, defend the poor and oppressed, and work toward the redemption of the whole of creation.

Addressing the Root Issues

As we begin to know our neighbors and hear their stories, we will realize that immigration is very often the consequence of difficult and sometimes unlivable conditions in other parts of the world. As long as the average salary of a worker in Mexico and Central America is a small fraction of what a worker in the United States earns, mass migration will continue, whatever border enforcement techniques we employ. As long as wars and persecution threaten the lives of people, there will be a constant supply of refugees to the United States and other safe havens. As long as environmental degradation threatens people's ways of life, there will be movement to other communities and then, often, to countries such as the United States. People on all sides of the immigration debate—those who want to welcome more immigrants and those who believe we should seal the borders entirely—can agree that we should address these root issues that motivate migration.

We believe very strongly, guided by Scripture, that immigrants and refugees should be welcomed into our society and treated with dignity and respect. Nevertheless, migration is a difficult, often traumatic event, and people ought to be able to live in dignity in their home countries, without being forced to migrate. Many Americans are only vaguely aware of the situations of poverty, conflict and environmental degradation that threaten the lives of billions of human beings around the world, particularly in Latin America, Africa and Asia. In a globalizing society, though, we no longer have the excuse of ignorance to keep us from action.

As our new immigrant and refugee neighbors tell us about their lives before they came to the United States, we are challenged to think about how our lifestyles—our consumption habits, our use of energy, our country's foreign policies—might affect how others live. Few young men eager to be married, for example, stop to think about where the diamond in their fiancée's engagement ring came from, and if it helped to fund a civil war in West Africa. Most would rather pay $1 less for a bag of coffee than spend the additional money for the assurance that the coffee farmer was paid a reasonable wage.* Few of us seriously consider the environmental impact on the poorest nations as we hop into our cars instead of using public transportation, walking or riding a bicycle. And not many take the time to investigate how U.S. trade policy, foreign aid policy, or support of a particular foreign political leader will affect individuals in other countries, and even fewer take the time to let their elected representatives know what they think.

Most of us think of ourselves as small, inconsequential actors on the global scene. Indeed, our individual lifestyle choices, when viewed in isolation, may not, in themselves, make a significant difference. Collectively, though, the potential for positive change is enormous. We can help to improve the situations in the countries from which most immigrants come if we examine and adjust our own lifestyles, advocate for just policies, and support churches and ministries doing important work abroad to support economic development, improve public health, protect and provide for children, increase education and empower women.†

---

*Justice-conscious consumers can look for conflict-free diamonds, which are carefully tracked from the mine to the jewelry store to ensure that they have not funded war or conflict. The Conflict-Free Diamond Council (www.conflictfreediamonds.org) can provide further information. Fair-trade coffee and other products are certified to provide a slightly higher wage to the producers than the market might otherwise provide; fair-trade coffee can now be purchased at many stores and is also available from organizations such as Pura Vida Coffee (www.puravidacoffee.com) and the Higher Grounds Trading Company (www.highergroundstrading.com).

†Appendix four provides a list of Christian organizations working throughout the Global South for holistic, transformational development.

Conclusion

This book has been the fruit of a journey for both of us as we have come into contact with immigrants in our respective neighborhoods, worked on immigration policy issues and began to question how God would have us respond. This book was born out of our own questions; we do not claim to have stumbled on the right, biblical answers to every question, but we think that we have learned a lot along the journey. Above all, we believe Scripture makes clear that immigrants are to be specifically included in the call to love our neighbors as ourselves. This love must be personal, and that means getting to know our immigrant neighbors.

When we begin to love our immigrant neighbors on a personal level, we will want to advocate for just, merciful and loving immigration policies as well. As we begin to converse and better understand the difficulties that these neighbors left in their home countries, we will also find our hearts stretching to other neighbors in need—the people still living in those places devastated by economic difficulties, war and environmental disaster—and we might, as the church, begin to do more to bring God's love into those situations as well.

Our prayer as we have embarked on this book has been that the church, particularly the evangelical arm of the church with which we both strongly identify, will take up this charge and even lead other faith communities to love our new immigrant neighbors. We believe that obedience to Christ means committing ourselves, not just as a few individuals, but united as God's people, to serving the sojourners among us and advocating on their behalf. That movement starts with individuals—with you—and grows through you to entire congregations and denominations until the church here in North America is known by its love for the immigrant and refugee. In the process, we have already begun to discover that God has provided his church in this country with a unique privilege to be blessed by our brothers and sisters from other parts of the globe.

APPENDIX 1

DISCUSSION QUESTIONS

These questions are designed to encourage discussion about and deeper reflection on the complexities surrounding immigration and the integration of this important issue with our Christian faith. We hope that they will be particularly useful for guiding small group discussions.

Chapter 1: The Immigration Dilemma

1. Two views were presented in the quotations at the beginning of the chapter. Which of these views have you heard the most?

2. The chapter says, "It is these 'easy' issues that often prove to be the most complex and the hardest to resolve, since our presumptions keep us from hearing the other side." What presumptions have you held regarding the issue of immigration?

3. The authors have shared their backgrounds and experiences with immigrants; spend some time sharing with the group your own experiences with immigrants and the debate.

4. C. S. Lewis says that humans are the "holiest object presented to your senses." How does this quote help us to begin to treat our neighbors in God's image?

5. Which aspect of the immigration debate either interests or confuses you the most? (Political, economic, spiritual, etc.)

6. What is one question concerning immigration that you would like to see answered in your study of this issue?

Chapter 2: Aliens Among You: Who Are Undocumented Immigrants?

1. The rhetoric surrounding undocumented immigrants is particularly fierce. How does the emotional rhetoric change the debate?

2. How do the stories of immigrants help us see the image of God in present-day circumstances?

3. Which story stands out to you as the most interesting story? Why are you drawn to that particular story?

4. In the story of Pedro and Martha, Social Security cards and taxes show the complexity of ethical dimensions in the issue of undocumented immigrants. If most undocumented immigrants pay taxes, what rights should they have under the law?

Chapter 3: Nation of Immigrants: A Historical Perspective on Immigration to the United States

1. God presents care for refugees as a justice issue while reminding the Hebrews that he was faithful to redeem their situation. How can the church remember its past in a productive way? How can we rehearse our own immigrant history both in a national and spiritual sense?

2. Historian Roger Daniels has proposed that Americans have a "dualistic" view of immigration. What does he mean? Do you think this is historical or hypocritical?

3. What are two or three goals that you find immigrants of the past and present share?

4. What does the ebb and flow of historical sentiment toward immigrants reveal about our country? Is it an encouragement or a discouragement to read the brief historical immigration summary of our nation?

5. In the section titled "The Church and Immigration History," what surprised you the most about the church's response to immigration in the past?

Chapter 4: Immigrating the Legal Way: Our Immigration System Today

1. Before reading this chapter, what were some common misconceptions that you have either heard or held with regard to the current immigration system?

2. Many say that undocumented immigrants should just "wait in line." How does this chapter shed light on this misconception? How has your understanding of the immigration system changed?

3. Have you ever known anyone who struggled with the process of obtaining a visitor's visa? What was their experience?

4. What surprised you the most about the path to legal status in the United States?

5. In your opinion, what role does the U.S. economy have on undocumented immigration?

6. Do you think that environmental or economic hardship should be added to the definition of a refugee? Why or why not?

Chapter 5: Thinking Biblically About Immigration

1. Share and reflect on a past experience of turning to Scripture for insight and principles regarding a particular social or political issue. How is this issue of undocumented immigration similar or different?

2. How should our heavenly citizenship dictate the way we view and treat immigrants in our churches? How about in our schools and in our communities?

3. Why do you think that God places special emphasis on the well-being of immigrants?

4. How does Jesus respond when he is asked, "Who is my neighbor?" How does his response inform how we view immigrants?

5. After reading this chapter, do you agree that there is a biblical mandate to care for immigrants? If so, what is one way you could begin to fulfill this calling during the next week?

Chapter 6: Concerns About Immigration

1. What were some of your primary concerns regarding this debate before reading this book? Who or what was your source for these concerns?

2. Do you think that we have an obligation to the poor living among us prior to the poor living abroad? What are some possible nuances to that argument?

3. Which argument of those against a more generous immigration policy—poverty already in our communities, creation care, national security, cultural identity, etc.—is most persuasive and compelling to you? Why?

4. Describe or reflect on a time when you were a minority. What was the most uncomfortable aspect of this experience?

5. What distinction do the authors make between "doing justice" and "acting justly"? How does this change or reinforce your own perception of the command?

6. Are there any immigrants or refugees in your daily path? At the end of your time together, take some time to pray for ways to reach out to immigrants and the foreign born in your own neighborhood.

Chapter 7: The Value of Immigration to the United States

1. What do you see as the impact of immigration on your local community? What are the benefits? What are the costs?

2. Do you think God's instructions to "welcome the stranger" trump any negative impact that immigrants might have on the economy? Why or why not?

3. What were a couple of the key take-away points from the section on global perspectives on immigration?

4. Over the last fifty years, immigrants have moved to more developed countries. What are the implications for the sending and receiving countries as well as for the immigrants themselves?

5. It is often difficult to understand the economic impact of immigrants. From this chapter, what is the ultimate impact contended to be?

6. Examine George Borjas's argument and the counterarguments discussed. Which makes more sense?

7. In your personal experience—or in those of your family or community—how have you observed the economic impact of immigrants?

8. Brainstorm together some of the possible "root causes" of why there are so many undocumented immigrants in America today.

Chapter 8: The Politics and Policies of Immigration Reform

1. Do you think that the issue of immigration has been used for political gain by members of Congress and those running for president?

2. Do you think that a path to earned legalization with the appropriate penalties is a fair consequence for the legal infraction of illegal presence in the United States?

3. How do you think the moral voice of the faith community can shape the immigration debate?

4. What factors have made immigration a "hot topic" in political circles?

5. After reading through the many pieces of legislation concerning immigration, what are the core elements that you believe immigration reform should include?

6. What further information would you need to know in order to advocate on behalf of immigrants?

7. As a follower of Christ, how can you encourage the people within your

sphere of influence toward a more godly view of undocumented immigrants?

Chapter 9: The Church and Immigration Today

1. How do you see your church ministering to "the least of these" in the United States?

2. How should ethnic majority churches respond to the rise in immigrant churches?

3. If your church were to create a statement on immigration, what would it say?

4. In his daily life, Jesus showed personal hospitality to outcasts, both ethnically with the Samaritan woman (John 4), religiously with the Roman centurion (Matthew 8), and socially with the woman caught in adultery (John 8). What can we do to show Christlike hospitality both personally and corporately?

5. Do you agree with the authors when they state that God is using cultural diversity to accomplish his greater purposes here on earth?

6. How does the fact that the immigrant church is the fastest growing evangelical church in America change the missions strategy of the church?

7. In the conclusion the authors remark, "correct obedience to God is submitting to what is essential to God's heart." After reading this chapter, what do you think is essential to God's heart in the midst of the immigration debate? What do you think God may be asking you to submit to while reading this book?

Chapter 10: A Christian Response to the Immigration Dilemma

1. The authors argue that we cannot really understand the immigration issue until we personally know and interact with immigrants in our communities. How could you begin to do this?

2. Is there a church or organization in your community that is actively serving the foreign born? How could you get involved?

3. What could you—individually or as a group—do to help educate your larger church community about this issue?

4. Many Christians are wary of meddling in politics. Why do you think this is? Do you think that there is a place for the church to be involved in political advocacy?

5. How could you personally and as a church community help your congressional representatives understand your position(s) on this issue?

6. What do the authors argue are some of the root causes of immigration? Do you agree? What part of the way that you live might contribute, either positively or negatively, to these situations?

7. What response do you believe that God is calling you to with this important and controversial issue? How will you respond to that call?

APPENDIX 2

WORLD RELIEF STATEMENT IN SUPPORT OF
COMPREHENSIVE IMMIGRATION REFORM*

World Relief is actively engaged in advocating for comprehensive immigration reform in Congress. This document explains why we believe advocacy on this issue is important and encourages other evangelicals to support comprehensive immigration reform. World Relief has a long history of resettling refugees in the United States and providing immigration legal services, English classes and other assistance to refugees and other immigrants. We are compelled to speak from our experience by engaging the Evangelical community on the issue of immigration reform.

How Can We Expand God's Kingdom by Accepting and Ministering to Immigrants?

The Bible commands us to welcome the stranger. Modern reality also requires us to embrace the immigrant population, many of whom are our brothers and sisters in Christ and a growing force in the church. Through immigration, God is bringing citizens of many closed and unreached countries into contact with American Christians. We therefore welcome

*©World Relief, February 27, 2006. This statement may be reproduced and distributed, with attribution to World Relief. World Relief is the humanitarian arm of the National Association of Evangelicals USA. In the United States and twenty-four countries around the world, World Relief works with local churches to create sustainable solutions that help the desperately poor. World Relief's programs include refugee and immigrant assistance, disaster relief, AIDS ministries, community health, agricultural development and community banking.

the opportunity to share our faith with people who might otherwise have no opportunity to hear the good news. The immigrant evangelical church is growing rapidly in the United States and around the world. Among evangelicals in the United States, "the fastest growing are found among the Independent immigrant churches. . . . In 20 years, African, Asian and Latin American Evangelicals . . . will likely be at the forefront of . . . global movements as well as their manifestations in the USA."*

In the Bible, God repeatedly calls us to show love and compassion to "aliens," or immigrants. In Deuteronomy 10:18-19,† we are told that "[God] defends the cause of the fatherless and the widow, and loves the alien, giving him food and clothing. And you are to love those who are aliens, for you yourselves were aliens in Egypt." Leviticus 19:33-34 teaches us that, "[w]hen an alien lives with you in your land, do not mistreat him. The alien living with you must be treated as one of your native-born. Love him as yourself, for you were aliens in Egypt. I am the LORD your God."

Love in the Christian tradition requires specific acts of care and respect. In the Gospel of Luke, Jesus answers the question of "who is my neighbor?" with the parable of the Good Samaritan (Luke 10:29-37). Part of what makes the Good Samaritan parable so compelling is that the Samaritan, who was a stranger or alien himself, was the one who stopped to help the Jewish man. This and other parables remind us that "we are all aliens sent out to help other aliens find a place of safety in this world."‡ God does not distinguish among arbitrary divisions such as country of origin. Instead, God desires to include all people in his kingdom, for "[t]here is neither Jew nor Greek, slave nor free, male nor female, for you are all one in Christ Jesus" (Galatians 3:28).

Evangelicals recognize that "[e]veryone must submit himself to the governing authorities, for there is no authority except that which God has

---

*Dr. Todd M. Johnson, Center for the Study of Global Christianity at Gordon-Conwell Theological Seminary, "USA Evangelicals/evangelicals in Global Context: Trends and Statistics."

†All Scripture references are taken from The Holy Bible, New International Version.

‡ Jonathan Robert Nelson, Remarks for The American Bar Association's, "Fortress America: The State and Future of U.S. Immigration Law and Policy," held at the National Press Club, January 26, 2006.

established" (Romans 13:1). Therefore we support the importance of following and enforcing laws, while simultaneously recognizing that laws were created for the well-being of human beings and society. Ultimately the laws must answer to God's higher law, which requires us to treat all human life with sanctity. All persons bear the image of Christ and thus should be treated with the dignity and respect that we would afford our Savior. Valuing persons includes doing what we can to preserve them, to care for them and to create fair systems that lead to healthy societies.* We must, from time to time, ask if our human-made laws create a just and better existence for those who are created in God's image.

Why Do Immigrants Come Here and What Do They Do for Society?

We at World Relief have worked to serve refugees and other immigrants for many years, and have found that they contribute to our society in countless ways. Immigrants often fill jobs that native-born Americans do not fill, such as jobs that require hard labor but less education. There are also many immigrants in medical and technical fields. Immigrants are also helping to fill the gap left by an aging population that is leaving the workforce. Immigrants pay taxes, participate in our communities, churches, schools and political systems. Immigrants are dedicated to their families and are hard-working.

We know that some immigrants have violated immigration law by entering this country illegally or overstaying a valid visa, and there are many reasons why they have done so. They may have had to flee quickly to escape persecution, civil strife, or natural disasters in their own countries. Many others came to this country because they needed to support their families, who are from countries where they cannot earn a living wage. Many immigrants have applied legitimately for the right to live in this country with their family members, but must wait for many years for final approval due to backlogs in the system.

---

*Evangelical Project for Public Engagement. National Association of Evangelicals, For the Health of the Nation: An Evangelical Call to Civic Responsibility, 8, 10 (2004).

The Need for Comprehensive Immigration Reform

Immigration is a defining feature of America's history and will continue to be an important issue for America's future. President Bush, members of both parties in Congress and the faith community have called for changes to our immigration system to address numerous problems.

World Relief believes that a comprehensive approach to immigration reform is required to address the complex and outmoded immigration system that currently exists. For example, current law has created numerous barriers for legitimate refugees abroad and seekers of asylum in the United States to receive the protection they deserve. Additionally, approximately 11 million undocumented immigrants currently live in the United States,* and more than 3 million U.S.-citizen children live in families headed by an undocumented immigrant.† An undocumented individual does not have current permission to work or live in the United States.

Many undocumented children are raised here but are unable to attend college or work legally. Individuals are risking their lives and literally dying to come to the United States. Families face inhumane waits of up to twenty years to reunify with family members. There are an inadequate number of visas for employers to hire the foreign workers necessary for jobs that they cannot find native-born Americans to fill. We have a growing black market characterized by widespread use of false documents, increasingly violent smuggling cartels and exploitation of undocumented workers.

Because many immigrants do not currently have a means by which to receive lawful status in the United States, they go undetected by living in the shadows. If they could apply for current lawful status, they would be much more likely to come forward, and the government could better target the small number of potential criminals and terrorists.

We do not condone any violations of the law, such as living in the United States illegally, but we recognize that our complex and inadequate

---

*pewhispanic.org/files/reports/44.pdf, stating that as of March 2005, there were nearly 11 million undocumented individuals in the United States.
†pewhispanic.org/files/reports/46.pdf.

immigration system has made it nearly impossible for many of the hard-working people that our country needs, to enter or remain in the country legally and/or reunite with family members.

What Are World Relief and Other Agencies Doing?

World Relief is actively advocating for comprehensive immigration reform at the federal level, cooperating with other faith-based agencies and working to engage the evangelical community. We approach comprehensive immigration reform as a nonpartisan issue, in which we feel called to engage based upon Scripture and our moral values.

We believe that a comprehensive approach is required that goes beyond border protection alone and addresses the current problems of our immigration system: by looking at root causes of immigration, developing workable solutions and providing dignified relief to the millions of immigrants who are contributing to our communities, despite their lack of legal status. We also advocate for reforms that better protect those seeking refugee and asylum status.

We advocate that any legislation that is passed include the following specific principles:

- Reforms in our family-based immigration system to significantly reduce waiting times for separated families who currently wait many years to be reunited;

- The creation of more responsive legal avenues for workers and their families who wish to migrate to the United States to enter our country and work in a safe, legal and orderly manner that prevents their exploitation and assures them due process;

- The option for those individuals and families who are already living in the United States, and working hard, to apply for permanent legal status and citizenship if they choose to do so, by meeting specific application criteria; and

- Border protection policies that are consistent with humanitarian values and with the need to treat all individuals with respect, while allowing the authorities to carry out the critical task of enforcing our laws.

What Can You Do? A Call to Action

- Ask your church and/or pastor to sign the attached letter to the president and Congress, in support of comprehensive immigration reform.

- Call or send a letter or e-mail to the president, your senators and representative, in support of comprehensive immigration reform. (See <www.whitehouse.gov/contact/>; <www.senate.gov/>; <www.house.gov/writerep/>.)

- Schedule an appointment with your senator or representative, or with their staff.

- Talk about immigrants and refugees in your church.

- Volunteer with a local refugee or immigration program, such as a World Relief office.

- Contact World Relief for more information.

Throughout the country, there are churches and Christian organizations working to serve, welcome and empower immigrants and refugees, and they very often need volunteers. We have listed several of the larger, national organizations below. Also many local organizations and individual churches are doing important work in Christ's name—so many that we cannot include contact information for each one here.

World Relief
7 E. Baltimore Street
Baltimore, MD 21203
443-451-1900 or 800-535-5433
www.wr.org

World Relief, our employer, a partner in the publication of this book and the recipient of the authors' portions of the royalties of this book, is the humanitarian arm of the National Association of Evangelicals. World Relief's mission is to empower the local church to serve the most vulnerable. Within the United States, we have various affiliate offices that partner on a local basis with churches to holistically assist immigrants, refugees and members of their communities to become fully integrated participants in society. World Relief's U.S. offices are listed below; you can call the office nearest you to ask about church partnership and volunteer opportunities. Our website also provides further information on our work in the United States and around the world, with links to the local websites of many of our individual affiliate offices.

California

Modesto	209-575-1132
Sacramento	916-978-2650
San Jose	408-729-3786
Southern California	714-210-4730
Stockton	209-943-6919

Florida

Jacksonville	904-448-0733
Miami	305-541-8320
Tampa	727-849-7900

Georgia

Atlanta	404-294-4352

Idaho

Boise	208-323-4964

Illinois

Aurora	630-906-9546
Chicago	773-583-9191
DuPage County	630-462-7566
Moline	309-764-2279

Indiana

Fort Wayne	(office pending)

Maryland

Baltimore	410-244-0002

Minnesota
Minneapolis-St. Paul   612-798-4332

North Carolina
High Point   336-887-9007
Durham   919-286-3496

Tennessee
Nashville   615-833-7735

Texas
Fort Worth   817-924-0748

Washington
Kent   253-854-7857
Richland   509-734-5477
Seattle   206-587-0234
Spokane   509-484-9829

Catholic Legal Immigration Network (CLINIC)
415 Michigan Avenue, NE
Suite 150
Washington, D.C. 20017
202-635-2556
www.cliniclegal.org

CLINIC, working through a network of local affiliates, including many Catholic charities and Catholic social services offices and individual Catholic parishes, provides immigration legal services to local offices located throughout the United States. Many of these local offices have volunteer opportunities. Look at <www.cliniclegal.org> for the Public Directory of CLINIC member organizations.

Christian Community Development Association

3555 W. Ogden Avenue

Chicago, IL 60623

773-762-0994

www.ccda.org

The Christian Community Development Association (CCDA) includes hundreds of member organizations, many of which work directly with immigrants and refugees. See their website for a directory of member organizations.

Church World Service

28606 Phillips Street

P.O. Box 968

Elkhart, IN 46515

574-264-3102 or 1-800-297-1516

www.churchworldservice.org

Church World Service, which is affiliated with about thirty-five Protestant and Orthodox denominations in the United States, provides a number of services, including programs for refugees and immigrants. Their website can help you to connect with a local office in your area.

Episcopal Migration Ministries

815 Second Avenue

New York, NY 10017

800-334-7626

www.episcopalchurch.org/emm

A ministry of the Episcopal Church in the Unites States, Episcopal Migration Ministries provides refugee resettlement and immigration services at locations throughout the country. For information on local affiliates, see their website.

Lutheran Immigration & Refugee Service
700 Light Street
Baltimore, MD 21230
410-230-2700
www.lirs.org

Lutheran Immigration & Refugee Service (LIRS) also serves refugees and immigrants in many communities throughout the United States, working through affiliated offices. It is associated with several Lutheran denominations in the United States. Their website includes a full list of affiliate offices.

APPENDIX 4

MINISTRIES AND ORGANIZATIONS ADDRESSING
THE ROOT CAUSES OF IMMIGRATION

There are literally thousands of excellent Christian ministries and organizations seeking to act out of God's love in order to assist and empower those facing situations of poverty, unemployment, war and conflict, and environmental degradation. Though we cannot mention all of them here, we have provided the names and website addresses of several reputable organizations engaged in this work, through direct service or through advocacy, that you could choose to support in various ways.

A Rocha (www.arocha.org)
Agros International (www.agros.org)
Baptist World Aid (www.bwanet.org/default.aspx?pid=13)
Bread for the World (www.bread.org)
Catholic Relief Services (www.crs.org)
Christ for the City International (www.cfci.org)
Christian Reformed Church World Relief Committee (www.crcna.org/pages/crwrc.cfm)
Compassion International (www.compassion.com)
Congo Initiative (www.congoinitiative.org)
Covenant World Relief (www.covchurch.org/cwr)
Floresta (www.floresta.org)
Food for the Hungry (www.fh.org)

Habitat for Humanity (www.habitat.org)
InnerCHANGE (www.crmleaders.org/ministries/innerchange)
International Justice Mission (www.ijm.org)
Lutheran World Relief (www.lwr.org)
Mennonite Central Committee (www.mcc.org)
The Micah Challenge (www.micahchallenge.org)
The ONE Campaign (www.one.org)
OxFam International (www.oxfam.org)
Samaritan's Purse (www.samaritanspurse.org)
Salvation Army World Service (www.salvationarmy.org)
Servants to Asia's Urban Poor (www.servantsasia.org)
Sojourners (www.sojo.net)
Tear Fund (www.tearfund.org)
World Concern (www.worldconcern.org)
World Relief (www.wr.org)
World Vision (www.worldvision.org)

For more resources on immigration, visit
www.welcomingthestranger.com

APPENDIX 5

SELECTED RESOURCES FOR LEARNING MORE
ABOUT THE IMMIGRATION ISSUE

Please note that some resources may contain language or other content that some readers may find offensive.

BOOKS

Christian Perspectives on Immigration

Bulls, Bears & Golden Calves: Applying Christian Ethics in Economics by John E. Stapleford (Downers Grove, Ill.: InterVarsity Press, 2009). (See particularly chapter sixteen.)

Christians at the Border: Immigration, the Church, and the Bible by M. Daniel Carroll R. (Grand Rapids: Baker Academic, 2008).

Good Intentions: Nine Hot-Button Issues Viewed Through the Eyes of Faith by Charles M. North and Bob Smietana (Chicago: Moody Publishers, 2008). (See particularly chapter nine.)

Re-Creating America: The Ethics of U.S. Immigration Policy in a Christian Perspective by Dana Wilbanks (Nashville: Abingdon Press, 1996).

Santa Biblia: The Bible Through Hispanic Eyes by Justo González (Abingdon Press, 1996). (See particularly chapter four.)

Immigrant and Refugee Stories

Brother, I'm Dying by Edwidge Danticat (New York: Alfred A. Knopf, 2007).

Enrique's Journey by Sonia Nazario (New York: Random House, 2006).

The New Americans: Seven Families Journey to Another Country by Rubén Martínez (New York: New Press, 2004).

Of Beetles & Angels: A Boy's Remarkable Journey from a Refugee Camp to Harvard by Mawi Asegdom (New York: Little, Brown and Company, 2001).

The Story of My Life: An Afghan Girl on the Other Side of the Sky by Farah Ahmedi and Tanim Ansary (New York: Simon Spotlight Entertainment, 2005).

On Serving Immigrants and Refugees

The Middle of Everywhere: Helping Refugees Enter the American Community by Mary Pipher (Eugene, Ore.: Harvest Books, 2003).

History of Immigration to the United States

Driven Out: The Forgotten War Against Chinese Americans by Jean Pfaelzer (New York: Random House, 2007).

Guarding the Golden Door: American Immigration Policy and Immigrants Since 1882 by Roger Daniels (New York: Hill and Wang, 2004).

Harvest of Empire: A History of Latinos in America by Juan Gonzalez (New York: Viking Penguin, 2000).

Immigrants, Baptists, and the Protestant Mind in America by Lawrence B. Davis (Champaign: University of Illinois Press, 1973).

Strangers in the Land: Patterns of American Nativism, 1860-1925 by John Higham (New Brunswick, N.J.: Rutgers University Press, 2002).

Websites

American Immigration Law Foundation
www.ailf.org

America's Voice
www.americasvoiceonline.org

Christians for Comprehensive Immigration Reform
www.sojo.net/immigration

Immigration Advocates Network
www.immigrationadvocates.org

Immigration Policy Center
www.immigrationpolicy.org

Migration Policy Institute
www.migrationpolicy.org

National Immigration Forum
www.immigrationforum.org

Pew Hispanic Center
www.pewhispanic.org

U.S. Catholic Bishops' "Justice For Immigrants" Campaign
www.justiceforimmigrants.org

United States Citizenship & Immigration Services
www.uscis.gov

World Relief
www.wr.org

Films

Destination America, directed by David Grubin, Stephen Stept and Chana Gazit (PBS Films, 2005).

Dying to Get In: Undocumented Immigration at the U.S. Mexican Border, directed by Brett Tolley (Cape Cod, Mass.: Mooncusser Films, 2007).

Dying to Live: A Migrant's Journey, directed by Bill Groody (Groody River Films, 2005).

God Grew Tired of Us, directed by Christopher Dillon-Quinn and Tommy Walker (NewMarket Films, 2006).

The New Americans, miniseries edited by David E. Simpson (Chicago: Kartemquin Films, 2003).

Rain in a Dry Land, directed by Anne Makepeace (Lakeville, Conn.: Anne Makepeace Productions, 2006).

Under the Same Moon, directed by Patricia Riggen (Fox Searchlight, 2008).

The Visitor, directed by Thomas McCarthy (Beverly Hills, Calif.: Overture Films, 2008).

Wetback: The Undocumented Documentary, directed by Arturo Perez Torres (Washington, D.C.: National Geographic Video, 2007).

APPENDIX 6

TOOLS FOR POLITICAL ADVOCACY

Elected officials really do take very seriously the concerns of their constituents—if they know what they are. The debate over immigration policy in the United States over the past several years has been driven by a group of relatively small but very committed, persistent anti-immigration activists, who diligently have called their U.S. representatives and senators whenever legislation was being considered. Contacting your legislators is very important in order to ask for his/her support on a particular issue or piece of legislation, but phone calls and letters are equally as important when you want to thank your legislator for his/her vote or position on a particular issue.

Contacting your elected officials is really very easy. The first step is to know who they are. Each citizen of the United States is represented in Washington by one representative, who represents a congressional district, and by two senators, who each represent the entire state. To find out who your representative and senators are, simply call the congressional switchboard at 202-224-3121 or check online at <www.house.gov> and <www.senate.gov>. To contact the White House, call 202-456-1111.

When you call, simply state your name and where you are calling from and express your opinion. If there is a particular bill that you would like your elected representative to support or not support, be sure to mention the bill name or number.

Writing a letter, which can either be mailed or faxed to your elected officials, can also be a very effective way to let them know what you think about a particular issue (faxing is often preferable as it gets to the office quicker than snail mail). The mailing address and fax numbers for each official should be available on their website or by calling the congressional switchboard at 202-224-3121. When you write, be sure to include your name and address, express clearly the position or specific legislation that you would like your representative to support or not support, and perhaps provide some of the reasons that you would like him or her to take this position. For example, you may want to explain how your faith motivates you or to write about how a particular issue personally affects you, a neighbor or a member of your church community.

You can also ask in your telephone call or letter to meet with your congressperson or his/her staffer who focuses specifically on an issue. Be flexible in scheduling an appointment, and do your research beforehand! Know how the issue specifically affects your community and bring along materials that represent your viewpoint. You may also consider bringing to the meeting other people or leaders in your community who have a position similar to yours. Make sure to write a follow-up thank-you e-mail or letter after the meeting, and try to keep in touch.

To check the language or status of a piece of legislation, you can go to <thomas.loc.gov> which offers a comprehensive database of all current and past legislation.

You can also receive advocacy updates by e-mailing advocacy@wr.org or checking out our website at <www.wr.org/joinin> (click on the "Join In" section of the website, then click on "Advocacy").

ACKNOWLEDGMENTS

This book has also been blessed to be reviewed and critiqued by a number of patient and thoughtful friends scattered all over the world, particularly Anna Porter, Michael Kingsley, Brad Pritts, and Amy Tenney. Emily Snyder and Dawnielle Miller graciously assisted me with gathering interviews in their community—I'm so grateful for their commitment to their neighbors near Washington, D.C. Al Hsu and everyone at InterVarsity Press have patiently walked us through writing our first book, improving the manuscript significantly in the process.

My colleagues at World Relief DuPage have taught me much of what I know about immigration and have also been extraordinarily supportive of this book project. In particular, I'd like to thank Daniel Stutz, Hayley Meksi, Tanya Thomas, Damon Schroeder, Erika Miles, Maritza Velazquez and, at World Relief Aurora, Javier Rabadan and Susan Sosa. Jenna Liao was very helpful in writing the discussion questions at the back of the book—she's also who you should call if you live in DuPage County, Illinois, and this book inspires you to serve immigrants and refugees in your community through volunteering. Luke Niermann has been a particular help in working through some of the ideas in this text and in reminding me of the importance of prayer as we think about the immigration issue. And this book would probably still be an idea lingering in my mind were it not for Catherine Norquist, whose encouragement and assistance have been priceless.

A few professors of mine from my time at Wheaton College—particularly Lindy Scott, Sandra Joireman, Jeff Greenberg, Paul Robinson and Amy

Black—have helped me to integrate my Christian faith with the issues facing our world, including the topic of this book. They have taught me much about what it is to seek God's justice, to share with God's people both in joy and suffering, and to charitably engage even with those with whom I disagree.

My neighbors—whose names are mostly changed to protect their privacy—have contributed in countless ways to this text. Their stories make up the heart of this book. Their courage, perseverance and faith inspire me, and I also very much appreciate a few particular neighbors' cooking. The young men of my Thursday night Bible study have been eager to provide their input on and prayers for this book: I am so proud of each of you and eager to see what God does with your lives.

My three roommates over the past several years—Ryan Himes, Theogene Nishimwe and Jonathan Kindberg—have been faithful in prayer for our community as a whole and particularly for this book project. And my thoughts on immigration and justice have also been profoundly informed by the passion and zeal of my late friend and roommate, Luke Anderson, whose absence I have felt keenly in the process of writing.

Three Central American families—the Muñoz Montero family of Pavas, San José, Costa Rica, the Quiñónez Matute family of Ocotal, Nicaragua, and particularly the Pérez Gutiérrez family of Granada, Nicaragua—have taught me a great deal about authentic Christian hospitality by welcoming and embracing me as a member of their own families when I was a stranger in their respective lands. *Gracias por todo su amor para conmigo; nos vemos pronto, si Dios quiere.*

And, finally, my own family has nurtured my faith, challenged me to apply it to the difficult situations in our world and modeled Christlike service and compassion. They also endured countless e-mails and phone-call questions and read over various versions of this manuscript. I love you each so much!

Matthew Soerens
Wheaton, Illinois

My World Relief family has been instrumental in growing my knowledge of and love for immigrants and refugees throughout the world. Teaching that the social message in the gospel is central to Christian faith, World Relief has empowered the local church to alleviate suffering and poverty in the name of Jesus Christ. Dan Kosten, Joe Paschal, Amy Tenney, Meredith Long, Stephan Bauman and Sammy Mah are God-anointed leaders who have shaped World Relief's unique and prophetic voice in the immigration debate. Their constant support and belief that World Relief could be instrumental in changing the politics of an issue to reflect biblical concern for the least of these has allowed me to fully engage and believe that as Christians we have a unique role in bringing a moral message to an issue where Christian values are not often in play.

My colleagues in Washington, D.C., Kevin Appleby, Michelle Waslin and Cory Smith, offered their expertise and knowledge in helping edit the book to reflect how the debate has unfolded among our policymakers over the years. They make change happen every day in our nation's capital and have demonstrated to me how steadfast dedication and belief in a cause can create ripples of movement across the country.

My friends (you know who you are!) and church family, Grace Life Church in Baltimore, Maryland, constantly challenge me to "walk the talk" with a solid foundation in Christ. Pastor Roger and Ann Kim and Pastor Bill and Michelle Nelson have guided my spiritual growth and helped me think through the role of the church in social justice and ethnic ministries.

And finally, my family, Mom, Dad and Charlie, have always been my biggest source of encouragement and strength. Their love for me and belief that I can make the greatest impact by living to glorify God in all that I do has allowed me to realize that only when I am less, can God be more. I love you tremendously in ways words can never fully express!

Jenny Hwang
Baltimore, Maryland

NOTES

Chapter 1: The Immigration Dilemma

[1] Quoted in Alex Kotlowitz, "Our Town," *New York Times Magazine*, August 5, 2007.

[2] Elvira Arellano, "Statement of Elvira Arellano on August 15, 2007," Los Angeles Independent Media Center, August 15, 2007, accessed September 10, 2007, at <la.indymedia.org/news/2007/08/205070.php>.

[3] Amy E. Black, *Beyond Left and Right: Helping Christians Make Sense of American Politics* (Grand Rapids: Baker Books, 2008), p. 160.

[4] C. S. Lewis, "The Weight of Glory," *The Weight of Glory: And Other Addresses* (New York: HarperCollins, 2001), p. 45.

Chapter 2: Aliens Among You

[1] Jeffrey S. Passel, "The Size and Characteristics of the Unauthorized Migrant Population in the U.S.: Estimates Based Upon the March 2005 Current Population Study," Pew Hispanic Center, March 7, 2006, accessed December 29, 2007, at <pewhispanic.org/files/reports/61.pdf>, p. 2.

[2] Quoted in Chuck Colson, "Defending the Stranger in Our Midst," Townhall.com, June 6, 2006, accessed December 27, 2007, at <www.townhall.com/columnists/ChuckColson/2006/06/09/defending_the_strangers_in_our_midst>.

[3] Ibid.

[4] David Leonhardt, "Truth, Fiction, and Lou Dobbs," *The New York Times*, May 30, 2007, C1.

[5] Ibid.

[6] Ibid.

[7] Amy Goodman, "Dobbs Needs to Follow His Own Advice," *The Seattle Post-Intelligencer*, December 6, 2007, B6.

[8] Leonhardt, "Truth, Fiction, and Lou Dobbs."

[9] James C. Russell, *Breach of Faith: American Churches and the Immigration Crisis* (Raleigh, N.C.: Representative Government Press, 2004), pp. 3-5.

[10]Quoted in David Holthouse, "Arizona Showdown: High-Powered Firearms, Militia Maneuvers and Racism at the Minutemen Project," Southern Poverty Law Center's Intelligence Report, Summer 2004, accessed December 28, 2007, at <www.splcenter.org /intel/intelreport/article.jsp?pid=915>.

[11]Colson, "Defending the Stranger in Our Midst."

[12]Christians for Comprehensive Immigration Reform, "A House Divided: Why Americans of Faith Are Concerned About Undocumented Immigrants," November 2007, accessed December 27, 2007 at <www.sojo.net/action/alerts/CCIR_T_giving_Report .pdf>, p. 4.

[13]Jeffrey S. Passel, "Growing Share of Immigrants Choosing Naturalization," Pew Hispanic Center, March 28, 2007, accessed December 28, 2007 at <pewhispanic.org/files/ reports/74.pdf>, p. i.

[14]United Nations Development Programme, *Human Development Report 2007/2008: Fighting Climate Change—Human Solidarity in a Divided World,* 2007, accessed December 29, 2007, at <hdr .undp.org/en/media/hdr_20072008_en_complete.pdf>, p. 238.

[15]Eduardo Porter, "Illegal Immigrants Are Bolstering Social Security with Billions," *The New York Times,* April 5, 2006, Business/Financial section, p. 1.

[16]Ibid.

[17]Quoted in Nina Bernstein, "Tax Filings Rise for Immigrants in U.S. Illegally," *The New York Times,* April 16, 2007, sec. A1.

[18]Ibid.

[19]Jacqueline Maria Hagan, "The Church vs. the State: Borders, Migrants, and Human Rights," in *Religion and Social Justice for Immigrants,* ed. Pierrette Hondagneu-Sotelo (New Brunswick, N.J.: Rutgers University Press, 2007), p. 93.

[20]Passel, "The Size and Characteristics of the Unauthorized Migrant Population in the U.S," p. 5.

[21]Roger Waldinger, "Between Here and There: How Attached Are Latino Immigrants to Their Native Country?" Pew Hispanic Center, October 25, 2007, accessed December 31, 2007, at <pewhispanic.org/files/reports/80.pdf>, p. 11.

[22]Ruth Ellen Wasem, "Unauthorized Aliens in the United States: Estimates Since 1986," Congressional Research Service, September 15, 2004, accessed December 31, 2007, at <fpc.state.gov/documents/organization/39561.pdf>, p. 6.

[23]Pew Hispanic Center, "Modes of Entry for the Unauthorized Migrant Population," May 22, 2006, accessed December 26, 2007, at <pewhispanic.org/files/factsheets/19.pdf>, p. 1.

[24]Passel, "The Size and Characteristics of the Unauthorized Migrant Population in the U.S," p. 5.

[25]Ibid.

[26]*Immigration & Nationality Act: An AILA Primary Source Reference* (Washington, D.C.: American

Immigration Lawyers Association, 2006); INA § 212(a)(9)(B)(i)(II) and INA § 212(a)(9)(B)(v). The Immigration & Nationality Act (INA) is also available online at <www.uscis.gov>.

[27]Passel, "The Size and Characteristics of the Unauthorized Migrant Population in the U.S.," p. 8.

[28]Shirin Hakimzadeh and D'Vera Cohn, "English Usage Among Hispanics in the United States," Pew Hispanic Center, November 29, 2007, accessed December 31, 2007, at <pewhispanic.org/files/reports/82.pdf>, p. 4.

[29]Michael Fix and Jeffrey Passel, "The Scope and Impact of Welfare Reform's Immigrant Provisions," The Urban Institute, January 2002, accessed April 26, 2008, at <www.urban .org/UploadedPDF/410412_discussion02-03.pdf>, p. 6; Federal Emergency Management Agency, "Questions and Answers for Undocumented Immigrants Regarding FEMA Assistance," June 17, 2004, accessed April 26, 2008 at <www.fema.gov/news/newsrelease .fema?id=12562>.

[30]Fix and Passsel, "The Scope and Impact of Welfare Reform's Immigrant Provisions," p. 6.

[31]8 CFR: Code of Federal Regulations, Aliens & Nationality: An AILA Primary Source Reference (Washington, D.C.: American Immigration Lawyers Association, 2004); 8 CFR § 213a.4. The Code of Federal Regulations: Aliens & Nationality (8 CFR) is also available online at <www.uscis.gov>.

[32]Jeffrey S. Passel, Randy Capps and Michael Fix, "Undocumented Immigrants: Facts and Figures," The Urban Institute, January 12, 2004, accessed April 26, 2008, at <www.urban .org/UploadedPDF/1000587_undoc_immigrants_facts.pdf>, p. 1.

Chapter 3: Nation of Immigrants

[1]Rob Bell, "The Wandering Aramean Part I" (Mars Hill Bible Church, Grandville, Mich., October 26, 2007), accessed December 24, 2007, at <www.marshill.org/teaching/ download.php?filename=MTAyODA3LmlwMw percent3D percent3D>.

[2]Ibid.

[3]Nancy Foner, From Ellis Island to JFK: New York's Two Great Waves of Immigration (New Haven, Conn.: Yale University Press, 2000), p. 3.

[4]Roger Daniels, Guarding the Golden Door: American Immigration Policy and Immigrants Since 1882 (New York: Hill and Wang, 2004), p. 6.

[5]Benjamin Franklin, Franklin: Writings, ed. J. A. Leo Lemay (New York: Library of America, 1987), p. 374.

[6] Emma Lazarus, Selected Poems, ed. John Hollander (New York: Library of America, 2005), p. 58.

[7]Quoted in Gerald Neuman, "The Lost Century of American Immigration Law: 1776-1875," Columbia Law Review 93, no. 8 (December 1993): 1859.

[8]Immigrant Legal Resource Center, A Guide for Immigration Advocates (San Francisco: Immigrant Legal Resource Center, 2006), 2:21-22.

[9]Quoted in Daniels, *Guarding the Golden Door*, p. 7.

[10]Daniel Kanstroom, *Deportation Nation: Outsiders in American History* (Cambridge, Mass.: Harvard University Press, 2007), p. 52.

[11]Stephen Behrendt, "Transatlantic Slavetrade," in *Africana: The Encyclopedia of the African and African American Experience*, ed. Kwame Anthony Appiah and Henry Louis Gates Jr. (New York: Basic Civitas Books, 1999), p. 1867.

[12]Marcus Lee Hanson, *The Immigrant in American History* (Cambridge, Mass.: Harvard University Press, 1940), p. 162.

[13]James Ciment, ed., *Encyclopedia of American Immigration: Volume 1* (Armonk, N.Y.: Sharpe Reference, 2001), pp. 67-68.

[14]Brian N. Fry, *Nativism and Immigration: Regulating the American Dream* (New York: LFB Scholarly Publishing, 2007), p. 39.

[15]Daniels, *Guarding the Golden Door*, p. 5.

[16]William Craig Brownlee, *Popery, an Enemy to Civil and Religious Liberty; And Dangerous to Our Republic* (New York: Charles K. Moore, 1839), p. 4.

[17]Fry, *Nativism and Immigration*, p. 39.

[18]Ibid., p. 41.

[19]Daniels, *Guarding the Golden Door*, p. 178.

[20]Ibid.

[21]Orlando Crespo, *Being Latino in Christ: Finding Wholeness in Your Ethnic Identity* (Downers Grove, Ill.: InterVarsity Press, 2003), p. 147.

[22]Quoted in Juan Gonzalez, *Harvest of Empire: A History of Latinos in America* (New York: Penguin Books, 2001), p. 44.

[23]Quoted in David Herbert Donald, *Lincoln* (New York: Touchstone, 1996), pp. 123-24.

[24]Daniels, *Guarding the Golden Door*, p. 176.

[25]Jean Pfaelzer, *Driven Out: The Forgotten War Against Chinese Americans* (New York: Random House, 2007), pp. 3-4.

[26]Quoted in Pfaelzer, *Driven Out*, pp. 4-5.

[27]Daniels, *Guarding the Golden Door*, p. 12.

[28]Ibid.

[29]Ibid.

[30]Pfaelzer, *Driven Out*, pp. 256, 259-64, 268-73.

[31]Ibid., p. 257.

[32]Ibid.

[33]Quoted in Daniels, *Guarding the Golden Door*, pp. 17-18.

[34]Daniels, *Guarding the Golden Door*, p. 19.

[35]Ibid., p. 3.

[36]Ibid., pp. 92-93.

[37]Ibid., p. 24.

[38]Fred Tsao, "Making Sense of the Immigration Debate" (Wheaton College, Wheaton, Ill.: October 19, 2006), accessed December 24, 2007, at <www.wheaton.edu/CACE/audio downloads /06FALLTsao.mp3>.

[39]Daniels, *Guarding the Golden Door*, pp. 5, 30.

[40]Foner, *From Ellis Island to JFK*, p. 19.

[41]Ibid., p. 20.

[42]Ibid., p. 22.

[43]Quoted in Foner, *From Ellis Island to JFK*, p. 23.

[44]Ibid., p. 22.

[45]Daniels, *Guarding the Golden Door*, p. 31.

[46]Michael C. LeMay, *Guarding the Gates: Immigration and National Security* (Westport, Conn.: Praeger Security International, 2006), p. 22.

[47]The Immigration Commission, *Reports of the Immigration Commission: Emigration Conditions in Europe* (Washington, D.C.: Government Printing Office, 1911), p. 209; Toni Young, *Becoming American, Remaining Jewish: The Story of Wilmington, Delaware's First Jewish Community, 1879-1924* (Cranbury, N.J.: Associated University Presses, 1999), p. 189.

[48]The Immigration Commission, *Brief Statement of the Investigations of the Immigration Commission, with Conclusions and Recommendations and Views of the Minority* (Washington, D.C.: Government Printing Office, 1911), p. 48.

[49]Daniels, *Guarding the Golden Door*, p. 46.

[50]Ibid., pp. 51-52.

[51]Ibid., p. 52.

[52]Ibid., p. 53.

[53]Gonzalez, *Harvest of Empire*, p. 103; Daniels, *Guarding the Golden Door*, p. 143.

[54]Richard Griswold del Castillo and Richard A. Garcia, *Cesar Chavez: A Triumph of the Spirit* (Norman: University of Oklahoma Press, 1995), p. 29.

[55]Fry, *Nativism and Immigration*, p. 39.

[56]Robert Seager II, "Some Denominational Reactions to Chinese Immigration to California, 1856-1892," *The Pacific Historical Review* 28, no. 1 (February 1959): 65.

[57]Lawrence B. Davis, *Immigrants, Baptists, and the Protestant Mind in America* (Urbana: University of Illinois Press, 1973), p. 42.

[58]Ibid., pp. 90-94.

[59]Ibid., pp. 127-28.

[60]Howard B. Grose, *The Incoming Millions* (New York: Fleming H. Revell, 1906), pp. 106-7.

[61]Davis, *Immigrants, Baptists, and the Protestant Mind*, p. 189.

[62]National Association of Evangelicals, "Statement on the Immigration Laws of 1965," accessed December 26, 2007, at <www.nae.net/index.cfm?FUSEACTION=editor.page&

pageID=208&IDCategory=9>.

[63]Douglas A. Sweeney, *The American Evangelical Story: A History of a Movement* (Grand Rapids: Baker Academic, 2005), p. 182.

[64]Quoted in David M. Reimers, *Still the Golden Door: The Third World Comes to America* (New York: Columbia University Press, 1985), p. 63.

[65]Ibid., p. 68.

[66]John F. Kennedy, *A Nation of Immigrants* (New York: Harper Torchbooks, 1964), p. 82.

[67]Reimers, *Still the Golden Door*, p. 67.

[68]Lyndon B. Johnson, "Remarks at the Signing of the Immigration Bill" (New York: October 3, 1965), accessed December 24, 2007, at <www.lbjlib.utexas.edu/Johnson/archives.hom/speeches.hom/651003.asp>.

Chapter 4: Immigrating the Legal Way

[1]National Park Service, "Ellis Island," June 28, 2006, accessed December 26, 2007, at <www.nps.gov/archive/stli/serv02.htm#Ellis>.

[2]INA § 212.

[3]Pew Hispanic Center, "Modes of Entry for the Unauthorized Migrant Population," p. 1.

[4]INA § 237.

[5]U.S. Citizenship and Immigration Service, "USCIS Holds White House Naturalization Ceremony," January 18, 2008, accessed January 22, 2008, at <www.uscis.gov/files/pressrelease/WH_Natz_Ceremony_01-16-2008.pdf>.

[6]INA § 203(b)(5).

[7]INA § 201(d).

[8]INA § 203(b).

[9]INA § 201(c).

[10]INA § 202(a)(2).

[11]U.S. Department of State, "Visa Bulletin for February 2008" 8, no. 115, accessed May 7, 2008, at <travel.state.gov/visa/frvi/bulletin/bulletin_3925.html>.

[12]Ibid.

[13]Ibid.

[14]Ibid.

[15]Ibid.

[16]Migration Policy Institute, "Backlogs in Immigration Processing Persist," *Immigration Facts* 10 (June 2005): 1.

[17]Spencer S. Hsu and Darryl Fears, "Immigration Application Fees to Rise by 80 Percent," *Washington Post*, January 31, 2007, sec. A03.

[18]Ibid.; Kevin McCoy, "Complaints Cause Delays in Increased INS Fees," *Daily News* (New York), August 7, 1998, p. 38.

[19]U.S. Department of State, "Diversity Visas Lottery 2009 (DV-2009) Results," accessed August 9, 2008, at <travel.state.gov/visa/immigrants/types/types_4317.html>.

[20]Ibid.

[21]United Nations High Commission for Refugees, "Convention Related to the Status of Refugees," December 14, 1950, accessed January 30, 2008 at, <www.unhchr.ch/html/menu3/b/o_c_ref.htm>; see also INA § 101(a)(42).

[22]United Nations High Commission for Refugees, "UNHCR Global Report 2006," accessed January 22, 2008, at <www.unhcr.org/publ/PUBL/4666d25b0.pdf>.

[23]George W. Bush, "Presidential Determination No. 2008-29 of September 20, 2008," *Federal Register* 73, no. 5 (October 7, 2008); U.S. Department of State, Bureau of Population, Refugees, and Migration, "Emergency Refugee and Migration Assistance: Fiscal Year 2007," accessed January 29, 2008, at <www.state.gov/g/prm/rls/rpt/2006/66292.htm>.

[24]U.S. Office of Refugee Resettlement, "Fiscal Year 2006 Refugee Arrivals: By Country of Origin and State of Initial Resettlement for FY 2006," accessed January 29, 2008, at <www.acf.hhs.gov/programs/orr/data/fy2006RA.htm>.

[25]Dana Wilbanks, *Re-Creating America: The Ethics of U.S. Immigration & Refugee Policy in a Christian Perspective* (Nashville: Abingdon, 1996), p. 161.

[26]Kelly Jefferys, "Annual Flow Report: U.S. Legal Permanent Residents: 2006," U.S. Department of Homeland Security Office of Immigration Statistics, March 2007, accessed January 29, 2008, at <www.dhs.gov/xlibrary/assets/statistics/publications/IS-4496_LPR FlowReport_04vaccessible.pdf>.

Chapter 5: Thinking Biblically About Immigration

[1]R. J. D. Knauth, "Alien, Foreign Resident," in *Dictionary of the Old Testament: Pentateuch*, ed. David W. Baker and T. Desmond Alexander (Downers Grove, Ill.: InterVarsity Press, 2003), p. 29.

[2]Ethan Kapstein, "The New Global Slave Trade," *Foreign Affairs*, November/December 2006, p. 105.

[3]Justo L. Gonzalez, *Santa Biblia: The Bible Through Hispanic Eyes* (Nashville: Abingdon, 1996), pp. 96-97.

[4]M. Daniel Carroll R., *Christians at the Border: Immigration, the Church, and the Bible* (Grand Rapids: Baker Academic, 2008), p. 102.

Chapter 6: Concerns About Immigration

[1]Deut 15:11; Ps 82:3; Prov 14:31; Amos 5:12; Mt 19:21; Lk 12:33; and Gal 2:10, among many others.

[2]Carol Swain, "Love Thy Neighbor: Main Issues in Contemporary Immigration Debates" (Center for Applied Christian Ethics Spring 2006 Conference, Wheaton College,

Wheaton, Ill., March 23, 2006), accessed December 26, 2007, at <www.wheaton.edu/CACE/audiodownloads/06SCONCarolSwain2.mp3>.

[3]James Edwards, "Seeking Biblical Principles to Inform Immigration Policy," *Christianity Today,* September 2006, accessed November 1, 2007, at <www.christianitytoday.com/ct/2006/septemberweb-only/138-32.0.html>.

[4]Louis Uchitelle, "Nafta Should Have Stopped Illegal Immigration, Right?" *The New York Times,* February 18, 2007, section 4, p. 4.

[5]Krissah Williams, "An Advocate Rallies to Unify GOP," *Washington Post,* May 21, 2007, sec. A1.

[6]Quoted in Rob Reuteman, "Hiring Woes at Cargill Tied to Tougher Laws," *Rocky Mountain News,* May 9, 2008, accessed May 10, 2008, at <www.rockymountainnews.com/news/2008/may/09/reuteman-hiring-woes-at-cargill-tied-to-tougher/>.

[7]John Cobb, ed., *Progressive Christians Speak: A Different Voice of Faith and Politics* (Louisville, Ky.: Westminster John Knox Press, 2003), p. 160.

[8]Jim Jewell, "New Evangelicals: Green, Not Liberal," *The Atlanta Journal-Constitution,* August 31, 2007, sec. 15A.

[9]G. Marland, T. A. Boden and R. J. Andres, "Global, Regional, and National CO2 Emissions," *Trends: A Compendium of Data on Global Change,* Carbon Dioxide Information Analysis Center, Oak Ridge National Laboratory, U.S. Department of Energy, accessed October 15, 2007, at <cdiac.esd.ornl.gov/trends/emis/tre_coun.htm>.

[10]Mike Glover, "Buchanan Names New Campaign Head," Associated Press Wire, April 28, 1999.

[11]Eunice Moscoso, "As Immigration Booms, so Do English Classes," *Austin American-Statesman,* August 25, 2006, sec. A12.

[12]Patrick Buchanan, *State of Emergency: The Third World Invasion and Conquest of America* (New York: St. Martin's Press, 2006), p. 146.

[13]Quoted in Jonathan Alter and Michael Isikoff, "The Beltway Populist," *Newsweek,* March 4, 1996, p. 26.

[14]Alberto Guerra, "Immigration Issues and the Church's Response," (Missions on Your Doorstep conference, Wheaton Bible Church, Wheaton, Ill., March 1, 2008).

[15]Ibid.

[16]U.S. Constitution, Amendment 14.

[17]INA § 212(a)(9)(B)(i)(II).

[18]Passel, "The Size and Characteristics of the Unauthorized Migrant Population in the U.S.," p. 8.

[19]INA § 203.

[20]Lindsay Lowell and Micah Bump, "Projecting Immigrant Visas: Report on an Experts Meeting," October 2006, Georgetown University Institute for the Study of International

Migration, accessed June 10, 2008, at <isim.georgetown.edu/Publications/SloanMaterials/ Lowell, ProjectionsWorkshop.pdf>, p. 6.

[21]Family Research Council, "Marriage & Family" accessed on June 9, 2008, at <www.frc .org/marriage-family>.

[22]Translation by George Grant, *The Micah Mandate: Balancing the Christian Life* (Nashville: Cumberland House Publishing, 1999), p. 8, 10.

[23]Edwards, "Seeking Biblical Principles to Inform Immigration Policy."

[24]John Howard Yoder, *The Politics of Jesus* (Grand Rapids: Eerdmans, 1972), p. 207.

[25]Evangelical Project for Public Engagement, National Association of Evangelicals, *For the Health of the Nation: An Evangelical Call to Civic Responsibility,* 2004, accessed December 26, 2007, at <www.nae.net/images/civic_responsibility2.pdf>, pp. 8, 10.

[26]Pew Research Center for the People and the Press, "Strong Support for Stem Cell Research: Abortion and Rights of Terror Suspects Top Court Issues," August 3, 2005, accessed September 15, 2007, at <people-press.org/reports/pdf/253.pdf>.

[27]Swain, "Love Thy Neighbor: Main Issues in Contemporary Immigration Debates."

[28]Rob Bugh and Al Guerra, "Reporting of Illegal Immigrants Opposed," letter to the editor, *The Daily Herald,* April 20, 2006, news section, p. 14.

[29]Ronald J. Sider, "Justice, Human Rights, and Government" in *Toward an Evangelical Public Policy,* ed. Ronald J. Sider and Diane Knippers (Grand Rapids: Baker Books, 2005), p. 177.

[30]Carroll R., *Christians at the Border,* p. 95.

Chapter 7: The Value of Immigration to the United States

[1]Doris Meissner, *Immigration and America's Future: A New Chapter* (Washington, D.C.: Migration Policy Institute, 2006), p. 1.

[2]Susan B. Carter and Richard Sutch, "Historical Perspectives on the Economic Consequences of Immigration into the United States," in *The Handbook of International Migration: The American Experience,* ed. Charles Hirschman, Philip Kasinitz and Josh DeWind (New York: Russell Sage Foundation, 1999), p. 319.

[3]Betty W. Su, "The U.S. Economy to 2016: Slower Growth as Boomers Begin to Retire," *Monthly Labor Review* 130, no. 11 (November 2007): 13.

[4]Mitra Toossi, "Labor Force Projections to 2016: More Workers in Their Golden Years," *Monthly Labor Review* 130, no. 11 (November 2007): 33.

[5]Arlene Dohm and Lynn Schniper, "Occupational Employment Projections to 2016," *Monthly Labor Review* 130, no. 11 (November 2007): 87.

[6]Hugh Morton, "Housing Short-Handed Without Immigrant Workers," *Nation's Building News,* July 31, 2006, accessed January 18, 2008, at <www.nahb.org/news_details.aspx ?newsID=3010>.

[7]Tim Annett, "Illegal Immigrants and the Economy: Undocumented Workers Reduce the

Wages of Low-Income Workers; But How Much?" *The Wall Street Journal*, April 13, 2006, accessed September 3, 2008, at <online.wsj.com/public/article/SB114477669441223067 -sEhMH8CUN7F7ukBMWULwRxqTLNU_20070413.html?mod=tff_main_tff_top>.

[8]Roger Lowenstein, "The Immigration Equation," *The New York Times Magazine*, July 9, 2006, p. 36.

[9]Michael Fix and Jeffrey S. Passel, *Immigration and Immigrants: Setting the Record Straight* (Washington, D.C.: The Urban Institute, 1994), p. 58.

[10]Stephen Moore, *A Fiscal Portrait of the Newest Americans* (Washington, D.C.: Cato Institute and the National Immigration Forum, 1998), p. 20.

[11]George Borjas and Lawrence Katz, "The Evolution of the Mexican-Born Workforce in the United States," National Bureau of Economic Research Working Paper 11281 (April 2005): 37.

[12]George Borjas, *Heaven's Door: Immigration Policy and the American Economy* (Princeton, N.J.: Princeton University Press, 2005), p. 37.

[13]Julia Preston, "Short on Labor, Farmers in U.S. Shift to Mexico," *The New York Times*, September 5, 2007, sec. A1.

[14]David Card, "Is the New Immigration Really So Bad?" Institute for the Study of Labor (IZA) Discussion Paper 1119 (April 2004): 16.

[15]Eric Schlosser, "Penny Foolish," *The New York Times*, November 29, 2007.

[16]Eduardo Porter, "Cost of Illegal Immigration May Be Less Than Meets the Eye," *The New York Times*, April 16, 2006, accessed September 3, 2008, at <www.nytimes.com/2006/04/16/ business/yourmoney/16view.html?_r=1&scp=1&sq=eduardo%20porter%20cost%20 of%20illegal%20immigration&st=cse&oref=slogin>.

[17]Tamar Jacoby, "Immigrant Nation," *Foreign Affairs*, November/December 2006.

[18]I. P. Gianmarco and Peri Giovanni, "Rethinking the Gains from Immigration: Theory and Evidence from the U.S.," National Bureau of Economic Research Working Paper 11672 (September 2005): 12-13.

[19]Michael R. Bloomberg, Mayor, City of New York, Testimony before the Committee on the Judiciary, United States Senate, July 5, 2006, accessed January 30, 2008, at <judiciary .senate.gov/testimony.cfm?id=1983&wit_id=5493>.

[20]"Making the World's Information Accessible," *Academy of Achievement*, October 28, 2000, accessed May 12, 2008, at <www.achievement.org/autodoc/page/pag0int-1>.

[21]Gary D. MacDonald, Kingston Technology, testimony before the Immigration Subcommittee, United States Senate, Washington, D.C., April 15, 1997.

[22]Max Alexander, "An Illegal Immigrant Turned Brain Surgeon—with His Own Two Hands," *Reader's Digest*, February 2008, accessed September 3, 2008, at <www.rd.com /illegal-immigrant-turned-brain-surgeon/article51808.html>.

[23]Neeraj Kaushal and Michael Fix, "The Contributions of High-Skilled Immigrants,"

Migration Policy Institute Insight 16 (July 2006): 1.

[24]David H. Autor, Lawrence F. Katz and Melissa S. Kearney, "The Polarization of the U.S. Labor Market," National Bureau of Economic Research, Working Paper 11986 (January 2006).

[25]Arlene Dohm and Lynn Shniper, "Occupational Employment Projections to 2016," p. 4.

[26]National Science Board, "The Science and Engineering Workforce: Realizing America's Potential," National Science Board 03-69 (August 14, 2003): 9.

[27]Quoted in "U.S. Venture Capitalists Investing in Immigrant Businesses," November 27, 2006, accessed on December 14, 2007, at <www.workpermit.com/news/2006_11_27/us/ immigrant_business_venture_capital.htm>.

[28]William A. Wulf, President, National Academy of Engineering, the National Academies, "The Importance of Foreign-Born Scientists and Engineers to the Security of the United States," testimony before the Subcommittee on Immigration, Border Security, and Claims, United States House of Representatives, Washington, D.C., September 15, 2005, accessed January 30, 2008, at <www7.nationalacademies.org/ocga/testimony/ Importance_of_Foreign_Scientists_and_Engineers_to_US.asp>.

[29]Stuart Anderson and Michaela Platzer, "American Made: The Impact of Immigrant Entrepreneurs and Professionals on U.S. Competitiveness," National Venture Capital Association (November 2006): 6-7, accessed September 3, 2008, at <www.nvca.org/pdf/ AmericanMade_study.pdf>.

[30]William H. Gates, Testimony before the Committee on Health, Education, Labor, and Pensions, United States Senate, Washington, D.C., March 7, 2007, accessed January 30, 2008, at <help.senate.gov/Hearings/2007_03_07/Gates.pdf>.

[31]United Nations Children's Fund, "The State of the World's Children 2008: Child Survival," December 2007, p. 76.

[32]Richard B. Freeman, "Does Globalization of the Scientific/Engineering Workforce Threaten US Economic Leadership?" National Bureau of Economic Research Working Paper 11457 (July 2005).

[33]National Science Board, "Higher Education in Science and Engineering," in *Science and Engineering Indicators 2008*, 2 vols. (Arlington, Va.: National Science Foundation, 2008), 1:44.

[34]Inter-American Development Bank, *Sending Money Home: Leveraging the Development Impact of Remittances* (Washington, D.C.: Inter-American Bank), p. 4.

[35]Ibid.

[36]World Bank, "Income Generation and Social Protection for the Poor" (World Bank, 2004), p. 150.

[37]Pablo Fajnzylber and J. Humberto Lopez, "Close to Home: The Development Impact of Remittances in Latin America" (World Bank, 2007), p. 15.

[38]Richard H. Adams Jr. and John Page, "Do International Migration and Remittances Reduce Poverty in Developing Countries?" *World Development* 33, no. 10 (2005): 1645.

[39]Douglas Massey, "Five Myths About Immigration: Common Misconceptions Underlying U.S. Border-Enforcement Policy," *Immigration Policy in Focus* 4, no. 6 (August 2005): 5.

[40]International Organization for Migration, "International Migration Trends," *World Migration 2005* (Geneva, Switzerland: International Organization for Migration, 2005), p. 380.

[41]Ibid.

[42]James B. Davies, Susanna Sandstrom, Anthony Shorrocks and Edward N. Wolff, "The World Distribution of Household Wealth," United Nations University-Wider, December 5, 2006, p. 26.

[43]Ibid., p. 27

[44]Massey, "Five Myths About Immigration," p. 1.

[45]Tim Amstutz, *A Church Leader's Guide to Immigration* (Baltimore: World Relief National Immigration Resource Network, 2003), p. 3.

[46]Richard Mouw, *When the Kings Come Marching In* (Grand Rapids: Eerdmans, 2002), p. 11.

[47]Orlando Crespo, "Our Transnational Anthem." *Christianity Today* 50, no. 8 (2006): 32.

[48]Ibid.

[49]Richard Beattie, "Immigrant Art Exhibitions: Insights of Passage," *The New York Times*, May 19, 2006, sec. F2.

[50]John F. Kennedy, *A Nation of Immigrants* (New York: Harper Perennial, 2008), p. 36.

[51]Meissner, *Immigration and America's Future*, p. 13.

[52]Roger M. Mahoney, "The Challenge of 'We the People' in a Post-9/11 World: Immigration, the American Economy and the Constitution" (The Fifth Annual John M. Templeton, Jr. Lecture on the Constitution and Economic Liberty, Philadelphia, Penn., May 8, 2007).

Chapter 8: The Politics and Policies of Immigration Reform

[1]M. Daniel Carroll R. *Christians at the Border* (Grand Rapids: Baker Academic, 2008), p. 92.

[2]President George W. Bush, "President Signs Homeland Security Appropriations Act for 2006," October 18, 2005, accessed January 30, 2008, at <www.whitehouse.gov/news/releases/2005/10/20051018-2.html>.

[3]David Aguilar, testimony before the House Committee on the Judiciary, Washington, D.C., March 30, 2007, accessed on June 1, 2008 at <judiciary.house.gov/OversightTestimony.aspx?ID=814>.

[4]Alison Siskin et al., "Immigration Enforcement Within the United States," Congressional Research Service, April 6, 2006, p. 8.

[5]House bill HR 4437, Title II, Section 202, accessed on June 1, 2008, at <thomas.loc.gov/

cgi-bin/query/F?c109:11:./temp/~mdbsAXVZqS:e31959:>.

[6]Roger Mahoney, "Called by God to Help," *The New York Times*, March 22, 2006, accessed September 3, 2008, at <www.nytimes.com/2006/03/22/opinion/22mahony.html?scp =13&sq=cardinal%20mahoney&st=cse>.

[7]Editorial, "The Gospel vs. H.R. 4437," *The New York Times*, March 3, 2006.

[8]Richard Land, statement during a Capitol Hill Press Conference, Washington, D.C., September 26, 2006.

[9]Merriam-Webster's Online Dictionary, accessed January 30, 2008, s.v. "amnesty," at <www.m-w.com/dictionary/amnesty>.

[10]Richard Land, "Immigration Reform and Southern Baptists," April 3, 2007, accessed December 10, 2007, at <erlc.com/article/statement-by-richard-land-on-truly-comprehensive -immigration-reform>.

[11]*Time* magazine/SRBI, "January 24-26, 2006 Survey," January 27, 2006, accessed January 30, 2008, at <www.srbi.com/TimePoll3738-Final percent20Report-2006-01-27--8.05am.pdf>.

[12]Lake Research Partners and The Tarrance Group, "Key Findings from a Nationwide Survey of Registered Likely Voters," March 2006, accessed January 30, 2008, at <www .immigrationforum.org/documents/PressRoom/Summaryof3-06 percent20Poll.pdf>.

[13]Federation for American Immigration Reform website, accessed on June 2, 2008, at <www.fairus.org/site/PageServer?pagename=about_aboutlist1ce5>.

[14]Paul Taylor and Richard Fry, "Hispanics and the 2008 Election: A Swing Vote?" Pew Hispanic Center, December 6, 2007, p. 21.

[15]Pew Hispanic Center, "Latinos and the 2006 Mid-Term Elections," November 27, 2006, accessed November 20, 2007 at <pewhispanic.org/files/factsheets/26.pdf>.

[16]Stephen Kaufman, "Hispanic Americans' Political Clout Expected to Increase," U.S. State Department International Information Programs, October 11, 2007, accessed November 20, 2007, at <usinfo.state.gov/xarchives/display.html?p=washfile-english&x= 20071011113828esnamfuak0.9106256>.

[17]Charlie Savage, "Hispanic Evangelical Offering GOP a Bridge to Future," *Boston Globe*, March 6, 2006.

[18]*The New York Times*/CBS News, "Poll: May 19-23, 2007," accessed December 9, 2007, at <graphics8.nytimes.com/packages/pdf/national/20070525poll.pdf>.

[19]Kathy Kiely, "Public Favors Giving Illegal Immigrants a Break," *USA Today*, April 18, 2007.

[20]National Conference of State Legislatures, "State Laws Related to Immigrants and Immigration: January 1–June 30, 2008," accessed Septermber 3, 2008, at <www.ncsl.org/ print/immig/immigreportjuly2008.pdf>.

Chapter 9: The Church and Immigration Today

[1]Presbyterian Church USA, "Racial Ethnic Church Growth," accessed January 30, 2008,

at <www.pcusa.org/immigrant/pdf/growth-strategy.pdf>.

[2]International Mission Board, "Immigration: An Opportunity to Reach the Unreached," accessed January 2, 2008, at <www.sbc.net/redirect.asp?url=http percent3A percent2F percent2Fwww percent2Eimb percent2Eorg percent2Fcore percent2Fstory percent2Easp percent3FLanguageID percent3D1709 percent26StoryID percent3D726&key=minoritie s&title=Immigrationpercent3A+an+opportunity+to+reach+the+unreached+ perce nt2D+International+Mission+Board percent2C+SBC&ndx=SBC percent2C+IMB percent2C+NAMB percent2C+ANNUITY percent2C+LIFEWAY percent2C+WMU percent2C+ERLC percent2C+SEMINARIES>.

[3]Mickey Noah, "North American People Groups NAMB/IMB Website Launched," February 7, 2007, accessed January 29, 2008, at <www.bpnews.net/bpnews.asp?ID=24916>.

[4]North American Mission Board, *Annual Ministry Report 2007*, accessed January 30, 2008, at <www.namb.net/site/c.9qKILUOzEpH/b.245607/k.A9D1/Annual_Report.htm>.

[5]Jerry Porter, "Immigration: A Global and US Challenge," *MissionStrategy.org Magazine* (Summer 2007): 2.

[6]Joan Huyser-Honig, "New Ethnic Churches: Visit One Soon," Calvin Institute of Christian Worship, accessed January 27, 2008, at <www.calvin.edu/worship/stories/crc_ethnic.php>.

[7]Phone interview with author Jenny Hwang on January 25, 2008.

[8]E-mail correspondence with author Jenny Hwang on December 6, 2007.

[9]Todd Johnson, "USA Evangelicals/evangelicals in a Global Context," *Lausanne World Pulse* (January 2006), accessed September 3, 2008, at <www.lausanneworldpulse.com/pdf/issues/LWP0106.pdf>, p. 34.

[10]Conversation with author Jenny Hwang on December 18, 2007.

[11]Phone interview with author Jenny Hwang on January 25, 2008.

[12]Ibid.

[13]Jane Norman, "Immigrants Feel Distress, Shock, Nun Says," *Des Moines Register,* May 21, 2008, accessed September 3, 2008, at <www.desmoinesregister.com/apps/pbcs.dll/article?AID=/20080521/NEWS/805210358>.

[14]Interfaith Statement on Comprehensive Immigration Reform, October 18, 2005, accessed January 29, 2008, at <www.usccb.org/mrs/interfaith.shtml>.

[15]Jack Hayford, "Statement on Church and Immigration," accessed January 30, 2008, at <www.churchandimmigration.org/statements.htm>.

[16]Colson, "Defending the Stranger in our Midst."

[17]Southern Baptist Convention Resolutions, "Resolution 6. On the Crisis of Illegal Immigration," June 2006, accessed January 30, 2008, at <www.sbc.net/resolutions/amResolution.asp?ID=1157>.

[18]Luis Cortes, "An Open Letter to Evangelical Leaders on Comprehensive Immigration

Reform," accessed January 30, 2008, at <www.esperanza.us/atf/cf/ percent7bB793CA9C-D2B9-4E02-886B-E6DE52E04944 percent7d/Open percent20Letter percent20to percent 20Evangelicals.pdf>.

[19]Tim Stafford, "The Call of Samuel," *Christianity Today* 50, no. 9 (September 2006): 82.

[20]Korean Resource Center Los Angeles, "Letter to Feinstein on S.1348," accessed on June 9, 2008, at < krcla.org/blog/365/>.

[21]John M. Perkins, "Statement on Church and Immigration," accessed January 30, 2008, at <www.churchandimmigration.com/statements.htm>.

[22]Roberta Combs, "Washington Weekly Review: April 7, 2006," accessed January 30, 2008, at <www.cc.org/content.cfm?srch=immigration>.

[23]National Association of Evangelicals, "Resolution on Immigration," October 12, 2006, accessed January 30, 2008, at <www.nae.net/images/Resolution percent20on percent-t20Immigration percent20- percent20October percent202006.pdf>.

[24]Gregory A. Smith, "Attitudes Toward Immigration: In the Pulpit and the Pew," Pew Forum on Religion and Public Life, April 26, 2006.

Chapter 10: A Christian Response to the Immigration Dilemma

[1]Dietrich Bonhoeffer, *The Cost of Discipleship* (New York: Touchstone, 1995), p. 58.

[2]Henri Nouwen, Donald McNeill and Douglas Morrison, *Compassion: Reflections on the Christian Life* (New York: Doubleday, 1982), pp. 104, 116.

[3]Ibid., p. 104.

[4]Ibid., p. 109.

[5]Mary Pipher, *The Middle of Everywhere: The World's Refugees Come to Our Town* (New York: Harcourt, 2002), p. 331.

[6]Quoted in Nigel Rees, *Brewer's Famous Quotations: 5000 Quotations and the Stories Behind Them* (London: Weidenfeld & Nicolson, 2006), p. 119.

[7]National Association of Evangelicals, "For the Health of the Nation: An Evangelical Call to Civic Responsibility," accessed January 21, 2008, at <www.nae.net/images/civic_responsibility2.pdf>, pp. 2-3.

INDEX

Abel, 52

abortion, 110

Abraham, 83-84, 106

Abram. *See* Abraham

Abundant Life Church, 164

abuse, 39, 40

Achish (king of Gath), 85

Adams, John, 50

adjustment of status, 67-68, 76, 77

advocacy, 21, 60, 161, 177, 181-84, 193, 194, 205, 211, 212

Afghanistan, 79, 158

Africa, 37, 50, 62, 63, 79, 84, 86, 133, 165, 184

African American churches, 163, 172

African Americans, 16, 18, 90, 94, 157, 174. *See also* African American churches

aging of American workforce, 118-19

AgJOB. *See* Agricultural Job Opportunities, Benefits, and Securities Act

Agricultural Job Opportunities, Benefits, and Security Act, 143, 147, 155

agriculture, 56, 58, 59, 95, 116, 122, 123, 143

Aguilar, David, 144

Air Force, 30

Albright, Madeleine, 135

Albuquerque, New Mexico, 36

Aleman, Samuel, 166

Alexander II, Czar, 56

alien, 22

Alien and Sedition Acts of 1798, 50

amnesty, 79, 112, 142, 148-49, 151

anchor babies, 103-5

ancient Near Eastern law, 88

Anderson, Leith, 10, 169

anti-semitism, 56

Apostolic church, 41

Arellano, Elvira, 12

Arizona, 26, 30, 31, 32, 52, 152, 154

art, 135

Artaxerxes, 85

Arthur, Chester A., 54

Asia, 37, 47, 57, 62, 63, 65, 165, 184

Asia Pacific countries, 131

Asian American churches, 171

Asian immigrants, 17, 37, 55, 89, 90, 126, 134, 157

asylum, 39, 78, 105

Atlanta, Georgia, 159, 166

Atlantic Ocean, 9

Austin, Texas, 38

Australia, 131-32

baby boomers, 118

backlogs, 76

Baltimore, Maryland, 21, 167

Baptists, 60. *See also* Southern Baptist Convention

Beck, Roy, 150

Bell, Rob, 45-46

Bergdorff, Peter, 169

Berlin Wall, 145

Bible, 9, 17, 22, 24, 63, 81, 82, 83, 86, 88, 89, 91, 93, 94, 96, 100, 101, 106,107, 108, 109, 112, 113, 134, 137, 139, 166, 175, 117, 181, 184, 186, 189, 194, 195, 198, 207, 208, 214

Bin Laden, Osama, 152

birthright citizenship, 103-5

Black, Amy, 13

Bloomberg, Michael, 124

Board of Immigration Appeals, 38

Boaz, 85

Boca Raton, Florida, 9

Bonhoeffer, Dietrich, 177

Bonilla, Eliezer, 164, 165

border, 11, 15, 24, 30, 31, 33, 35, 36, 37, 51, 52,

62, 67, 75, 77, 83-85, 90, 93, 94, 96, 98, 103,
110-13, 125, 133, 137-41, 143-45, 147, 149-52,
154, 157, 168, 169, 172, 173, 184, 198, 207, 210
border patrol. *See* border security
Border Protection, Anti-terrorism, and
Illegal Immigration Control Act of 2005.
See HR 4437
border security, 31, 33, 35-36, 37, 98, 110-11,
140, 141, 143, 144, 147, 149, 151, 169
Borjas, George, 121-22
bracero program, 59
brain drain, 128
brain overflow, 128
Brazil, 115
Brin, Sergey, 125
Brownback, Sam, 151
Buchanan, Patrick, 99-100
Buddhism, 168
Bugh, Rob, 112
Burma, 18, 79
Burundi, 18, 79
Bush, George W., 78, 140, 151, 152, 153,
157, 197
California, 26, 27, 35, 40, 43, 52, 53, 54, 56,
115, 122, 126, 145, 146
Cambodia, 79, 161
Canaan, 83
Canada, 9, 37, 67, 74, 78, 89, 95, 132, 141
immigrants from, 58
Canton, 53
Caribbean, 100
Carpentersville, Illinois, 11
Carroll Rodas, Daniel, 88, 139
Catholic. *See* Roman Catholic Church
Catholic Charities USA, 161
Cato Institute, 121
Caucasian, 18, 90, 171, 173
Center for the Study of Global Christianity,
164-65
Central America, 17, 67, 79, 100

immigrants from, 36-37, 116
chain migration, 105-6, 155
Chavez, Cesar, 59
Chicago, Illinois, 12, 16, 31, 39, 43, 70, 146
Chihuahua, Mexico, 36
Child Status Protection Act, 73
children, 40, 72, 73, 77
Chile, 30
China, 74, 75, 78, 128
immigrants from, 53-55, 124
Chinese Exclusion Act, 48, 54, 60
Christian Coalition of America, 100, 169,
172
Christian Community Development
Association, 172
Christian Reformed Church of North
America, 163-64, 169
Christianity Today, 169
Christians at the Border (Carroll Rodas), 139
Christians for Comprehensive Immigration
Reform, 170
church, 24-25, 60, 81, 159-75, 180-81
Church of God (denomination), 164
Church of the Nazarene, 163
Church of the People. *See* Iglesia del Pueblo
Church World Service, 160
citizenship, 66, 69, 89
civil disobedience, 110
civil rights movement, 61, 110
Civil War, 49
Cizik, Richard, 11
climate change, 97
CNN, 27-28
college, 41-43
Colorado, 52, 93, 96, 157
Colorado Association of Commerce and
Industry, 96
Colson, Charles, 27-28, 168
Combs, Roberta, 172
complementarity, 123-25

Comprehensive Immigration Reform Act
of 2006. *See* S.2611
Comprehensive Immigration Reform Act
of 2007, 154-56
Comprehensive Immigration Reform,
principles of, 140-43
conflict-free diamonds, 185
Congo, Democratic Republic of, 14
CONLAMIC. *See* National Coalition of
Latino Clergy and Christian Leaders
Cornelius, 100
Cortes, Luis, 171
Costa Rica, 17
coyotes, 15, 31-32, 33, 37, 70
creation care, 96-97
criminals, 27-28, 67, 75, 98
Cuba, 67, 79
immigrants from, 79
cultural homogeneity, 99-100
Dallas, Texas, 146
Daniels, Roger, 47, 54
David, 84, 106, 181
Davis, Lawrence B., 60
De la Renta, Oscar, 135
Declaration of Independence, 135
Democracy in America (de Tocqueville), 135
Democrats, 26, 49, 150, 151-53, 157
Denver, Colorado, 159
Department of Homeland Security, 76, 147
Department of Justice, 38, 123
Department of Labor, 71
Department of State, 75
deportation, 68, 165, 171, 173
Development, Relief, and Education for
Alien Minors Act, 143, 147, 155
Dillingham Commission Reports, 57
Dillingham, William, 57
diversity, 133
immigration, 77-78
lottery. *See* diversity immigration

Dobbs, Lou, 27
Domingo, Placido, 135
DREAM Act. *See* Development, Relief, and
Education for Alien Minors Act
driver's licenses, 33, 138-39
drugs, 28, 41
earned legalization, 142, 147-48
eastern Europe, 55, 63, 79
economists, 119-20
education, 33, 41-42, 116
Edwards, James, 94, 108
Egypt, 45-46, 63, 83, 84-85, 86, 101-2, 134
El Paso, Texas, 35-36
El Salvador, 36-37, 78
elections
of 2006, 11, 148, 151-53
of 2008, 156-58
Ellis Island, 23, 47, 55, 63, 64-65
emissions, 97
employer verification, 34, 142, 154
employment-based immigration, 29, 71-72
enforcement-only bills, 143-46
England, 58, 78
English, 41, 68, 99-100, 129, 136, 148, 164
as official language, 99
as a Second Language, 60, 99, 136, 161,
166, 179
environmental degradation, 96-97, 184-85
Episcopal Church USA, 167
Episcopal Migration Ministries, 160
Esperanza USA, 170-71
Espin, Orlando, 82
Esther, 181
Ethiopian pilgrim, 86
Europe, 37, 47, 57, 62, 99, 131, 129, 132-33
immigration from, 50-51, 53, 55-56
Evangelical Free Church of America, 159,
162, 169
Evangelical Lutheran Church in America,
167

evangelicals, 16, 24-25, 40, 61, 96, 168-73
Evangelicals for Social Action, 113, 169
Ewing, Patrick, 135
Executive Office for Immigration Review, 38
Face the Nation (CBS News), 64
FAIR. *See* Federation for American Immigration Reform
fair-trade coffee, 185
false documents, 32, 34-35, 70, 197
family, 106-7
Family Research Council, 93, 107, 173
family-based immigration, 30, 72-77, 105-7, 141, 155-56
famine, 50
fatherless. *See* orphans
fear, 102, 160, 167
federal government, 120-21
Federalist Party, 50
Federation for American Immigration Reform (FAIR), 149
fees. *See* filing fees
Feinstein, Dianne, 171
fence, 144
filing fees, 76
Filipino immigrants, 37-39, 73-75
First Baptist Hispanic Church of Metro Atlanta. *See* Primera Iglesia Bautista Hispana de Metro Atlanta
first preference (family-based immigration), 73
Fix, Michael, 120
Flake, Jeff, 154
Florida, 9, 26, 56, 123, 157, 169
Focus on the Family, 173
Foner, Nancy, 47
food stamps. *See* public benefits
"For the Health of the Nation: An Evangelical Call to Civic Responsibility," 182

Ford Motor Company, 19
Fort Worth, Texas, 161
Fountain Valley, California, 126
fourteenth amendment, 69, 103
fourth preference (family-based immigration), 75
Fox, Michael J., 135
France, 50, 58
Franklin, Benjamin, 48, 49
fraud, 55
Frisco, Colorado, 159
Gad, 98
Gates, Bill, 127
Gath, 85
Gaza, 86
Gentile, 89-90, 100, 134
Georgia, 159, 166
ger, 82-83
Germany, 58
immigrants from, 48, 50, 60
Ghana, 74, 128
Giffords, Gabrielle, 26
giving, 179-80
Global South, 95, 97, 184
globalization, 118, 131-32
gold rush, 53
Gonzales, Javier, 166
González, Justo, 84
Google, Inc., 125, 127
Gordon-Conwell Theological Seminary, 108-9
grace, 46, 89, 112, 114. *See also* amnesty
Grant, Ulysses, 52
green card. *See* Lawful Permanent Resident
Grose, Howard, 60
Guatemala, 37, 79
Guerra, Al, 112
Guerrero, Mexico, 70
guest worker program, 147
Gutierrez, Luis, 154

Haiti, 9, 78, 130

Hamel, William, 169

Hansen's Disease. *See* leprosy

Haran, 83

Harlingen, Texas, 111

Harvard Medical School, 126

Harvard University, 56

Hayek, Salma, 135

Hayford, Jack, 168

health care, 16, 27, 42, 64, 75, 117-18

Hebrew Scriptures. *See* Old Testament

Herod, 85

Herrera, Carolina, 135

high-tech jobs, 126-29

Hispanics, 37, 41, 53, 62, 90, 94, 133-34, 150, 152-53, 157-58, 164, 166

    churches, 164-66

history, 23, 45-63

Hmong, 17

Holland, 17

Holy Spirit, 134

homeland security, 97-99

Honduras, 130

Horsham, Pennsylvania, 165

hospitality, 83, 88-89, 139

Houston, Texas, 111

HR 1645, 154

HR 4437, 143-46, 148, 151, 154

Hudson Institute, 94

Human Rights First, 149

human trafficking, 50, 84, 105

Hunter, Joel, 169

Hurricane Katrina, 42, 165

Idaho, 26

identity, 23, 86, 99-103

Iglesia Cristiana Misericordia, 170

Iglesia del Pueblo, 170

illegal, 22. *See also* undocumented immigrants

illegal aliens. *See* undocumented immigrants

illegal immigrants. *See* undocumented immigrants

Illinois, 76, 12, 16, 31, 33, 39, 43, 70, 76, 146, 170

Immanuel Fellowship Church, 159

immediate relatives, 72-73

immigration

    consultants. *See notarios*

    environmental concerns over, 96-97

    law, 23-24, 65-79

    root issues of, 184-85

Immigration Act of 1924, 57-58

Immigration and Nationality Act, 67

Immigration and Naturalization Service. *See* United States Citizenship and Immigration Service

Immigration Reform and Control Act (1986), 79

Immigration Restriction League, 56-57

India, 18, 29, 74, 75, 78, 97, 128

Individual Taxpayer Identification Numbers, 35

integration, 136

Intel Corporation, 128

Interfaith Coalition for Comprehensive Immigration Reform, 167

Internal Revenue Service, 35

International Church of the Foursquare Gospel, 168

International Mission Board (Southern Baptist Convention), 163

International Organization for Migration, 131

InterVarsity Christian Fellowship, 175

investors, 71

Iowa, 26, 116, 167

Iran, 74, 79

Iraq, 79, 151, 153, 158, 166

Ireland, 50

Irish immigrants, 49, 50, 60

Irish potato famine, 50
Iron Curtain, 145
IRS. *See* Internal Revenue Service
Islam, 168
Israelites, 45-46, 63, 83-85, 86-88, 98, 102, 113
Italian immigrants, 55-58, 60, 74, 124
ITINs. *See* Individual Taxpayer Identification Numbers
Jacob, 102
Japan, 19, 30, 131
Jerusalem, 85-86, 98, 134
Jesus, 85-86, 89, 91, 182
Jewish immigrants, 55-56, 58, 60
Jews, 89-90, 134
Johns Hopkins University, 126
Johnson, Lyndon, 62
Johnson, Todd, 164
Jordan River, 98
Joseph, 84, 101-2
Judah, 85
Judaism, 168
Judea, 134
judgment on those who mistreat immigrants, 87-88
justice, 109-10, 113-14, 181
Justice for Immigrants Campaign, 161
Kennedy, Edward, 147, 154
Kennedy, John F., 61-62, 135
Kenya, 128
kingdom of God, 90, 137, 170, 175, 182
Kingston Technology, 126
Kissinger, Henry, 135
Know Nothing Party, 51
Korean American church, 171
Korean War, 18
Kwon, Danny, 165
Kyl, Jon, 154
labor conditions, 59, 123
Lambert, Charles, 164
Land, Richard, 148

Laos, 17
Laredo, Texas, 170
Latin America, 47, 63, 135, 165, 184
Latinos. *See* Hispanics
law. *See* immigration, law
Lawful Permanent Resident, 29, 40, 43, 66, 68-69
Lazarus, Emma, 48-49
legalization, 15, 24, 142, 147-48, 149, 154
leprosy, 27
Levites, 87
Lewis, C. S., 22
Liberia, 79
Lincoln, Abraham, 52
local governments, 120-21, 157
Los Angeles Times, 27
Los Angeles, California, 26, 27, 145, 146
low-education workers, 71-72, 121-23
low-skill workers. *See* low-education workers
Lutheran Immigration and Refugee Service, 160
Ma, Yo-Yo, 135
Madrid, Spain, 21
Mahoney, Roger, 137, 145
mainline Protestantism, 25, 167, 168
Manifest Destiny, 52
Manila, Philippines, 39
marches, 146
marriage, 72-73
Massey, Douglas, 130, 132
McCain, John, 138, 151, 154, 157
McCain-Kennedy, Bill, 147
Medicaid. *See* public benefits
Medicare, 32, 34
Mediterranean Sea, 133
mercy, 108. *See also* grace
Mexican immigrants, 17, 30-35, 53, 58, 59, 62, 73-75, 94, 116, 126
Mexican-American War, 52

Mexico, 15-16, 18-31, 37, 40, 52-53, 59, 64-65, 67, 73, 75, 77-78, 89, 94, 95, 97, 111, 116, 122, 130, 132, 141, 145, 162, 179
Miami, Florida, 26
Michigan, 30, 163
Microsoft Corporation, 127
Middle East, 79
Midianite, 134
Migration and Refugee Service (U.S. Conference of Catholic Bishops), 161
migration, motivations for, 30, 47
military service, 30, 143, 166
Ming, Yao, 135
Minnesota, 169
Minuteman Project, 28
misinformation, 27, 64-65
missions, 19, 110, 161-62, 165
Moab, 85
Moore, Jan, 161
Moore, Stephen, 120
Morelos, Mexico, 31, 33
Mormonism, 168
Morton, Hugh, 119
Moses, 84-85, 88, 134, 181
Motorola, 128
Mouw, Richard, 133
Muslims. *See* Islam
NAE. *See* National Association of Evangelicals
NAFTA. *See* North American Free Trade Agreement
Naomi, 85, 106
Nation of Immigrants (Kennedy), 135
National Association of Evangelicals, 10, 61, 161, 169, 172, 182
National Association of Home Builders, 119
National Coalition of Latino Clergy and Christian Leaders, 170
National Council of Churches, 160
National Hispanic Christian Leadership Conference, 153, 170-71

national origins systems, 57-58, 61
Native Americans, 46, 53, 90, 94, 174
native-born poor, 94
native-born workers, 94, 118-19, 121-23
nativism, 51, 56-57, 60
naturalization, 38, 68-69, 76, 89-90
naturalized citizens, 29
Navratilova, Martina, 135
Neenah, Wisconsin, 17
Neff, David, 169
Nehemiah, 85, 98
neighbor, 82, 91-92
Nelson, Bill, 175
Nevada, 52, 157
New Mexico, 33, 36, 52, 53, 157
New Testament, 82, 88-89, 100, 107, 134
New York Times, 35, 146, 156
New York City, 26, 55-56, 60, 62, 124-25, 146
Nicaragua, 17, 80
    immigrants from, 79
Nigeria, 128
Nile River, 102
Nobel Prize, 127
non-immigrant visas, 66-67
North American Free Trade Agreement, 95, 132
North American Mission Board (Southern Baptist Convention), 163
North Carolina, 26
northern Europe, 58, 117
Northland, A Church Distributed, 169
notarios, 38
Nouwen, Henri, 177-78
Numbers USA, 150
Obama, Barack, 138, 157-58
Obed, 106
obedience, 176-77
oikonomia, 137
Old Testament, 82-85, 87, 89, 100, 107
open borders, 90, 112, 137

orphans, 87
overstayers, 37, 67
paper sons, 55
Passel, Jeffrey, 120
paths to legal status, 70-78
Patterson, Paige, 163
Paul, 86, 89-90, 94-95, 134
payroll taxes. *See* taxes
Pennsylvania, 9, 18, 45, 165
Perkins, John, 172
persecution, 56, 78, 86
Persia, 85
Peter, 86, 100
Pew Research Center, 29
Pfaelzer, Jean, 54
Pharaoh, 102, 134
Philadelphia, Pennsylvania, 9, 18, 165
Philip, 86
Philippi, 86
Philippines, 38, 39, 73-75, 78
Phillips, Judy and Mike, 159
Phoenix, Arizona, 32
Pilcher, Dan, 96
Pipher, Mary, 178
Plyler v. Doe, 42
Pol Pot, 161
Poland, 55, 78, 89
    immigrants from, 55-56, 64-65
politics, 137-58
Polk, James K., 52
polls. *See* public opinion
pollution, 97
poor, 94. *See also* poverty
Porter, Jerry, 163
Postville, Iowa, 167
poverty, 80, 184
prayer, 177-78
preference system. *See* family-based
    immigration
prejudice, 27-28, 150, 181

Presbyterian Church USA, 162, 167
Presbyterians, 5, 60, 79. *See also* Presbyterian
    Church USA
Primera Iglesia Bautista Hispana de Metro
    Atlanta, 166
Princeton University, 130, 132
priorities of obligation, 94-95
prison, 27-28
Prison Fellowship, 168
processing delays, 21, 73, 76
Protestants, 25, 60, 167
public benefits, 27, 34, 41-42
public charge, 49, 67
public housing. *See* public benefits
public opinion, 149-50, 156, 173
Pueblos en Acción Comunitaria, 17
Puritans, 117
Quinones-Hinojosa, Alfred, 126
quotas, 57-58, 59
railroad. *See* Union Central Pacific Railroad
Rankin, Jerry, 163
Reagan, Ronald, 79
reciprocal relationships, 179
reconciliation, 90, 100, 174-75
Reform Party, 99
refugees, 15, 66, 78, 84-85, 134-35
remittances, 130
Republicans, 64, 49, 93, 150, 151-53, 156-57
restoration, 112-14
Restoration Church, 166
restrictionists, 57, 139, 149, 172
Reuben, 98
Rights Working Group, 149
Rio Grande River, 17, 140
Rodriguez, Samuel, 153, 171
Roe v. Wade, 110
Roman Catholic Church, 15, 25, 28, 51, 60,
    100, 115, 145, 149, 161, 163, 167, 168
Russell, James, 28
Russia, immigrants from, 55-56, 60, 125

Ruth, 85, 106
Rwanda, 14, 18, 79, 179
S.2611, 146-51
Salvadoran immigrants, 79
Samaria, 134
San Antonio, Texas, 164
San Diego, California, 35
San Francisco, California, 40, 43
San Jose, Costa Rica, 17
Santa Cruz, California, 54
Sarconi, Steve, 122
Saul, 85
SBC. *See* Southern Baptist Convention
schools. *See* education
Schwarzenegger, Arnold, 135
Scripture. *See* Bible
Seattle, Washington, 30
second preference (family-based
    immigration), 73-74
Secure Fence Act, 151
Security Through Regularized
    Immigration and a Vibrant Economy
    (STRIVE) Act. *See* HR 1645
Sensenbrenner Bill. *See* HR 4437
Sensenbrenner, James, 64, 143
September 11, 2001, 97
Sider, Ronald, 113, 169
Sierra Leone, 18, 79
Simcox, Chris, 28
slavery, 50, 63, 84. *See also* human trafficking
smugglers. *See coyotes*
Social Security, 32, 34-35, 43, 64, 118, 120
Sojourners, 170
Somalia, 18, 79
South Africa, 128
South Carolina, 166
South Korea, 18-19, 78
Southeast Asia, 9, 79
Southern Baptist Convention, 148, 163,
    169-70

southern Europe, 63
Soviet Union (former), 79
Spain, 21
Spanish, 17, 99-100, 133, 164
Spartanburg, South Carolina, 166
Spurgeon, Charles, 181
Stanford University, 43
Stapleford, John, 115
state governments, 120-21, 157
statelessness, 104-5
statistics, 28-29
Statue of Liberty, 48, 62
Stephen, 86
STRIVE Act. *See* HR 1645
student visas, 30
Sudan, 18, 79, 179
Sun Microsystems, 127
Sun, David, 126
Supreme Court, 42
surveys. *See* public opinion
Swain, Carol, 94, 110
Sweeney, Douglas, 61
Switzerland, 132
Tancredo, Tom, 93
Tanzania, 14, 128
taxes, 32, 34-35, 64, 120
Taylor, Elizabeth, 135
temporary visas. *See* non-immigrant visas
terrorism, 97-98
Texas, 35-36, 38, 52, 111, 140, 161, 164, 170
Thill, Kathy, 167
third preference (family-based
    immigration), 73, 75
Tijuana, Mexico, 115
Tocqueville, Alexis de, 135
Treaty of Guadalupe Hidalgo, 51-53
Truman, Harry, 59, 61
Tsao, Fred, 55
Tu, John, 126
U.S. Conference of Catholic Bishops, 161

U.S. Consulate, 66, 80

Ukraine, 39-40

undocumented immigrants, 22, 26-44, 69, 98-99, 108, 111-12, 121-23, 142, 145, 151-52, 159-60, 169, 173, 180

Union Central Pacific Railroad, 53

United Farm Workers, 59

United Kingdom, 128. *See also* England

United Methodist Church, 167. *See also* Methodists

United Nations High Commission for Refugees, 78

United States Citizenship and Immigration Service, 65, 76

unlawful presence, 75, 104, 144

Ur, 83

USCIS. *See* United States Citizenship and Immigration Service

Utah, 52

Valley Harvesting and Packaging, 122

Vietnam, 18, 79, 89, 166

visitor visas. *See* non-immigrant visas

Volkswagon, 19

volunteering, 161, 176-79

wait times, 73-36

wall, 89-90

Wall Street Journal, 120

Wallis, Jim, 170

Washington (state), 30

Washington, D.C., 21, 24, 36, 54, 81, 150, 167

Washington, George, 49

Washington Times, 11

welfare. *See* public benefits

West Africa, 185

western Europeans, 63, 67, 89

Wheaton College, 43

Wheaton, Illinois, 170

whites. *See* Caucasians

widows, 87, 94-95

Wilbanks, Dana, 79

Wisconsin, 17, 26

Wooddale Church, 169

World Relief, 13, 17, 21-22, 24, 44, 160, 161-62, 169, 181, 183

World War I, 57

World War II, 59

Wyoming, 52

Yahoo, 127

Yang, Jerry, 127

Yoder, John Howard, 109

Yugoslavia (former), 79

Yuong-Sang Korean Presbyterian Church, 165

Zambia, 14